# Courts at War

# Courts at War

## EXECUTIVE POWER, JUDICIAL INTERVENTION, AND ENEMY COMBATANT POLICIES SINCE 9/11

Gregory Burnep

University Press of Kansas

Published by the University Press of Kansas (Lawrence, Kansas 66045), which was organized by the Kansas Board of Regents and is operated and funded by Emporia State University, Fort Hays State University, Kansas State University, Pittsburg State University, the University of Kansas, and Wichita State University.

Library of Congress Cataloging-in-Publication Data

Names: Burnep, Gregory, author.
Title: Courts at war : executive power, judicial intervention, and enemy combatant policies since 9/11 / Gregory Burnep.
Description: Lawrence : University Press of Kansas, [2021?] | Includes bibliographical references and index.
Identifiers: LCCN 2020024368
ISBN 9780700630479 (cloth)
ISBN 9780700630486 (epub)
Subjects: LCSH: Detention of persons—United States—History. | Terrorism—Prevention—Law and legislation—United States—History. | Combatants and noncombatants (International law)—History. | Judicial power—United States. | War and emergency powers—United States. | Executive power—United States. | National security—Law and legislation—United States. | Detention of persons. | Terrorism—Prevention—Law and legislation.
Classification: LCC KF9625 .B87 2021 | DDC 345.73/0527—dc23
LC record available at https://lccn.loc.gov/2020024368.

British Library Cataloguing-in-Publication Data is available.

Printed in the United States of America

10 9 8 7 6 5 4 3 2 1

The paper used in this publication is recycled and contains 30 percent postconsumer waste. It is acid free and meets the minimum requirements of the American National Standard for Permanence of Paper for Printed Library Materials Z39.48-1992.

*For my parents*

# *Contents*

Acknowledgments, *ix*

Introduction *1*

1 "The Least Worst Place": Detention in the Early Bush Administration (2001–2004), *19*

2 Detaining Enemy Combatants amid Legal Uncertainty (2005–2008), *42*

3 Detention Policy in a Post-*Boumediene* World (2009–2017), *67*

4 "Kangaroo Courts?" The Troubled Beginnings of Military Commissions (2001–2005), *93*

5 The Supreme Court Intervenes: Military Commissions, Version 2.0 (2006–2008), *114*

6 Litigation without End: Military Commissions after *Hamdan* (2009–2017), *133*

Conclusion, *158*

Timeline of Significant Events, *167*

Notes, *171*

Cases Cited, *209*

Bibliography, *211*

Index, *231*

# *Acknowledgments*

I almost wrote that this project began as a dissertation, but its origins are more complicated than that. My study of American government started at the College of the Holy Cross, where I now teach, under the tutelage of so many extraordinary professors whom I now call colleagues (and friends). In particular, I thank Daniel Klinghard and Don Brand, who taught most of the American government courses I took as an undergraduate. They ignited in me a passion for thinking about American government that has only grown with time. I am also grateful to Ward Thomas, who took me under his wing and made me his research assistant during my sophomore year. Ward showed me the ropes and answered many of my earliest questions about a potential career in academia. Daniel, Don, and Ward were not only wonderful teachers, but also mentors as I struck out on the path to graduate school. I am so lucky to remain the recipient of their patient and thoughtful mentorship even now.

Returning to Holy Cross as a faculty member has been a dream come true in so many respects. For the purposes of completing this project, Holy Cross was an incredibly supportive environment in which to work. I thank the entire Department of Political Science, which is filled with remarkable individuals. Our chairpersons over these past few years, first Vickie Langohr and now Maria Rodrigues, have been especially helpful, always lending an ear to their new tenure-track colleague. I greatly appreciate their leadership and support. Outside my department, Tony Cashman, Ed O'Donnell, and Steve Vineberg have been excellent mentors. I also thank the generous donors to the Robert L. Ardizzone Fund for Tenure Track Excellence, which provided financial support during my fall 2018 research leave. And no ode to Holy Cross would be complete without a heartfelt shout-out to my amazing students, whose enthusiasm for studying political science continually energizes and inspires me. They remind me each and every day how lucky I am to do what I do.

My largest intellectual debt was incurred during my time as a graduate student at Boston College. Shep Melnick was the greatest dissertation advisor I could ever have asked for, and I owe him far more than I could ever hope to repay. Shep indelibly shaped the way I think about virtually every aspect of American politics, and no individual has more directly influenced the course of this project than he has. I also benefited greatly from the advice of my other dissertation committee members, Marc Landy and Ken Kersch, whose insightful feedback made this a much more well rounded book than it otherwise would have been. I consider myself very fortunate to have spent six years in the PhD program at Boston College, where so many faculty, staff, and fellow graduate students made it a terrific place to study.

Some of the material from my chapters on military commissions previously appeared in my article "Military Commissions and the War on Terror: A Separation of Powers Tug-of-War," *Polity* 49, no. 2 (April 2017): 270–300 (© 2017 Northeastern Political Science Association. All rights reserved.). I presented rough drafts of portions of this project at multiple academic conferences, and I am therefore thankful for the feedback I received from fellow panelists, panel chairs, and discussants at annual meetings of the New England Political Science Association (NEPSA) and the Northeastern Political Science Association (NPSA). Especially notable in this regard was a NEPSA roundtable on Jeb Barnes and Thomas Burke's *Varieties of Legal Order,* where I had the opportunity to interact with a number of scholars whose work I greatly admire, including Tom Burke, Rebecca Hamlin, Bob Kagan, Lynn Mather, and Paul Nolette. I am enormously grateful to my editor at the University Press of Kansas, David Congdon, who guided this project along with such great care. Thanks as well to Colin Tripp, who moved it through the production phase to completion, and to Carol Kennedy for copyediting the manuscript. The final product is significantly improved because of the input from two reviewers, Jeb Barnes and Chris Edelson, who read the entire manuscript and offered countless suggestions for making it better. Any shortcomings that remain are certainly my own.

This book is dedicated to my parents, Cindy and Jon, who have given me so much. I love them dearly. So many friends and family members supplied encouragement, laughter, and much-needed companionship at various stages of this process. I can scarcely believe how fortunate I am to have so many wonderful people in my life. It always amazed me how sure they all were that I could actually write a book. The only downside of having such a large cheering section, I have now learned, is the risk of leaving someone out in the acknowledgments section. I wish to give special thanks to my brother, Ben Burnep, and all of my aunts and uncles and cousins. Special thanks as well to the Berrys, the Campolettanos, the Craigs, the Davises, the Johnsons/Sperlings, the Montines, the NeCastros, the Powells, and the Worcester crew. Many other extraordinary people have helped me along the way; they are too numerous to mention but know who they are. Finally, there is Abby. You appeared in the summer of 2019, as I was putting the finishing touches on the first draft of this manuscript, and you changed my life forever. You were there every step of the way as I finished this book, offering me boundless love and support. Never could I have imagined a more perfect partner. I can't wait to spend the rest of my days with you.

# Introduction

On the second to last day of its 2003–2004 term, the US Supreme Court handed down decisions in six cases. Two of these cases concerned Miranda rights, and one dealt with a state court's denial of postconviction relief in a murder case.[1] The three cases were standard fare for the nation's highest judicial body—the sorts of cases that Americans have long come to expect their Supreme Court to decide. But the other three cases were a different matter. On June 28, 2004, the Court became an important actor in an armed conflict, delivering rulings in a trio of cases involving wartime detainees held by the US military. By wading into a war and declining to rubber-stamp the executive branch's actions, the Court broke with a long-standing tradition of deference to the executive in wartime national security cases.[2] Henceforth, judges would play a major role in shaping national security policies in what President George W. Bush dubbed the "war on terror." After the September 11, 2001, terrorist attack, lawyers, lawsuits, and court decisions have repeatedly altered the policy landscape in a variety of policy areas, including detention, interrogation, military trials, surveillance, and targeted killing. After 9/11, lawyers and judges became deeply involved in an armed conflict, with important consequences for presidential authority, the separation of powers, and the treatment of individuals suspected of posing a threat to the United States.

This is a book about courts at war.[3] By courts at war, I primarily mean that courts have become heavily involved in the post-9/11 armed conflict. However, as the reader will soon see, the phrase also applies to the position of courts vis-à-vis the other branches of government (courts in conflict with the executive, the legislature, or both)—and even courts in conflict with other courts. But this is more than just a book about courts. Scholars of public policy and public law have used terms such as "judicialization," "adversarial legalism," "legalization," "juristocracy," and "juridification" to describe the penetration of law and courts into a wide array of policy areas, and those terms might be equally fitting for this study.[4] But rather than getting bogged down in a debate about terminology, I follow Jeb Barnes and Thomas Burke in referring more broadly to lawsuits and court decisions—or, in their words, "rights, courts, and litigation."[5] And—again like Barnes and Burke—I adopt Martin Shapiro's approach to courts, treating them as one actor or policy maker among many, with what Barnes and Burke call "their own tilts and tendencies."[6] In the pages that follow, I examine the role of lawsuits and courts in shaping national security policy from September 11, 2001, through the beginning of the Trump presidency. I focus in particular on two wartime policy areas: detention and military commissions. By investigating these domains in detail, we gain a rich understanding of the effects of litigation and judicial intervention since 9/11. In an age when courts have become increasingly involved in war, we must ask: What are the consequences for those in the legislative and executive branches? And what are the consequences for those on the receiving end of American military might? These are the questions this book seeks to answer.

Some might object at the outset to my claim that courts have gone to war by asking whether the United States is really "at war"—or whether the current struggle against terrorist groups and their supporters is something different altogether. But President Bush's initial characterization of the 9/11 attack as an act of war necessitating a wartime response has repeatedly found widespread support across the federal government. Within a week of the attack, Congress authorized the president to use "all necessary and appropriate force" against the individuals, groups, and nations responsible for it, along with those who harbored them.[7] That statute, the 2001 Authorization for Use of Military Force (AUMF), remains on the books, and it continues to provide the primary legislative underpinning for the ongoing war against al-Qaeda (the terrorist organization responsible for the 9/11 attack), the Taliban (the organization that harbored al-Qaeda in Afghanistan), and associated terrorist groups.[8] Furthermore, in case after case, courts have accepted the proposition that the United States is at war with al-Qaeda and associated forces.[9] And although President Bush's successor, Barack Obama, stopped using the term "war on terror" to refer to the conflict, the Obama administration consistently maintained the Bush administration's position that the United States was engaged in a war against a set of terrorist groups. The Trump administration has adopted the same stance.[10] All three branches of government have repeatedly agreed that the 9/11 terrorist attack ushered in a period of extended armed conflict that continues to this day. They have all called it a war, and we should take them at their word.

## THE ARGUMENT

At the most basic level, this book argues that litigation and courts have had a significant impact on the laws and policies surrounding detention and military commissions since 9/11. Policies regarding who can be detained as an enemy fighter, who can be prosecuted in military commissions and for what crimes, and the procedures for detaining and prosecuting suspected terrorists have been greatly influenced by myriad lawsuits and court decisions. The same is true of other wartime policy areas: though they are largely beyond the scope of this book, policies around interrogation, surveillance, and targeted killing have also been reshaped by legal challenges and judicial intervention. In short, litigation and court rulings have frequently spurred policy change. This finding challenges scholars like Gerald Rosenberg who have argued that the litigation route is a largely ineffective one for those who desire significant reform.[11] Even in a realm where the authority of the elected branches is assumed to be at its apex, lawsuits and court rulings have had important effects on policy making.[12]

The precise consequences of litigation and judicial intervention have been complex, but they can be summarized here. After 9/11, policies surrounding detention and military commissions—what I refer to as enemy combatant policies—have been subject to recurring legal challenges, and as a result they have evolved in two major ways. First, enemy combatant policies have become increasingly insulated from presidential control. Decisions about how to handle suspected enemy fighters are subject to checks and balances, and the policies reflect the input of a variety of actors and institutions. As the American military response to 9/11 got underway, President George W. Bush initially moved swiftly and unilaterally to deal with captured belligerents. He issued an executive order in November 2001 outlining two policy tools: detention in military custody for enemy combatants and military commission trials for those enemy fighters suspected of having committed war crimes. In the months and years that followed, many fretted about the reemergence of an "imperial presidency."[13] In part, these concerns reflected long-standing fears of presidential overreach in times of war. The idea that war enhances executive authority has a long and rich historical pedigree: it was none other than the father of the Constitution himself, James Madison, who once observed, "War is in fact the true nurse of executive aggrandizement."[14] American history contains examples of extremely broad assertions of presidential power in wartime, including Abraham Lincoln's suspension of habeas corpus during the Civil War, Franklin Delano Roosevelt's internment of Japanese Americans during World War II, and Presidents Lyndon Johnson's and Richard Nixon's aggressive uses of executive power in the Vietnam War. Moreover, because the conventional wisdom holds that the legislative and judicial branches will typically be deferential on matters of war and peace, many observers worried that the post-9/11 presidency would have a blank check.

Fears of an imperial presidency were also partly attributable to factors specific to the conflict at hand. The seemingly indefinite duration of the war caused some to worry that unbridled presidential power would become a permanent feature of the American political system. The Bush administration's legal theories also raised alarms. Those theories, predicated on an extraordinarily expansive interpretation of presidential power under Article II of the Constitution, included claims that President Bush possessed virtually unchecked authority to wage a global war on terror.[15] In this way, the nature of the conflict, President Bush's early assertions of power and his administration's legal theories, and enduring concerns about executive overreach and a dearth of checks and balances in wartime combined to generate widespread fears of an unlimited, all-powerful presidency.

My account challenges this view. A failure to distinguish the Bush administration's legal arguments, which in some cases were quite radical, from the actual policies that were enacted, implemented, and later reformed has caused many observers to overstate the unilateralism and aggressiveness of the administration's response to 9/11. I will show that after President Bush's initial executive order on enemy combatant policies, the process for implementing and altering those policies featured very little presidential unilateralism. Instead, policies emerged from an extended back-and-forth involving a variety of actors—or what Mark Miller and Jeb Barnes have called "a continuous dialogue among the institutions of government."[16] The president is one important voice in this dialogue, and he may even speak the loudest from time to time—especially in the immediate wake of an attack like 9/11. But enemy combatant policies ultimately emanated from a lengthy series of interactions between what Richard Neustadt termed "separated institutions sharing powers," not edicts from the White House.[17] And lawsuits and court decisions were a key factor in ensuring this was the case.

A close examination of the creation, implementation, and reform of enemy combatant policies after 9/11 demonstrates that other voices in the policy-making "dialogue" have mattered a lot. The judiciary repeatedly entered the fray, and its rulings helped Congress and members of the bureaucracy narrow the scope of presidential discretion. Lawsuits and court decisions gave reform proponents in Congress and the executive branch leverage for advancing their position. Lawmakers armed with court rulings enacted restrictions on presidential authority. In this regard, post-9/11 policy development resembled what Gordon Silverstein describes as a "complex iterated game," where "a judicial decision responds to legislative choices, and the next round of legislative choices is built on that legal ruling, leading to yet another round of legal rulings and legislative actions."[18] This process, which Silverstein calls "juridification," is evident in the evolution of enemy combatant policies.[19]

Even within the president's own branch, bureaucratic actors were sometimes able to extract concessions and limit White House control over enemy combatant policies. As James Q. Wilson's work on bureaucracy demonstrated, the executive branch is not a unitary actor, but rather a sprawling collection of departments and agencies with varying perspectives, interests, cultures, and professional norms.[20] It is also full of lawyers, whose presence and influence in national security agencies has continued to grow—a trend that began in the 1970s, but has picked up steam since 9/11. As recent accounts by Jack Goldsmith and Charlie Savage have shown, virtually every major decision in the war on terror involves a remarkable amount of input and oversight from executive branch lawyers.[21] In the chapters to come, we will see that at various points in the development of enemy combatant policies, disagreements inside the executive branch—among cabinet secretaries, agency lawyers, or both—were important drivers of policy change and a source of limitation on the president's freedom of action. In short, lawsuits and court rulings proved to be a useful tool for reform proponents inside and outside the executive branch, who wielded them to their advantage in the policy process.

In light of these developments, I conclude that our decentralized system of checks and balances has worked to limit presidential authority in this policy area and that fears of an unfettered wartime presidency are largely unfounded.[22] I am not the first person to make this claim. Jack Goldsmith's 2012 book *Power and Constraint* has already gone a long way toward refuting those who argue that wartime checks and balances are dead or on life support. But where Goldsmith's account primarily examines extraconstitutional actors as crucial sources of constraint on presidential authority, this book focuses on the more traditional constitutional actors—Congress, the bureaucracy, and especially the courts—and pays special attention to interactions across institutions. Furthermore, unlike Goldsmith's work, which takes a broad view of the entire wartime landscape, this account ventures deep into the weeds of one part of that landscape. I prioritize thick description and in-depth analysis, and by doing so I hope to complement the important work already done by Professor Goldsmith.

The second way in which enemy combatant policies have evolved since 9/11 involves the actual substance of the policies. Litigation and court decisions have helped generate multiple waves of reform that appear to have made US enemy combatant policies more hospitable to the interests of suspected adversaries. Early on in the conflict, the Bush administration claimed virtually unreviewable authority to detain and prosecute individuals it deemed to be part of or associated with al-Qaeda. In the first iteration of detention and military commissions, those designated as "enemy combatants" could be held indefinitely with no opportunity to challenge their confinement, and "unlawful" enemy combatants—those suspected of committing violations of the laws of war—could be prosecuted in military commissions that offered defendants few of the protections accorded to ordinary criminal defendants. But lawsuits and court rulings soon produced a host of changes.

Over time, those subject to detention without charges gained access to increasingly robust administrative review procedures, giving them an opportunity to contest their "enemy combatant" classifications and increasing their chances of being freed. Detainees held inside the United States and at Guantánamo Bay won the right to have their detentions reviewed by an Article III court as well. Litigation and court decisions also reshaped the military commission system: today, commission defendants enjoy many of the same protections present in the American criminal justice system. These policy changes emerged gradually, the product of an ongoing give-and-take between policy makers located in different institutions of government. Sometimes, the changes were made under the threat of litigation or in hopes of averting an unfavorable judicial ruling; other times, they were made in response to court decisions. Some of these changes were undertaken by the executive branch acting without Congress, while others featured significant involvement from the legislature. But most if not all of these changes gave detainees and military commission defendants access to heightened levels of due process. They received opportunities to challenge their detentions or demonstrate their innocence before bodies that are largely insulated from presidential control and feature enhanced safeguards for those who appear before them.

But if it sounds like these policy changes have been beneficial for suspected enemy fighters, the reality is a bit more complicated. My investigation also highlights some of the ways in which the use of litigation as a policy tool may have backfired. Here, I find Robert Kagan's work on adversarial legalism to be particularly helpful. In Kagan's telling, adversarial legalism is the product of two major forces: the United States' fragmented political structure and profound distrust of centralized authority and the increasing demands that Americans place on their government. When these two forces collide, the government takes on more responsibilities, but the political system retains its decentralized structure and becomes progressively more legalized. Government action is vigorously contested by a variety of actors in different, overlapping arenas, and one of these arenas is the courtroom.

Kagan's framework and insights have been applied to many domestic policy areas, but they also fit policy making in the war on terror quite well.[23] For example, Kagan points to entrepreneurial lawyers as leading promoters of adversarial legalism. He writes, "The United States has by far the world's largest cadre of special 'cause lawyers' seeking to influence public policy and institutional practices by means of innovative litigation."[24] This is precisely what attorneys working for organizations such as the Center for Constitutional Rights (CCR) and the American Civil Liberties Union (ACLU) have done since 9/11. Creative lawyering can also emerge from the legal academy, as law professor Neal Katyal's role in the litigation challenging military commissions demonstrates. It is not surprising that many judges, educated in these same legal academies, have been receptive to entrepreneurial litigation and willing to adopt novel legal interpretations and arguments in a variety of post-9/11 cases.[25] Kagan has also noted that the decentralized structure of the judiciary gives lower court judges plenty of leeway to improvise from the bench—something that has happened over and over again in enemy combatant cases.[26] And judges have ample opportunity to do so, for as Kagan has stated, American courts are remarkably open: "Even the lowest and most despised of citizens, convicted felons, feel entitled to petition a court for relief."[27] It turns out that Kagan actually understated the accessibility of US courts: "even the lowest and most despised" of *noncitizens*—suspected terrorists—felt "entitled to petition a court for relief" after 9/11. And on several occasions, these noncitizen terrorist suspects won their cases! The litigation pathway has proven to be highly responsive, flexible, and open—qualities that Kagan ascribes to adversarial legalism.[28]

Other key features of adversarial legalism are evident throughout my account, and they highlight some of the potential perils of turning to the courts.[29] Three of these drawbacks are on display repeatedly in the story I tell:

delay, legal uncertainty, and unintended consequences. Litigation is slow: it typically takes years for a legal challenge to reach the Supreme Court (if it ever does), as cases must first wend their way through the lower courts. Sometimes lawsuits are dismissed for lack of jurisdiction and must be reconceived and refiled. Courts may issue narrow rulings that settle very little—creating, or at least failing to resolve, legal uncertainty, and thereby encouraging more litigation. Although the procedures for detention and military commissions have become more favorable to detainees, those changes took years to develop. In perhaps the starkest example of delay, the military commission for those individuals directly tied to the 9/11 plot is still mired in pretrial proceedings. Enemy combatant policies continue to be litigated nearly two decades after the events of 9/11, and much legal uncertainty remains.

Litigation and court decisions have also produced unintended consequences. Here, Gordon Silverstein's work is again relevant: as Silverstein has observed, "Policy that is driven in large measure by litigation and judicial rulings . . . can and often does limit, direct, shape, and constrain those policies in the longer run in ways quite different from what might have been expected by those who chose a judicial route in the first place."[30] In the area of enemy combatant policies, delay and uncertainty have meant prolonged detention for some individuals who might otherwise have received military commission trials featuring a growing array of protections for defendants. Continued litigation directed at the military commission system has pushed trial dates further and further into the future, and in the meantime detainees are kept in limbo. So too are the families of the victims of 9/11. And the effects go beyond detention and military commissions: for policy makers charged with managing the conflict, judicial intervention has made some policy options more appealing than others. As litigation and court decisions have made sustaining detentions and military commission prosecutions more difficult, the executive branch has increasingly utilized other mechanisms for removing suspected belligerents from the battlefield.

As others have documented, the United States has in recent years relied more heavily on drone strikes and proxy detention—detention by other countries, often with poorer human rights records than the United States—to incapacitate suspected enemy fighters.[31] For human rights–focused groups like the CCR and the ACLU, those hardly seem like desirable alternatives to detention or prosecution by the US military. A similar trend played out in the early years of the conflict: when judges claimed the power to review detentions at

Guantánamo Bay, the United States began holding more individuals in Afghanistan, beyond the reach of the courts—and in worse conditions than those detained at Guantánamo. None of these alternatives to detentions or military trials at Guantánamo Bay are preferable from the standpoint of protecting the rights of suspected enemy combatants.

There are also costs for the government. The United States loses potentially valuable intelligence sources when it kills individuals instead of capturing them. Uses of lethal force—whether by drone or by other means—create the possibility of civilian casualties, a lamentable development in its own right that also undermines the United States' effort to prevent radicalization by winning hearts and minds. Turning captured individuals over to other countries with interests that may diverge from American interests poses risks as well: other countries may not share vital information, or they may free the individual sooner than the United States would like. And we know that a number of individuals released from Guantánamo Bay have gone on to reengage in the conflict.[32] Clearly, policy tools that have in many instances been elevated over detention and military commissions have drawbacks for the government too—not just for the individuals it seeks to combat.

One other policy alternative must be mentioned here: criminal prosecution in Article III courts. All three presidential administrations since 9/11 have utilized this option at times, and it has generally been a highly effective way to neutralize suspected terrorists. The government's success rate in these terrorism prosecutions is very high, and Article III courts have handed down sentences that are on average longer than those delivered by military commissions.[33] Moreover, defendants in Article III terrorism trials enjoy all of the rights and protections embedded in the American criminal justice system. This may seem like an ideal policy solution for both parties, but it too has potential downsides. Evidence collected in the fog of war may not be admissible in court. Others may worry that judges and juries will cut corners to secure guilty verdicts in high-profile terrorism cases, creating precedents that water down various due process protections for ordinary criminal defendants. And the two most common terrorism charges—conspiracy and material support—are broad, "catch-all" offenses that encompass lots of behavior, leading to potential concern that the bar for convicting individuals of these crimes might be too low. Article III trials might be the best way forward in some situations, but they are hardly a magic bullet. The question of how to deal with suspected enemy fighters has no clear, easy answers.

In sum, while changes in enemy combatant policies may have appeared to benefit suspected belligerents, the consequences are actually more mixed. For those already in American custody, the benefits would seem to outweigh the costs. Though some have remained in limbo as they awaited judicial review of their detentions or trials before a military commission, many were released from custody. Those who got their day in court won substantial victories: individuals detained without charges received multiple layers of review, and those prosecuted in military commissions were granted numerous protections and guarantees. But as detention and military commissions have tilted more and more in this direction, policy makers have turned to other options, some of which seem less likely to protect the rights of suspected adversaries and fulfill the government's security objectives.

Whether these two developments—limits on presidential discretion and the substantive policy changes described above—ought to be celebrated or decried depends on one's perspective. Defenders of a strong presidency in wartime might lament the rise of national security litigation and judicial involvement in the war, on the grounds that it unduly restricts presidential authority. But those who worry about an imperial presidency may be mollified. Security hawks may be uncomfortable with policy changes that increase the likelihood of suspected enemy fighters being released or acquitted, but human rights advocates will cheer these same developments. This account is primarily descriptive in nature, so I generally avoid reaching normative judgments on these issues. But these are important debates, and it is my hope that this book will enlighten and enliven them.

## CAUSES

Another big question lurks behind this study: Why? Why have lawsuits and court decisions played such an important role in the current conflict? Though this book focuses on the effects of litigation and judicial intervention rather than its causes, some brief thoughts are in order. In short, I suspect that there are many explanations for the proliferation of litigation and judicial involvement since 9/11. We can divide these explanations into two basic categories: (1) explanations that center on the specific—perhaps even unique—characteristics of this war and (2) broader explanations that are largely divorced from the particulars of the present conflict. Both are persuasive.

The first set of explanations for widespread litigation and an expanded judicial role focuses on the nature of the conflict. These explanations start from a simple premise: the war against al-Qaeda, ISIS, and assorted other terrorist organizations differs from the wars of the past. The United States is at war with a shadowy array of nonstate actors, not another nation. Adversaries in the current conflict do not wear uniforms, and they intentionally blend in with—and target—the civilian population. Furthermore, this war has no obvious endpoint. In armed conflicts between nation-states, wars end when one side formally surrenders. But in the present conflict, it is virtually impossible to imagine al-Qaeda and other terrorist groups surrendering in their entirety—and even if they did, individuals who adhere to their ideology would likely remain dangerous. It is also true that this war is closer to home than most have been: the events of 9/11 occurred on US soil and were carried out by men who had been living inside the country. And some US citizens have been linked to terrorist organizations with whom the United States is at war.

These distinctive qualities of the current war—its indefinite duration, the blurry line between combatants and noncombatants, and its close connection to the home front—help explain judicial involvement since 9/11. When it is difficult to distinguish a combatant from a civilian, the risk of mistakenly capturing or killing noncombatants is much greater. And the war's indefinite duration means that incorrectly classifying someone as an enemy fighter may result in decades of detention. Add to this that some of the individuals the United States may wish to hold are citizens or residents with a strong claim to constitutional protections, and it is not surprising that courts have entertained a wide array of lawsuits and generally demanded higher levels of due process and more constraints on presidential power than in past wars.

Other possible explanations for these developments similarly emphasize contingent factors. For example, one might concentrate on the Bush administration's controversial legal theories and view the judiciary's enemy combatant jurisprudence as a repudiation of those expansive theories of presidential power. On this view, if the Bush administration had sought and secured clear legislative approval for its national security policies, judges might have stayed on the sidelines. Or perhaps judges were affected by things they saw on television and read in the newspaper: grisly images of prisoner abuse at Abu Ghraib in Iraq, leaked legal memos arguably authorizing torture, and reports that the Bush administration was engaged in warrantless surveillance on American soil.[34] It is also worth keeping in mind that the Supreme Court and lower courts have often been closely and sharply divided in post-9/11 cases, such that a shift in just one vote could completely alter an outcome.

These conflict-specific or contingent explanations are undoubtedly part of the story. But treating the present war as uniquely prone to litigation and judicial involvement misses broader tendencies and forces that also help to explain these developments. The burgeoning role of lawyers and judges in war ought to be understood, at least in part, as a natural outgrowth of what C. Neal Tate and Torbjörn Vallinder have called "the global expansion of judicial power."[35] Other scholars have described this development in more general terms—as a sweeping increase in law or legalization.[36] As comparative studies make clear, the United States has long been a leader on this front. It is, in the words of one scholar, "the land of law."[37]

For our purposes, the general trend can be summed up this way: over the past several decades law, litigation, and courts have penetrated sphere after sphere of public policy in the United States, leaving almost no area untouched. Alexis de Tocqueville's famous remark that in America almost every political question eventually becomes a judicial one rings truer now than ever before. As Thomas Burke puts it, "There are few litigation-free zones in twenty-first century American life."[38] Thomas Keck's recent work on the judiciary demonstrates just how common the use of litigation has become for policy advocates across the political spectrum.[39] According to Keck, litigation is "an ever-present tool."[40]

The United States has long had a powerful, independent judiciary and a tendency to frame political disputes or policy issues in terms of rights.[41] The use of litigation and the resulting judicial intervention after 9/11 is consistent with twentieth-century developments commonly known as the "rights revolution." As Charles Epp has noted, as late as the 1930s most of the judiciary's work did not involve rights, and cases that did primarily concerned property rights. That changed over the next few decades, so that by the 1960s a clear majority of Supreme Court cases revolved around rights, and civil rights and civil liberties became the central preoccupation of federal judges.[42] Many members of the legal profession adopted what Robert Kagan calls a "heroic view of the judiciary's role."[43] Beginning with *Brown v. Board of Education*, courts came to be seen as protectors of disadvantaged or marginalized groups. The NAACP's litigation campaign on behalf of the rights of African Americans became a model for subsequent movements to secure expanded rights for a variety of groups, including women, individuals with disabilities, homosexuals, and prisoners.[44]

Court decisions since 9/11 that have sought to safeguard or expand the rights of terrorist suspects fit comfortably within the framework of the rights revolution. When Malcolm Feeley and Edward Rubin wrote their account of judicially driven prison reform, they cast the litigation and court rulings as an effort to protect "America's final minority."[45] They could not have foreseen the developments described in this book: suspected enemy belligerents in an ongoing war—many of whom were noncitizens held outside sovereign US territory—claiming rights and winning protections from courts. Groups such as the CCR and ACLU—part of what Charles Epp refers to as the "support structure" for the rights revolution—used litigation to promote policy changes that were unlikely to emerge from the democratic process.[46] After all, it is difficult to imagine a constituency with less political clout than noncitizen terrorist suspects. But through lawsuits, advocates for these individuals won favorable court rulings, and those rulings invigorated the interbranch tug-of-war that our decentralized system of checks and balances so often produces.[47] The resulting institutional interactions yielded policy outcomes that were favorable to terrorist suspects.

Another general explanation for the post-9/11 developments described here revolves around the growth of law in the national security realm. The sheer number of laws touching on war and foreign affairs has increased over time, particularly after the Vietnam War and Watergate led to a legislative backlash against presidential war powers and higher levels of distrust in the executive.[48] Furthermore, there are multiple sources of law in this area: in addition to domestic statutory and constitutional law, there is also international law. As we will see, the Geneva Conventions were critically important in the litigation involving military commissions. Law's expansion has created an opportunity for lawyers and judges to increase their involvement in these matters, and they have seized this opportunity. We see this most obviously in the barrage of lawsuits filed since 9/11 and the judicial response to them. But we also see it in the growing presence and influence of lawyers inside the executive branch, where they shape policies in accordance with the law before they are challenged in court.[49] As the national security space has become more legalized and rule-bound, it is not surprising that lawyers and judges have come to play a greater role.

Finally, as Mark Graber and others have shown, policy makers in the elected branches sometimes encourage litigation and judicial intervention.[50] Members of Congress or officials in the executive branch may find it advantageous to punt certain politically sensitive questions to the courts. On occasion they sidestep issues entirely, producing a policy vacuum that judges later fill. Or they may enact policies that explicitly create or enlarge a role for the judiciary. These tendencies have been on display in the evolution of enemy combatant policies. Judicial involvement in policy making is not just a consequence of entrepreneurial lawyering and activist judging. Sometimes, it is at least partly attributable to the actions—or inaction—of other players in the policy process.

Regardless of its precise causes, this much is clear: one of the most notable developments in American governance since September 11, 2001, has been the widespread success that litigants have had in convincing courts to get deeply involved in reshaping national security policies. In an area where judicial deference has long been the rule, lawyers and judges have now become crucial actors. This book is an effort to assess the consequences of courts at war.

## A QUICK WORD ABOUT METHODS

In order to accurately describe and analyze the creation and evolution of law and policy in the United States, it is necessary to use a wide lens. Though I am concerned here with the role of courts and litigation in the policy-making process, one cannot understand or evaluate that role without adopting a broader perspective that includes the White House, the bureaucracy, and Congress. This book envisions the policy-making process as an ongoing set of interactions between different actors and institutions—an interplay that may be cooperative or conflictual. Because policies emerge from "the ongoing interaction among overlapping and diversely representative forums," an interbranch perspective is required.[51] This perspective recognizes that the American political system disperses power across a variety of institutions and that focusing on one moment in time or a single institution will yield an incomplete picture of the policy process.[52]

Like my emphasis on the importance of litigation and courts in the policy-making process, this conception of policy making as an extended conversation involving a long cast of characters is not a new one. But existing scholarship that utilizes an interbranch perspective focuses almost exclusively on domestic policy. For too long now, those who study American politics, public policy, and public law have neglected to apply their insights to national security policy. They have drawn a sharp dividing line between wartime and peacetime policy making. Now, nearly two decades removed from the events of 9/11, it is time to overcome this barrier and begin systematically evaluating the impact of litigation and judicial involvement in the national security sphere.

This endeavor requires going beyond Supreme Court rulings. For one thing, it requires paying close attention to lower court rulings. In our decentralized judicial system the Supreme Court is one court among many, yet it garners almost all of commentators' attention.[53] It is true that the Supreme Court has issued a few very significant rulings on enemy combatant policies, and those are included in this account. But federal district and appellate courts have repeatedly weighed in on national security matters since 9/11, and those interventions form a significant part of my study.

This is not enough, however. In order to fully appreciate the policy impact of lawsuits and court decisions, one must pay attention to the before and after—that is, the actions and developments that predate and postdate events in the courtroom. As Jeb Barnes has noted, focusing only on a court ruling "isolates judicial decisions from the broader political and policy-making processes that lead up to and flow from court decisions."[54] Before a court reaches a decision—indeed, before any lawsuit is even filed—policy makers regularly account for the prospect of an adverse judicial decision.[55] They may create or alter policies in ways that make favorable judicial outcomes more likely—or judicial intervention in the first place less likely. Moreover, even after a court rules, there are often disagreements among policy makers about how to interpret and implement the decision. Some may favor only narrow compliance with the ruling, while others urge a broader reading that calls for more substantial policy change. It can be difficult to document these subtler, more indirect effects of litigation and court decisions. However, by canvassing journalistic and newspaper accounts and policy makers' memoirs, I am able to find several instances in which lawsuits and court rulings had these sorts of indirect influences on policy makers.

Because the policy-making process is best understood as an ongoing series of interactions between different actors and institutions, my adoption of an interbranch perspective and my approach of process tracing through detailed case studies is necessary. Focusing entirely on a single institution or point in time would likely lead to a distorted view of the post-9/11 policy landscape. For example, an account that looked only at the presidency might conclude that we are witnessing the return of an imperial presidency with unchecked authority. Instead, by utilizing an interbranch perspective and prioritizing careful description through case studies, we learn that an increase in presidential power is only part of the story.[56] We witness the growing involvement of other actors in the executive branch, Congress, and especially the courts, and we come to appreciate the ways in which interactions across institutions reshaped enemy combatant policies and limited presidential unilateralism.

## PLAN OF THE BOOK

The first three chapters of the book focus on detention policies. Chapter 1 covers the creation and implementation of detention policies in the early years of the conflict. It begins with President Bush's November 2001 executive order authorizing the detention of suspected enemy combatants and then explores the first wave of lawsuits challenging these policies. Those lawsuits resulted in a series of lower court and Supreme Court rulings that generated important changes to detention operations inside the United States and at Guantánamo Bay. The policy changes narrowed presidential discretion over detention matters, added new administrative review mechanisms and enhanced procedural protections for detainees, and spurred a shift in detention operations away from Guantánamo Bay to other locations.

Chapter 2 describes detention policy developments during President George W. Bush's second term. The first part of the chapter focuses on the back-and-forth between Congress and the courts: Congress responded to Supreme Court rulings in 2004 and 2006 by passing two major pieces of national security legislation touching on detention policy—the Detainee Treatment Act of 2005 and the Military Commissions Act of 2006. Both statutes further limited presidential control over detention. Now, all three branches of government had placed their imprint on detention policies. The second part of the chapter traces the litigation that culminated in the Supreme Court's landmark 2008 decision in *Boumediene v. Bush.* The Court ruled that noncitizens detained at Guantánamo Bay have a constitutional right to habeas corpus and that existing administrative review procedures were an inadequate substitute for habeas corpus review in federal court. The consequences of these changes tracked the first round of changes: detention policies became more insulated from presidential control, detainees held at Guantánamo received more due process, and the population at Guantánamo continued to dwindle, as hundreds of detainees were transferred out of the facility and the arrival of new individuals stopped entirely.

Chapter 3 investigates the evolution of detention policies after President Bush left office. I point out that the status quo at Guantánamo Bay has been highly resistant to change: President Barack Obama, who vowed to close the facility within his first year as president, was unable to do so before he left office, and President Donald Trump has not brought a single new person to Guantánamo Bay despite a campaign promise to significantly increase the detainee population there. That neither Obama nor Trump was able to fulfill these objectives is further evidence of detention policy's growing independence from presidential control. Still, important developments occurred in this period. The *Boumediene* ruling did little to resolve legal uncertainty about who could be detained and under what procedures, and the result of the Supreme Court's intervention was more litigation. Detainees held at Guantánamo filed habeas corpus challenges, and detainees held by the US military in Afghanistan filed a lawsuit aimed at extending *Boumediene* to US-run detention facilities in Afghanistan. Litigation and court rulings led to more releases from Guantánamo and to policy changes in Afghanistan giving detainees held there access to more rigorous review procedures.

Chapters 4–6 explore a different element of enemy combatant policy: military commissions. Chapter 4 examines the creation and implementation of military commissions in the first four years of the war. In November 2001, President Bush acted unilaterally to create a system of military commissions to prosecute certain captured individuals for war crimes. Several months later, however, implementing regulations emerged that made the commission system more favorable to defendants and more insulated from presidential direction than Bush's initial order suggested it would be. Internal executive branch divisions were a key cause of these changes, and it was military lawyers called judge advocates general (JAGs) who proved particularly influential. Later, as a lawsuit challenging military commissions began moving through the courts, supporters of defendant-friendly reforms were able to use the litigation as leverage to secure additional policy changes.

By the time the litigation challenging military commissions reached the Supreme Court in 2006, then, military commissions already looked somewhat different from President Bush's initial vision for them. Despite these adjustments, however, the Court found the commission system unlawful. Chapter 5 begins by considering the Court's decision in *Hamdan v. Rumsfeld.* It then examines the legislative response to the ruling: in October 2006, four months after the Supreme Court ruling, Congress passed the Military Commissions

Act (MCA). Although Congress was controlled by President Bush's own party, key lawmakers who favored reforms pushed for and won policy changes opposed by the Bush administration. The MCA contained new protections for commission defendants and further circumscribed presidential authority. But despite congressional action, litigation persisted.

Chapter 6 focuses mainly on these ongoing legal challenges and their effects on the commission system. First, though, the chapter details another round of reform by Congress, undertaken at the request of President Obama. In 2009, a Democratic Congress amended the MCA to make it even more protective of military commission defendants. Even so, litigation has continued unabated, and the US Court of Appeals for the District of Columbia Circuit has issued a series of rulings in recent years that have narrowed the jurisdiction of military commissions and overturned convictions. As with detention, legal and policy developments surrounding military commissions produced mixed results. On one hand, military commission defendants received more protections and fairer trials. But litigation also caused interminable delays, and military commissions became a less appealing tool for policy makers. This latter point is confirmed by early experiences in the Trump administration: despite his vowing to use military commissions more often, not a single individual taken into custody on President Trump's watch has been placed into the system.

The concluding chapter does three things. First, it considers the future role of detention and military commissions. Though the two policy options have been used sparingly by Presidents Obama and Trump, this war is likely to span several more presidential administrations and will continue to evolve. Policy makers will keep facing hard questions about how to handle suspected belligerents, and they may sometimes find that detention or military prosecution suits their objectives better than the alternatives. Second, the conclusion briefly describes four other national security policy areas—surveillance, interrogation, targeted killing, and President Trump's travel ban—that have been similarly influenced, either directly or indirectly, by litigation and court decisions. These other examples indicate that the argument I am making here is generalizable to policy areas other than detention and military commissions. In closing, I step back and reflect on the big-picture lessons of the book, offering a generally optimistic take on our political system's performance after 9/11 and some thoughts about the future.

# 1. "The Least Worst Place": Detention in the Early Bush Administration (2001–2004)

Detention policies in the war on terror look much different today than they did in the immediate wake of the 9/11 attacks. They reflect input from a variety of actors—especially the courts—and feature more due process protections for detainees. The litigation that began shortly after the first group of detainees was flown to the detention facility at Guantánamo Bay, Cuba, led to important policy changes. Some of these policy changes were the direct result of court decisions, while others were driven at least in part by the ever-present threat of lawsuits and judicial intervention. Litigation and court rulings gave rise to a long and messy back-and-forth between different institutions, producing detention policies that are considerably more legalized and insulated from presidential control than the policies initially pursued in 2001. These developments have generated a complex array of costs and benefits for both suspected enemy combatants and the government that seeks to combat them.

At the outset, decisions to subject battlefield captures to military detention featured a high degree of presidential unilateralism, very few review procedures or oversight, and little law. But litigation soon changed that. As lawsuits challenging detentions at Guantánamo Bay and inside the United States proliferated during the first two years of the war, policy change began to occur in the shadow of litigation. Executive branch actors dissatisfied with the White House's approach pushed for enhanced screening and review procedures and more detainee releases from US custody. Aided by the presence of litigation, those actors won important victories. Detainee lawsuits also had a more direct impact on the shape of detention policies. Lower federal courts issued a medley of rulings in 2002 and 2003—some favorable to the government, others favorable to detainees—and these court decisions further unsettled the status quo.

The Supreme Court's intervention in 2004 had an even more decisive effect on detention policies. Even before the Court handed down its landmark detainee decisions in the summer of 2004, its grants of certiorari in those cases helped convince the executive branch to begin developing more formalized review panels, called administrative review boards (ARBs), for detainees held at Guantánamo Bay. Then, after the Supreme Court issued a pair of rulings allowing Guantánamo detainees to file habeas corpus petitions in federal court (*Rasul v. Bush*) and requiring more due process for American citizens held in military detention on US soil (*Hamdi v. Rumsfeld*), the Bush administration adopted a surprisingly broad reading of the decisions and instituted a second type of review body, known as combatant status review tribunals (CSRTs), for noncitizens held at Guantánamo Bay. The creation of two new review mechanisms, combined with an impending flood of habeas corpus petitions in the US District Court for the District of Columbia, generated considerable momentum for reducing the population at Guantánamo Bay. By making the process for detaining individuals at Guantánamo more onerous and therefore less attractive for the government, litigation also produced unintended consequences. Although fewer detainees were brought to Guantánamo beginning in 2004, detention elsewhere—closer to the battlefield in Afghanistan and, to a lesser extent, in the CIA's secret rendition, detention, and interrogation (RDI) program—received a boost. Unlike those at Guantánamo Bay and inside the United States, these detentions remained outside the purview of the federal courts, largely untouched by the forces of legalization during this period.

## INITIAL DETENTION DECISIONS AFTER 9/11

The Bush administration's decision to treat the 9/11 terrorist attack as an act of war necessitating a military response was highly consequential. By placing the nation on a war footing, President Bush activated a number of wartime authorities that would become central to his administration's efforts to combat terrorism. One of these wartime policy options was detention. The laws of war have long permitted the detention of enemy fighters for the duration of an armed conflict to prevent them from returning to the battlefield and taking up arms again.[1] As military operations against al-Qaeda (the terrorist organization responsible for 9/11) and the Taliban (the group that governed Afghanistan and harbored al-Qaeda) commenced pursuant to the 2001 Authorization for Use of Military Force (AUMF) passed by Congress, the United States began detaining individuals captured in the course of the fighting.

Initial statements by Secretary of Defense Donald Rumsfeld indicated that he did not view long-term detention as a leading tool in the military's arsenal. As the Bush administration began debating what to do with the first group of detainees, Rumsfeld pressed his position that the Pentagon—and the United

States more generally—should avoid becoming "the world's jailer." Rumsfeld thought that captures should be followed by a review process intended to ensure that the United States detained individuals only when it was absolutely necessary. And for those detainees who had to be kept in US custody, Rumsfeld favored either prosecuting them in military commissions or transferring or releasing them as soon as possible.[2] National Security Advisor Condoleezza Rice agreed with this position.[3] Rumsfeld, Rice, and other detention skeptics in the executive branch would continue to push these arguments over the coming months.[4]

Despite the existence of these misgivings from some administration officials, US forces soon wound up with a multitude of presumed al-Qaeda and Taliban members in their custody. Under an executive order issued by President Bush on November 13, 2001, these suspected belligerents could be detained by the military. The November order, which also announced the creation of military commissions to prosecute captured individuals for war crimes, made the secretary of defense the "detention authority" tasked with fleshing out the policy details. Early on, as debates unfolded inside the executive branch over what to do with them, detainees were held in makeshift Afghan facilities by allied Afghan forces or aboard American ships.[5] But this ad hoc approach to detention quickly proved unsustainable. In late November 2001, a large uprising at a temporary detention site called Qala-i-Jangi led to the first American combat death in the war. The prison riot and ensuing battle at Qala-i-Jangi helped convince the Bush administration that it needed to find a secure location further from the battlefield where it could hold and interrogate those detainees deemed the most dangerous and the most knowledgeable about future terrorist activities.[6]

By late December, after considerable internal discussion, the Bush administration settled on what Rumsfeld soon dubbed "the least worst place": the US-controlled naval outpost at Guantánamo Bay, Cuba.[7] Its remote location made it an attractive spot for holding the most threatening enemy fighters, and the administration's assumption that Guantánamo was beyond the reach of the judiciary seemed to give the executive branch much discretion in dealing with individuals detained there.[8] An Office of Legal Counsel (OLC) memo on the matter canvassed relevant precedents and concluded that courts were unlikely to assert jurisdiction over the military base at Guantánamo Bay. Moreover, because the territory was, under the terms of a long-standing agreement between the United States and Cuba, subject to "complete [US] jurisdiction and control," Cuban law also would not apply.[9] Though the OLC memo focused specifically on the legal status of Guantánamo, executive branch lawyers were also animated by a more general belief that judges would be hesitant to second-guess the commander in chief's wartime decisions.[10]

Detainees began to arrive at Guantánamo in January 2002. The first group of twenty arrived on January 11, and within a week and a half the number of Guantánamo detainees surpassed one hundred. The Bush administration's move garnered widespread attention. Scrutiny from the International Committee of the Red Cross and the media began immediately. Critics focused on detainee treatment and confinement conditions as well as the uncertain legal status of the captives.[11] At first, the Bush administration's plan was to begin prosecuting these detainees in military commissions as soon as possible for violations of the laws of war. Less than two weeks after the first group of detainees arrived at Guantánamo, the White House asked Department of Defense (DOD) officials to fill out documents for each detainee in order to begin the military commission process.

The Bush administration initially labeled Guantánamo detainees "unlawful enemy combatants." As Adam Pearlman has noted, the choice of terminology was telling: the use of the word "unlawful" reflected the administration's intent to prosecute detainees for war crimes. So too did President Bush's repeated public vows to "bring [the perpetrators of 9/11] to justice."[12] But logistics quickly got in the way. It became clear early on that DOD lacked crucial information about many detainees and their activities; without this information, it was impossible to start charging and prosecuting detainees in military commissions. So DOD shifted gears: in March 2002, it announced that it would instead hold many of the detainees without charges as "enemy combatants"—a new category that deemphasized the traditional distinction between lawful and unlawful combatants. The government might not have specific evidence directly linking detainees to war crimes for which they could be prosecuted, but it argued that some evidence of mere membership in al-Qaeda or the Taliban would be sufficient grounds for detaining someone while hostilities are ongoing. Long-term detention at Guantánamo, then, was less a conscious policy choice than a fallback position compelled by practical considerations. DOD general counsel William Haynes summed up the administration's position: "We are within our rights, and I don't think anyone disputes it, that we may hold enemy combatants for the duration of the conflict. And the conflict is still going and we don't see an end in sight right now."[13]

Not everyone agreed with Haynes. It was one thing to claim that enemy combatants could be detained without trial while hostilities were ongoing (though some even objected to this idea). But Haynes's statement glossed over the central, and most controversial, questions: what was the definition of "enemy combatant" and what sort of process was required before an individual could be determined to have met the criteria for enemy combatancy? These questions became the subject of litigation right away, kicking off several years of court rulings and complicated interbranch interactions. Just days after the first group of detainees reached Guantánamo Bay, a group calling itself Coalition of Clergy, Lawyers, and Professors filed a lawsuit in federal district court in Los Angeles challenging the detentions in general terms.[14] A month later, the Center for Constitutional Rights (CCR) brought a lawsuit on behalf of specific named detainees: an Australian named David Hicks and two British citizens, Asif Iqbal and Shafiq Rasul.[15] Lawyers had now become involved at Guantánamo Bay, and judges would soon follow.

## EARLY DETENTION LITIGATION IN FEDERAL DISTRICT COURTS: A MIXTURE OF DEFERENCE AND PUSHBACK

Neither of the two Guantánamo lawsuits went anywhere at the district court level, where they were dismissed for lack of jurisdiction. In *Coalition of Clergy v. Bush* (February 2002), Judge A. Howard Matz ruled that the plaintiffs lacked standing and went on to suggest that even with standing no federal court would have jurisdiction to entertain habeas corpus petitions from noncitizens detained at Guantánamo Bay.[16] The crucial precedent was a World War II–era case called *Johnson v. Eisentrager.*[17] In that case, the Supreme Court held that noncitizen enemy fighters captured, tried, and imprisoned abroad were not entitled to have their confinement reviewed by US courts. The petitioners in *Eisentrager* were German soldiers who had been convicted by a military commission for war crimes and imprisoned in US military custody in postwar Germany. For Judge Matz, the Guantánamo litigation raised the same basic issues: "In all key respects, the Guantanamo detainees are like the petitioners in *Johnson.*"[18] He dismissed the argument that the United States' lease agreement with Cuba essentially converted Guantánamo Bay into sovereign US territory, and for additional support he cited a US Court of Appeals for the Eleventh Circuit decision finding no federal court jurisdiction over Guantánamo.

The DC District Court handed down a similar ruling approximately five months later in *Rasul v. Bush.*[19] Judge Colleen Kollar-Kotelly also found the *Eisentrager* precedent to be decisive. Unimpressed by the petitioners' efforts to distinguish *Eisentrager* from the present case, Judge Kollar-Kotelly argued that *Eisentrager* stood for the proposition that aliens held outside the sovereign territory of the United States had no recourse to US courts. Like Judge Matz, she was unwilling to equate the United States' "complete jurisdiction and control" over Guantánamo with sovereignty. Thus, the outcome was the same: no habeas corpus rights for noncitizens detained at Guantánamo Bay.

Two other detention cases reached the federal district courts in 2002, though they did not concern detentions at Guantánamo Bay. The plaintiffs in these two lawsuits, Yaser Hamdi and Jose Padilla, were American citizens being detained as enemy combatants inside the United States by the US military. Hamdi was allegedly captured on the battlefield in Afghanistan fighting alongside the Taliban; after a brief detention in Afghanistan, he was transferred to Guantánamo Bay. Soon after he arrived at Guantánamo the government learned that Hamdi was born in Louisiana, and he was moved to a military facility in Virginia in April 2002 and held there without charges as an enemy combatant.[20] Jose Padilla was linked to al-Qaeda and suspected of plotting bombings inside the United States. Unlike Hamdi, who was captured abroad, Padilla was taken into custody on American soil. Federal law enforcement officers nabbed him at O'Hare International Airport in May 2002, pursuant to a material witness warrant. Padilla was originally held in New York by the Department of Justice (DOJ), but in June he was transferred to DOD custody and detained as an enemy combatant at a military brig in South Carolina.[21] Both Hamdi and Padilla sued, claiming that their detentions were unlawful.

The *Hamdi* litigation generated an extended colloquy between the US District Court for the Eastern District of Virginia and the US Court of Appeals for the Fourth Circuit. The first controversy, called *Hamdi I*, revolved around two questions: First, whether the public defender for the Eastern District of Virginia, Frank Dunham, had standing to file a habeas corpus petition on Hamdi's behalf, and second, whether Dunham should be permitted to meet with his client, who was being denied access to counsel. District Judge Robert Doumar answered both questions in the affirmative.[22] Dunham would qualify as Hamdi's "next friend" for the purposes of filing a habeas petition, and Hamdi was constitutionally entitled to meet with his lawyer. The government immediately appealed, and the Fourth Circuit reversed on the question of standing, finding that Dunham did not qualify as Hamdi's next friend because he did not have a "significant relationship" with the detainee.[23]

Shortly after the Fourth Circuit's ruling, Yaser Hamdi's father filed a habeas corpus petition on his son's behalf. This removed the next-friend issue from the litigation, and District Judge Doumar again ordered the government to allow the public defender unmonitored access to Hamdi. The government appealed again, and in *Hamdi II* the Fourth Circuit rebuked Judge Doumar for giving insufficient consideration to the sensitive national security issues involved in the case.[24] Stressing that this was a war powers dispute during a time of ongoing hostilities, the Fourth Circuit panel counseled deference to the government. It took the district court to task for deciding the access-to-counsel question "without proper benefit of briefing and argument" and for failing to properly consider the implications of Hamdi's designation as an enemy combatant.[25] Despite these admonishments, however, the Fourth Circuit declined to endorse the government's position that courts should grant complete deference to the executive branch's decision to classify Hamdi as an enemy combatant. Instead, the court remanded the case to Judge Doumar and asked for additional proceedings on that issue. As the two courts volleyed back and forth, legal uncertainty persisted.

In an August 2002 ruling, *Hamdi III*, the district court found that the government had not adequately demonstrated that Hamdi was properly classified as an enemy combatant subject to detention without trial. The government had submitted to Judge Doumar a two-page document from a Defense Department official named Michael Mobbs describing the government's decision to classify Hamdi as an enemy combatant. Mobbs, a special advisor to the under secretary of defense for policy, stated that he had worked on detention policy matters and reviewed "relevant records and reports" surrounding Hamdi's capture.[26] The DOJ's litigating position was that the "Mobbs Declaration" ought to be the end of the matter, because courts were bound to defer to the executive branch's finding. Judge Doumar disagreed, writing that the Mobbs Declaration "falls far short" of providing Hamdi with even a minimal version of "meaningful judicial review."[27] Criticizing the document's lack of detail regarding Hamdi's capture and status, Doumar insisted that the court would need to see more information. The government would have to turn over the "screening criteria" it used to classify Hamdi as an enemy combatant, as well as records of the detainee's statements to interrogators. The brief summaries contained in the Mobbs Declaration were insufficient; according to Judge Doumar, the document reflected "little more than the government's 'say so.'" Accepting it as an appropriate basis for continuing to detain Hamdi would turn the court into "a rubber-stamp."[28] Once again, the government appealed.

The other lawsuit involving a citizen detainee, *Padilla v. Bush*, reached federal district court not long after Hamdi's. Like the *Hamdi* litigation, Padilla's challenge drummed up legal uncertainty and led to a protracted back-and-forth between two courts, as well as between the executive branch and the judiciary. In December 2002, Chief Judge Michael Mukasey of the US District Court for the Southern District of New York ruled in *Padilla I* that the government had the authority to detain Padilla as an enemy combatant, but only if he was given the opportunity to rebut the government's claims about him in a habeas corpus proceeding.[29] For this to occur, Judge Mukasey found, Padilla must have access to a lawyer.

Before reaching those conclusions, Mukasey had to resolve a pair of jurisdictional issues. Padilla's lawsuit was filed by Donna Newman, a lawyer who represented Padilla prior to his transfer from DOJ to DOD custody. After President Bush designated Padilla an enemy combatant, Newman was no longer permitted to meet or communicate with her client. Rejecting the government's argument that Newman did not have standing, Judge Mukasey ruled that Newman's relationship with Padilla prior to his military detention allowed her to bring the suit. After that, Mukasey rebuffed the government's claim that the habeas petition was filed in the wrong court. He stated that the ordinary rule—that the proper respondent for a habeas petition is a detainee's "immediate custodian" (in Padilla's case, the commander of the South Carolina brig)—did not obtain here. Given the extraordinary circumstances and Secretary Rumsfeld's personal involvement as head of DOD, Mukasey held that Rumsfeld could be the respondent and was within the jurisdiction of his court.

Judge Mukasey then proceeded to the merits. Here, he awarded the government a partial victory. He ruled that an American citizen could be detained as an enemy combatant pursuant to the president's constitutional authority as commander in chief and under the 2001 Authorization for Use of Military Force (AUMF) passed by Congress, which authorized the president to use "all necessary and appropriate force" against those connected to the 9/11 attack.[30] However, Mukasey also held that the federal habeas corpus statute guaranteed Padilla the opportunity to present facts challenging the government's allegations against him. And in order to do this, Mukasey insisted that Padilla would need to have access to counsel: "Padilla's need to consult with a lawyer to help him do what the statute permits him to do is obvious. He is held incommunicado at a military facility."[31] Notably, the government also received from Judge Mukasey an indicator of the evidentiary standard that courts might insist on before signing off on military detention of a US citizen. At the end of his opinion, Mukasey suggested that the proper standard for judicial review of an enemy combatant designation was "some evidence," meaning the government would face a low bar for proving enemy combatancy. Of course, the opinion of one judge in this one case did little to ameliorate the legal uncertainty swirling around the issue. The *Hamdi* and *Padilla* lawsuits, though similar in some respects, also had important differences, and they generated different answers in different courts.

Litigation and the tug-of-war between the executive branch and the courts continued into 2003. Unhappy with Judge Mukasey's ruling in *Padilla I*, the government asked him to reconsider. The decision could have disastrous consequences for its ongoing efforts to interrogate Padilla, the government warned. Judge Mukasey was unmoved: in an opinion brimming with frustration, he refused to yield.[32] First, he scolded the government for dragging its feet on filing the motion to reconsider. Next, he confronted a statement from the head of the Defense Intelligence Agency alleging that granting a detainee access to a lawyer could undercut the application of "psychological pressure" and the development of "trust and dependency" between detainee and interrogator, hindering the government's efforts at intelligence collection. Unwilling to defer to the government's position, Judge Mukasey dismissed the claims as "speculative" and "only plausible."[33] He concluded his opinion in *Padilla II* in the strongest of terms: "Lest any confusion remain, this is not a suggestion or a request that Padilla be permitted to consult with counsel, and it is certainly not an invitation to conduct a further 'dialogue' about whether he will be permitted to do so. It is a ruling—a determination—that he will be permitted to do so."[34] The government appealed the ruling.

By early 2003, then, the hallmarks of adversarial legalism were clearly on display. Litigation moved slowly and generated legal uncertainty. Judges entertained the claims of enemy combatants and issued a welter of decisions on the government's detention policies. Viewed as a whole, these early rulings featured some deference to the executive but contained a surprising degree of resistance. On a core national security policy, and with a war still in its early stages, courts pushed back. Rather than deferring to policy makers in the executive branch, judges involved themselves in the details of detention policy.

To date, judicial intervention came exclusively in the citizen-detainee cases, where district court judges evinced substantial skepticism of the government's arguments. But even though the district court cases dealing with detention of noncitizens at Guantánamo Bay were dismissed for lack of jurisdiction, the Bush administration's approach there soon began to evolve. Policy changes were a response to a variety of factors, including negative media coverage, persistent criticism from various civil society groups, and growing dissension within the executive branch itself. But the ongoing pressure of litigation was a factor as well. As of September 2002, one year after the 9/11 attack, the Guantánamo population stood at approximately six hundred, and only two detainees had been sent away: one was Hamdi, who was relocated to American soil, and the other was a mentally unstable individual who was repatriated to Afghanistan.[35] But pressure began to build inside the executive branch, with officials at DOJ, DOD, and the State Department pushing for enhanced screening and review processes and reductions in the detainee population.[36]

In October 2002, a National Security Council meeting on detention policy produced some changes.[37] DOD announced that more releases would begin to occur, and it instituted occasional ad hoc reviews of ongoing detentions.[38] The initial screening procedures for sending detainees captured in Afghanistan to Guantánamo were also quietly revamped in December 2002.[39] In March 2003, a group of nearly two dozen Afghans were sent back to their home country.[40] Even with these changes, however, the review and release processes were slow and haphazard at this point in time. The State Department struggled to convince countries to take custody of former detainees.[41] And despite the releases that did occur, the overall detainee population at Guantánamo was growing, not shrinking. By April 2003 it was nearing seven hundred.[42]

## DETENTION LITIGATION IN THE CIRCUIT COURTS

As these policy changes unfolded in late 2002 and early 2003, the detention litigation continued to move forward. In November 2002, a unanimous panel of the Ninth Circuit Court of Appeals upheld the district court's decision in *Coalition of Clergy*, finding that the petitioners did not have standing.[43] However, deeming it unnecessary to go any further and address whether Guantánamo Bay was within the jurisdiction of the federal judiciary, the Ninth Circuit vacated the portion of the lower court opinion finding no jurisdiction. A few months later, the DC Circuit Court of Appeals confronted the jurisdictional question head-on. In a 3–0 decision handed down in March 2003, the DC Circuit affirmed the DC District Court ruling: the judiciary could not entertain habeas corpus petitions from noncitizens held at Guantánamo Bay.[44] Like the court below, it relied heavily on the *Eisentrager* precedent. The United States' "control" over Guantánamo was, in the DC Circuit's view, insufficient to give courts jurisdiction over what went on there. Sovereignty, not control, was the relevant criterion.

The government also received a favorable ruling in the *Hamdi* litigation. In January 2003, the Fourth Circuit reversed the district court's decision in *Hamdi III*. A unanimous panel held that the alleged circumstances and location of Hamdi's capture combined with the government's submission of the Mobbs Declaration formed an adequate basis to detain him pursuant to the 2001 AUMF.[45] Declaring it "undisputed that Hamdi was captured in Afghanistan during a time of armed hostilities there," the panel viewed Hamdi's classification as an enemy combatant as the sort of wartime decision that judges ought to accord a great degree of deference. Under the Fourth Circuit ruling, Hamdi was entitled to judicial review of his detention, but that review would be severely circumscribed. He could even be denied access to a lawyer.

In the other citizen-detainee case, however, the outcome was different. The Second Circuit Court of Appeals issued a 2–1 decision finding Jose Padilla's detention unlawful.[46] The majority held that neither the AUMF nor the president's powers under Article II of the Constitution authorized Padilla's detention. Coming on the heels of the Fourth Circuit's pro-government ruling in the *Hamdi* litigation, the *Padilla* decision seemingly injected renewed uncertainty into detention policy. The Second Circuit opinion did repeatedly emphasize a distinguishing factor, however: unlike Hamdi, Jose Padilla was taken into custody on US soil, far from a foreign battlefield. While the president's authority might be expansive in battlefield situations, the majority concluded that it was more limited in the domestic context. Authorizing the detention of individuals like Padilla was a job for Congress, the court said, and Congress had not clearly exercised that authority. The majority could not believe that the legislature would "leave unstated and to inference something so significant and unprecedented as authorization to detain American citizens under the

Non-Detention Act."[47] The Non-Detention Act, a 1971 law, stated that "no citizen shall be imprisoned or otherwise detained by the United States except pursuant to an Act of Congress."[48] Reading this statute alongside the AUMF, the Second Circuit majority concluded that even if the AUMF might arguably be construed to authorize detentions like Hamdi's—a nod to the Fourth Circuit's decision—it did not constitute the sort of clear and specific authorization required to detain Padilla. The majority opinion ended by noting the existence of alternative methods for lawfully incapacitating Padilla: he could be held as a material witness; he could be charged with a crime and prosecuted; or the executive branch could go to Congress to ask for additional detention authority. Otherwise, Padilla would have to be released. Judge Richard Wesley dissented, arguing that the president's constitutional authority and the AUMF permitted Padilla's detention.

As these various strands of detention litigation moved through the federal courts, detention policies continued to evolve. Members of Congress, including Republican senators Lindsey Graham (SC) and John McCain (AZ), began calling for more robust review procedures.[49] The legal confusion surrounding Guantánamo increased further in the waning weeks of 2003, when the Ninth Circuit became the first court in the country to rule that Guantánamo detainees could challenge their detentions in federal court. Although the Supreme Court had already agreed to hear *Rasul v. Bush*, which raised the same question, the Ninth Circuit went ahead with its decision. The 2–1 decision in *Gherebi v. Bush* exacerbated the existing judicial muddle on detention matters.[50] Then, in early 2004, the Supreme Court added *Hamdi* and *Padilla* to its docket. Before the trio of detention cases was decided, the Bush administration began setting up a more formalized review process for detainees held at Guantánamo Bay. As Neal Katyal has suggested, the timing of the executive branch's decision was no coincidence. DOD's announcement of the new review process occurred on the same day that the government's brief in *Rasul* was due at the Supreme Court, making this an important example of policy change driven at least in part by the ongoing pressure of litigation.[51] The government's brief cited the new procedures, and the topic was raised at oral argument as well.[52]

In May 2004—one month before the Supreme Court delivered decisions in the detention cases—DOD started implementing the new review mechanism. Deputy Secretary of Defense Paul Wolfowitz issued an order establishing ARBs—military-staffed panels tasked with examining whether or not detainees could be safely released from US custody.[53] Comparable to parole boards, ARBs were not designed to review or second-guess enemy combatant designations. Rather, an ARB would make a prospective judgment about whether a detainee brought before it was too dangerous to release or could be safely resettled.[54] The creation of ARBs brought a new level of formality to the review procedures employed at Guantánamo Bay and increased the likelihood that more releases would occur. Even before the Supreme Court could weigh in, then, litigation helped prompt alterations to the government's detention policies. Supreme Court decisions would soon spawn more policy changes.

## DETAINEE CASES IN THE SUPREME COURT

In late June 2004, the Supreme Court delivered its decisions in the three detention cases. The Bush administration obtained something close to a draw, winning on some crucial points and losing on others. The Supreme Court's rulings led to significant changes in detention policies. The first round of reform following the Court's intervention was undertaken by the executive branch acting alone. But Congress soon got involved as well, passing the first major piece of legislation explicitly dealing with detainees. In this way, the first wave of detention litigation—culminating in the 2004 Supreme Court decisions—not only resulted in substantive policy changes, but also narrowed the scope of presidential discretion. After a brief period of presidential unilateralism immediately following the 9/11 attack, detention policies quickly became subject to the usual push-and-pull of the policy-making process. Buffeted by lawsuits and judicial intervention, policy development in this area resembled the "ongoing, interbranch dialogue" identified by Jeb Barnes and Mark Miller as central to the making of public policy in the United States.[55]

*Rasul v. Bush* was a loss for the Bush administration. In a 6–3 ruling, the Court held that detainees at Guantánamo Bay could challenge their detentions in US courts.[56] Writing for the majority, Justice John Paul Stevens interpreted the federal habeas corpus statute to include Guantánamo Bay. He distinguished the case from *Eisentrager*, claiming that Guantánamo detainees and the World War II detainees in *Eisentrager* differed from one another in key respects: Guantánamo detainees did not hail from nation-states deemed to be at war with the United States; they denied that they were enemy fighters; they had not been charged with any offense and had not been able to challenge their confinement before any sort of tribunal; and they were being held in a place where the United States exercised "plenary and exclusive jurisdiction." Briefly canvassing the history of the writ of habeas corpus, Stevens argued that "plenary and exclusive jurisdiction," not just sovereignty, was sufficient to confer jurisdiction.[57] In a concurring opinion, Justice Anthony Kennedy agreed: Guantánamo Bay was "in every practical respect a United States territory, and . . . one far removed from any hostilities."[58] Kennedy also zeroed in on the details of detention policy, noting that Guantánamo detainees had not received any hearing or "legal proceeding" regarding their status as enemy combatants. And he expressed discomfort with the length of the detentions. While detention without a hearing might be acceptable for a period of weeks or months, Kennedy suggested, these "indefinite" detentions were different.

The ruling provoked a vigorous dissent from Justice Antonin Scalia, which Chief Justice William Rehnquist and Justice Clarence Thomas joined.[59] According to the dissenters, the Court's extension of jurisdiction to Guantánamo violated long-standing precedent. And it was doing so in a highly sensitive area involving wartime military operations, where judges should tread lightly. Justice Scalia thought that unsettling precedents upon which the executive branch relied in fashioning its detention policies amounted to pulling the rug out from under the government on a key matter of national security: "Today, the Court springs a trap on the Executive, subjecting Guantanamo Bay to the oversight of the federal courts even though it has never before been thought to be within their jurisdiction—and thus making it a foolish place to have housed alien wartime detainees."[60] In a nod to the coming spate of lawsuits, the dissent bemoaned the introduction of the "cumbersome machinery of our domestic courts into military affairs."[61]

Though litigation had already indirectly influenced detention policies before *Rasul*, it now appeared that federal judges would be playing a central role in the handling of enemy combatants. But the Supreme Court's decision in *Rasul* left many questions unanswered. These questions included the following: How long could the government hold individuals at Guantánamo as enemy combatants without judicial review? What kind of showing would the government need to make in order to satisfy a judge that an individual at Guantánamo is properly detained as an enemy combatant? Could a different sort of nonjudicial process be substituted in lieu of habeas corpus review in federal court? If Congress amended the federal habeas statute to expressly exclude Guantánamo Bay, what if any recourse to the courts would Guantánamo detainees have? Could they claim a constitutional right to habeas corpus? Would noncitizen detainees held closer to the battlefield, in Afghanistan, also be entitled to judicial review of their detentions? As of mid-2004, then, the Guantánamo litigation yielded clarity on only one very narrow issue: whether noncitizens detained as enemy combatants at Guantánamo Bay had a statutory right to habeas corpus review. The answer was yes, but lots of legal uncertainty remained.

*Hamdi v. Rumsfeld*, handed down the same day, was a different story. Whereas *Rasul* dealt exclusively with a question of jurisdiction, *Hamdi* appeared to contain partial answers to some of the questions left open by *Rasul*. But there was a crucial distinction between the two cases: *Rasul* concerned noncitizens held at Guantánamo Bay, while the *Hamdi* litigation focused on a citizen detained inside the United States. It was therefore far from clear that some of the answers the Court provided in *Hamdi* would apply to the detention of noncitizens at Guantánamo. However, as the following discussion will show, the Bush administration opted for a surprisingly broad application of *Hamdi* that led to significant changes in detention policies at Guantánamo Bay. Many of these changes were not strictly compelled by the Supreme Court's decisions in *Hamdi* and *Rasul*. But those rulings shook up the status quo, generating unpredictable policy responses that reflected, at least in part, a strong desire to stave off further litigation.

The Supreme Court confronted two fundamental questions in the *Hamdi* case.[62] The first was whether a US citizen could be designated an enemy combatant, placed in military custody, and detained without criminal charges. Because five justices answered this in the affirmative, the Court had to answer a second question: what sort of opportunity would a citizen detainee have to receive, pursuant to the due process clause, to challenge his detention? Eight justices—all except Justice Thomas—maintained that the minimal amount of due process given to Hamdi to date was constitutionally insufficient. Thus, the Bush administration won on the first question but lost on the second one.

The controlling opinion, written by Justice Sandra Day O'Connor and joined by Justices Stephen Breyer, Rehnquist, and Kennedy, held that the 2001 AUMF provided legislative authorization for detaining enemy fighters, including citizens. On this point Justice Thomas agreed, providing the crucial fifth vote.[63] In her plurality opinion, Justice O'Connor confined her analysis to the allegations against Hamdi: that he was "'part of or supporting forces hostile to the United States or coalition partners' in Afghanistan" and "had 'engaged in an armed conflict against the United States' there." She concluded that the government could detain an individual who met these criteria. Although the text of the AUMF did not explicitly mention detention, O'Connor reasoned that it was "so fundamental and accepted an incident to war" that it was implicit in the AUMF's grant of "all necessary and appropriate force."[64] The AUMF superseded the Non-Detention Act's bar on detaining citizens. Nor was the indefinite nature of military detention a stumbling block, according to the plurality. The law of war was clear: belligerents could be held until the end of an armed conflict, and the conflict was ongoing.[65]

The plurality opinion then moved to the due process issue. Using a balancing test from a case called *Mathews v. Eldridge*, O'Connor observed that there were extremely significant interests on both sides—Hamdi's interest in liberty versus the government's interest in keeping the country safe.[66] She rejected the district court's approach because it imposed too heavy a burden on the government's security efforts. She also ruled out the position adopted by the government (and accepted by the Fourth Circuit) for being insufficiently protective of Hamdi's rights. Declaring that "a state of war is not a blank check for the President," Justice O'Connor offered a general statement of what was constitutionally required: "We therefore hold that a citizen-detainee seeking to challenge his classification as an enemy combatant must receive notice of the factual basis for his classification, and a fair opportunity to rebut the Government's factual assertions before a neutral decisionmaker."[67]

Similar to the uncertainty generated by *Rasul*, O'Connor's formulation left a host of questions unanswered. How much "notice" would the government have to provide? Could some information be kept from the detainee, on the grounds that revealing it might imperil national security? What constituted a "fair opportunity" to challenge one's classification? Who qualified as a "neutral decisionmaker"? The plurality opinion offered some suggestions. For example, it stated that "enemy combatant proceedings may be tailored to alleviate their uncommon potential to burden the Executive at a time of ongoing military conflict."[68] Hearsay evidence could be allowed in. The government might use a military tribunal instead of an Article III court to conduct these proceedings. The government might benefit from a presumption in favor of its evidence.

Despite these suggestions, much uncertainty remained. And the splintered decision in the case added to the muddle. Justice Thomas objected to the plurality's approach to the due process issue, arguing instead for heavily circumscribed review as endorsed by the Fourth Circuit.[69] Even without Thomas's vote, though, O'Connor's approach to the due process issue garnered a majority, because Justices Ruth Bader Ginsburg and David Souter added their votes to this portion of her opinion. Ginsburg and Souter dissented from the first holding on the grounds that the AUMF did not constitute the sort of "clear congressional authorization" they believed necessary to override the Non-Detention Act.[70] However, because they favored giving Hamdi greater due process than he had received to date, they were willing to support that part of the plurality's opinion, realizing that without their votes there would be no controlling opinion on this point. But they refused to endorse the plurality's suggestions about how the government might tailor detention proceedings to help its cause, leaving those suggestions without clear majority support on the Court. The remaining two justices, Scalia and Stevens, also objected to the government's handling of Hamdi. Like O'Connor, they stressed the importance of the separation of powers. But Scalia and Stevens took a different tack: in a dissenting opinion, they argued that the government had only two options for keeping Hamdi in custody. With a US citizen like Hamdi, the government could either bring criminal charges or suspend the writ of habeas corpus. Anything else was a violation of the Constitution, in their view.

The third detention case, *Rumsfeld v. Padilla*, offered even less clarity than the other two. Unlike Hamdi, Jose Padilla was picked up at O'Hare International Airport as he stepped off an airplane. Could he and Hamdi be handled the same way, or did the location and circumstances of Padilla's capture necessitate different treatment? The Court did not answer this question. Instead, a majority of five justices issued a highly technical ruling, finding that Padilla had filed his habeas corpus petition in the wrong court.[71] The four dissenters objected strenuously to this purely jurisdictional holding, highlighting the case's "profound importance" and proclaiming it the Court's "duty" to reach the merits.[72] The 5–4 ruling in *Padilla* left unresolved whether a citizen taken into custody on US soil could be detained as an enemy combatant. But based on the vote breakdown in *Hamdi* and *Padilla*, it looked like the government might eventually lose on the merits in the latter case. It was obvious, in light of their votes in *Hamdi*, that Justices Scalia, Stevens, Ginsburg, and Souter would rule against the government, and in *Padilla* Justice Breyer provided one of the four dissenting votes—a strong indicator that he harbored objections to Padilla's detention.

By the summer of 2004, lawsuits brought by citizen detainees held inside the United States and noncitizen detainees held at Guantánamo Bay produced a jumble of judicial decisions. Lower court rulings and the specter of additional litigation had already generated momentum for policy change, and there would soon be more reforms undertaken in response to the Supreme Court rulings. Still, many legal questions remained partly or wholly unanswered following the Supreme Court's intervention. Lawsuits would continue to proliferate. The *Rasul* decision promised to unleash a torrent of habeas corpus petitions from Guantánamo Bay. The *Padilla* litigation would restart in a different district court. To comply with the *Hamdi* ruling, the Bush administration would have to give Hamdi and Padilla more due process if the government wished to continue detaining them. And in the meantime, in the face of persistent adversarial legalism and its attendant uncertainty, unpredictability, and delay, policy makers would need to make a number of decisions about how to carry out detentions—not only for those already in custody, but also for any other individuals who might come into custody in the future.

## THE EXECUTIVE BRANCH RESPONDS TO THE SUPREME COURT

With the Supreme Court joining the conversation, the Bush administration's rejoinder was remarkably swift. As noted above, the executive branch had already set up one type of review mechanism, ARBs, while the first wave of detention litigation was ongoing. On July 7, 2004—less than two weeks after the Supreme Court handed down its rulings—Deputy Secretary of Defense Wolfowitz issued an order announcing the creation of a second type of review body, CSRTs.[73] Like ARBs, CSRTs were administrative panels run by the military. But unlike ARBs, which made only prospective assessments about the future dangerousness of each detainee, CSRTs were tasked with a retrospective function. The tribunals would review whether each individual detainee at Guantánamo was properly classified as an enemy combatant. The Wolfowitz order offered the following definition of enemy combatant: "an individual who was part of or supporting Taliban or al Qaeda forces, or associated forces that are engaged in hostilities against the United States or its coalition partners. This includes any person who has committed a belligerent act or has directly supported hostilities in aid of enemy armed forces."[74] Modeled after military hearings for prisoners of war, CSRTs were not designed to adjudicate guilt or innocence in the manner of a criminal proceeding. Rather, they were confined to determining whether an individual was a combatant (who could be subject to continued detention) or a noncombatant (who must be released).[75]

The secretary of the navy, Gordon England, was charged with fleshing out the details for CSRTs. He issued implementing regulations in late July. Although the *Hamdi* ruling ostensibly applied only to citizen detainees, the CSRTs—which would be utilized for noncitizen detainees at Guantánamo—conformed closely with the review process sketched by the *Hamdi* plurality in that case. The Bush administration was going above and beyond what the Court said in its 2004 decisions. Each CSRT would be staffed by three military officers, at least one of whom would be a judge advocate general (JAG).[76] Detainees would not be given a lawyer, but would be assigned a "personal representative"—a member of the military charged with guiding them through the CSRT process. Hearsay and classified evidence were allowed, and the government would receive a presumption in favor of the accuracy of its evidence. Detainees could be present at their hearings and were permitted to call witnesses and produce exculpatory evidence, subject to limitations designed to protect sensitive information. When the government relied on classified information, detainees would be given access to unclassified summaries of it.[77] The standard for upholding an enemy combatant classification was a preponderance of the evidence—a significantly lower bar than the "beyond a reasonable doubt" standard used in criminal cases, but higher than the "some evidence" standard first adopted by Judge Mukasey in the *Padilla* litigation. In response to critics of CSRTs, Secretary England stressed that the tribunals were not meant to function like courts in criminal proceedings. England summed it up this way: "This is a fact-based determination. This isn't guilt or innocence. This is a look at facts. Here's a person: are they, or are they not, an enemy combatant?"[78]

Behind the Bush administration's rapid response to the Supreme Court decisions lay a hope that CSRTs might convince judges to limit their own independent inquiries into detentions.[79] In a world where adversarial legalism was not so entrenched and ubiquitous, perhaps CSRTs would have short-circuited the litigation route and become a substitute for habeas review in the federal courts. The tribunals were, after all, modeled after panels used to review combatant designations in past armed conflicts.[80] But lawyers representing Guantánamo detainees inundated the DC District Court with habeas corpus petitions anyway. They complained that CSRTs were essentially rubber stamps created primarily to allow the government to evade serious review of its detention decisions.[81] The Bush administration countered that CSRTs provided more protections and more rigorous review procedures than the Geneva Conventions contemplated and pointed out that CSRTs were in line with the

*Hamdi* plurality's suggestions.[82] If the procedures sketched by the *Hamdi* plurality were good enough for citizens held on US soil, surely they must be good enough for noncitizens held at Guantánamo Bay. Lawyers for the detainees disagreed, and they began filing lawsuits almost immediately.

In addition to spurring the creation of ARBs and CSRTs, litigation engendered ongoing pressure to release detainees when possible. In October 2004, despite having claimed that he was a dangerous enemy combatant, the Bush administration elected to release Yaser Hamdi to Saudi Arabia rather than continue to defend his detention.[83] In early 2005, Secretary of Defense Rumsfeld issued a memo to other executive branch agencies calling for more releases, and the pace of releases from Guantánamo increased.[84] Rumsfeld and some others inside the executive branch had long favored a policy of fewer detentions and more releases, but that position received a boost from the Supreme Court decisions.[85] The Court rulings had altered the politics of the issue inside the executive branch. As one administration official stated, "It's fair to say that the calculus now is different than what it was before, because the legal landscape has changed and those are factors that might be considered."[86] Each Guantánamo detainee would be able to file a lawsuit and receive his day in court, where the executive branch would be forced to defend its decisions before federal judges.

Furthermore, as Michael Greenberger has noted, detention policy decisions were now also being made in the shadow of the new administrative review procedures.[87] Although some questioned the rigor of CSRTs and CSRTs ultimately found that only a little more than 30 out of approximately 550 detainees had been improperly classified as enemy combatants, their mere existence, alongside ARBs, loomed over current and future detention decisions.[88] The specter of having to endure both kinds of review—review by multiple military panels and by Article III courts—had a significant impact on detention policies. It not only generated an increase in releases from Guantánamo Bay, but also led to fewer detainees being brought to the facility in the first place. By early 2005 more than 200 detainees had left Guantánamo Bay, and the flow of new detainees into the facility slowed to a trickle.[89]

The declining population at Guantánamo did not mean the United States had reduced its detention operations everywhere, however. The Supreme Court's assertion of jurisdiction over detentions at Guantánamo Bay produced an unintended but easily foreseeable consequence: newly captured enemy combatants were increasingly detained somewhere else, with fewer protections than Guantánamo detainees now enjoyed. Many were held overseas by the US military at the American-controlled Bagram detention facility in Afghanistan. Unlike Guantánamo, the Bagram facility appeared safely beyond the reach of the judiciary, at least for the time being.[90]

The CIA's RDI program for high-value detainees was also indirectly affected by the detention litigation and court rulings. The secret CIA program, which later became extremely controversial for employing extraordinarily harsh interrogation practices, arguably rising to the level of torture, apparently had its life extended by the 2004 rulings. According to long-time CIA lawyer John Rizzo, the agency had been looking to jettison its detention responsibilities. But the *Hamdi* and *Rasul* decisions drummed up uncertainty about what sorts of rights or protections the high-value detainees would receive if they were transferred to DOD custody and brought to Guantánamo Bay.[91] Concerned that some of these particularly dangerous detainees might be freed by adverse court rulings, the CIA detention program continued.

## CONCLUSION

The United States responded to the 9/11 terrorist attack by using military force against those deemed to have participated in the plot or to have harbored those responsible for it. These combat operations led to the capture and detention of hundreds of individuals suspected of being part of or fighting alongside enemy forces. Initially, determinations about the status of these individuals were made by the executive branch, which was subject to little or no oversight and possessed virtually unlimited discretion. But litigation quickly altered this state of affairs. A number of district and circuit court judges were open to innovative legal arguments and willing to break with a long-standing tradition of judicial deference to the executive in wartime. With lower courts issuing a complicated hodgepodge of rulings, the Bush administration began to institute enhanced screening and review procedures for detentions.

The procedures, informal and ad hoc at first, became increasingly formalized as detention litigation progressed through the courts. Before the Supreme Court found the federal habeas corpus statute applicable to Guantánamo Bay, the executive branch had already created ARBs. Following the Court's *Rasul* and *Hamdi* decisions, the Bush administration erected a second layer of review via CSRTs. These two institutions introduced more decision makers and more checks into the detention process, reducing the president's control over detention policies. The impending involvement of federal judges through habeas corpus proceedings promised to further limit presidential authority. Judicial intervention—already present, as we have seen, from the very beginning of the war—was about to deepen considerably. Those worried about indefinite detentions by presidential fiat could rest easier. Even in the early stages of the war, presidential power was constrained.[92]

The policy outcomes that emerged from this flurry of lawsuits, court decisions, and responses to these court decisions embodied a complex array of costs and benefits for both suspected enemy fighters and the government trying to neutralize them. Yaser Hamdi and approximately two hundred detainees released from Guantánamo Bay had reason to cheer, while the government that let them go may have harbored fears that some would later pose a security threat. For detainees held elsewhere, however—and for individuals who might enter US custody or arouse government suspicion sometime in the future—the consequences were quite different. Detention at Guantánamo and inside the United States was now a more arduous endeavor for the US government. Facing multiple layers of review and the potential for years of litigation, policy makers had strong incentives to find other places to house detainees. A greater share of detentions were conducted overseas, where detainees would face worse conditions, receive less attention, and enjoy fewer protections than detainees held at Guantánamo Bay or on American soil.

Key features of adversarial legalism were on display throughout the first three years of the war on terror. Entrepreneurial legal advocacy on behalf of highly unpopular plaintiffs—not garden-variety criminals, but suspected terrorists, including noncitizens—received a surprisingly warm reception in some courts. Judges seriously entertained novel legal arguments, showed lots of flexibility, and acted in unpredictable ways. The litigation moved slowly in volleys between district court and circuit court judges, before eventually reaching the Supreme Court. Delay and legal uncertainty prevailed throughout this period, and even the Supreme Court's first crack at the issues resulted in little clarity, setting the stage for further litigation. Still, by late 2004, lawsuits and court decisions had wrought significant changes in detention policies. They made the government's job at Guantánamo more difficult, giving scores of detainees their freedom and others who remained there enhanced protections. They circumscribed the president's powers over the handling of enemy combatants. And they incentivized the government to detain other individuals in different locations under different rules and procedures. But legal challenges and judicial involvement in the war on terror were just beginning.

# 2. Detaining Enemy Combatants amid Legal Uncertainty (2005–2008)

The initial policy responses to detention litigation were, as we have seen, centered in the executive branch. Administrative review boards (ARBs) and combatant status review tribunals (CSRTs) were created through administrative regulations. This chapter moves the story forward by examining developments in detention policies during the second half of the Bush administration, beginning with the flood of habeas corpus petitions in the DC District Court. Judges had their hands full right away, entertaining dozens of habeas corpus petitions from Guantánamo Bay in late 2004 and early 2005. Then in December 2005 Congress joined the fray, passing a law called the Detainee Treatment Act (DTA). In part a response to the Supreme Court's decision in *Rasul v. Bush*, the DTA made two key changes to detention policies. First, it amended the federal habeas corpus statute to override the Supreme Court's statutory interpretation in *Rasul.* But even as it stripped habeas jurisdiction over Guantánamo, Congress was unwilling to remove the judiciary entirely from detention matters. The DTA established a review process for CSRT decisions in the US Court of Appeals for the District of Columbia Circuit.

Although the DTA had something to say about detention, it was far from a comprehensive statute. Many of the questions left unanswered by the Supreme Court's 2004 rulings were still unanswered after Congress legislated. The interbranch back-and-forth over detention policies persisted. Now, it was Congress and the courts engaged in a contentious tug-of-war over the reach and scope of habeas corpus. Litigation also continued, and the detainee population at Guantánamo kept shrinking. Very few new detainees were brought to Guantánamo during the second half of the Bush presidency. Among the handful of exceptions were a group of high-value detainees formerly held in CIA custody, including 9/11 mastermind Khalid Sheikh Mohammed. That group came to Guantánamo largely as a result of a 2006 Supreme Court decision—another example of judicial intervention producing policy change. But with combat operations ongoing, the number of newly captured individuals held in US custody in Afghanistan swelled.

It was not until June 2008 that the Supreme Court finally brought some clarity to the legal situation at Guantánamo Bay. *Boumediene v. Bush* became the starkest example yet of the judiciary's assertiveness in wartime. In a 5–4 ruling, the Court held that the Constitution itself guarantees habeas corpus rights at Guantánamo Bay. And it struck down the detention review mechanisms established by Congress and the executive branch, on the grounds that they were an inadequate substitute for habeas corpus. *Boumediene* said almost nothing about how those habeas corpus proceedings should play out, however. Questions about the scope of the government's detention authority, the standard of review, the treatment of evidence, and many other issues were left unresolved. Answers would emerge, not through edicts from the Supreme Court, a comprehensive piece of legislation from Congress, or detailed executive branch regulations, but from federal judges on the US District Court for the District of Columbia and the DC Circuit Court of Appeals. These judges handled scores of lawsuits over a period of several years, becoming key actors in the policy-making process.[1] Detention operations at the Guantánamo Bay detention camp continued under the cloud of litigation, but that facility was increasingly confined to housing detainees brought there in the early years of the war. By the end of George W. Bush's second term, presidential discretion over detention had been narrowed even further.

## HABEAS CORPUS LITIGATION IN THE DC DISTRICT COURT

Habeas corpus petitions from detainees held at Guantánamo Bay inundated the DC District Court immediately after the Supreme Court's decision in *Rasul v. Bush.* In early 2005, a pair of rulings from two different judges reached diametrically opposed conclusions on a number of key issues. The first of these rulings came in a case called *Khalid v. Bush.*[2] At issue were habeas petitions from seven Guantánamo detainees, six of whom had been captured in Bosnia and one of whom had been captured in Pakistan. Judge Richard Leon sided with the government in sweeping terms. He rejected the petitioners' argument that individuals captured in places other than Afghanistan could not be detained under the 2001 Authorization for Use of Military Force (AUMF), noting that the statute did not contain geographical limits on the use of force. Giving the Supreme Court's *Rasul* decision an extremely narrow reading, Judge Leon held that there was "no viable legal theory" under which the detainees might win their challenges.[3] Their claim that their constitutional rights were being violated was denied; relying heavily on the World War II–era case *Johnson v. Eisentrager*, Judge Leon concluded that the petitioners had no constitutional rights because they were nonresident aliens captured and held outside of sovereign US territory. There was no need to go further and delve into the factual issues surrounding each detainee's challenge. Under this highly deferential approach, Judge Leon granted the government's motion to dismiss the habeas corpus petitions.

Less than two weeks later, District Judge Joyce Hens Green issued a decision completely at odds with her colleague's ruling in *Khalid*.[4] The case before Judge Green, *In re Guantánamo Detainee Cases*, featured a slew of habeas petitions brought on behalf of more than fifty Guantánamo detainees. The petitions had been consolidated for the sake of efficiency and uniformity, and Judge Green was tasked with deciding the legal questions common to these various lawsuits. Initially, the post-*Rasul* influx of habeas petitions was spread out across eight different district court judges, but each of these judges—except Judge Leon, who refused to relinquish *Khalid*—agreed to turn the common legal questions over to a single judge.

At the heart of the case was the same question Judge Leon had confronted: how to construe the Supreme Court's decision in *Rasul*. Judge Leon gave it the narrowest of readings, arguing that *Rasul* extended only statutory habeas jurisdiction, and not constitutional rights, to Guantánamo Bay. Judge Green, after bemoaning the Supreme Court's vagueness, settled on a much broader interpretation of the decision. In her view, *Rasul* was best read to grant Guantánamo detainees "enforceable constitutional rights," including a Fifth Amendment right to due process.[5] Having reached this conclusion, Judge Green then had to address the government's contention that if the Fifth Amendment due process clause applied, CSRTs satisfied its requirements without the need for independent review by a federal court. In this portion of her opinion, Judge Green relied heavily on Justice Sandra Day O'Connor's plurality opinion in *Hamdi*, which had mandated that citizen detainees receive notice of the facts surrounding their enemy combatant classification and a meaningful chance to rebut that classification before a neutral decision maker. Although the detainees in the case before her were noncitizens, Judge Green applied the test anyway and held that CSRTs came up short. The primary problem was the government's reliance on classified evidence that detainees could not see, and thus could not adequately rebut. In Judge Green's view, the unclassified summaries of evidence that CSRTs provided to detainees were insufficient, particularly in light of detainees' lack of access to a lawyer.

Judge Green's opinion expressed other misgivings about the government's detention policies. She expressed discomfort with the indefinite length of detentions. She worried about CSRTs using evidence obtained involuntarily through the use of coercive interrogation methods. She also drew attention to the formal definition of enemy combatant promulgated by DOD in its orders creating CSRTs: "an individual who was part of or supporting Taliban or al-Qaeda forces, or associated forces that are engaged in hostilities against the United States or its coalition partners. This includes any person who has committed a belligerent act or has directly supported hostilities in aid of enemy armed forces."[6] Judge Green criticized this definition for being significantly broader than the definition considered and endorsed by the Supreme Court in the *Hamdi* case. There, the plurality confined itself to deciding that an individual who was "part of or supporting forces hostile to the United States or coalition partners' in Afghanistan and who 'engaged in an armed conflict against the United States' there" could be detained as an enemy combatant.[7] DOD's subsequent definition was more expansive: it included "associated forces," and it was not limited to individuals who fought against the United States in Afghanistan. Finally, Judge Green found fault with CSRTs for not affording alleged Taliban fighters all the protections she determined the Geneva Conventions required.

It is difficult to imagine a better example of adversarial legalism's tendency to produce unpredictable outcomes and legal uncertainty. Two judges—serving on the same court, deciding the same issues at the same time—handed down rulings that were poles apart. The dueling decisions in *Khalid* and *In re Guantánamo* were swiftly appealed, with the DC Circuit Court slated to hear oral argument in late summer of 2005. Against this backdrop, the Bush administration proceeded with its efforts to winnow down the population at Guantánamo. But even the administration's attempts to release detainees were affected by litigation. In March 2005, DC District Court judge Gladys Kessler blocked the repatriation of a group of Yemeni detainees who feared being mistreated upon returning to their home country. Though ostensibly motivated by concern for the detainees' well-being, the ruling had the effect of prolonging their indefinite confinement at Guantánamo.[8] And it added yet another legal consideration to policy makers' detention calculus. Another stream of litigation began shortly thereafter, challenging the government's use of force-feeding procedures to combat detainee hunger strikes.[9] As all of this Guantánamo litigation inched forward, Congress got involved.

## CONGRESS TAKES ITS SEAT AT THE TABLE

The Detainee Treatment Act (DTA) represented Congress's first clear attempt to shape detention policies. Until the enactment of the DTA in December 2005, Congress's main contribution had been the 2001 AUMF. At most, that brief statute only implicitly authorized the detention of enemy combatants: its vague grant of "all necessary and appropriate force" was interpreted by the executive branch to include detention, and the Supreme Court endorsed this construction of the AUMF in *Hamdi.* Because Congress did not amend the law, the Court's interpretation prevailed. The details of detention policy had emerged from a back-and-forth between the executive branch and the courts, and for years Congress remained on the sidelines.

That changed in the summer of 2005. Lawmakers began debating a measure that would first and foremost limit the use of certain harsh interrogation techniques on individuals in US custody. These interrogation techniques—some of which appeared to many observers to rise to the level of torture—had been exposed in the media and generated widespread controversy. The backlash included members of President Bush's own party—most notably the influential Republican senator from Arizona, John McCain, himself a victim of torture during the Vietnam War. After months of debate, the DTA passed and was signed into law on December 30, 2005.[10] The lion's share of attention was focused on the DTA's prohibition of "cruel, inhuman, or degrading treatment or punishment" and President Bush's provocative signing statement indicating that his authority as commander in chief might permit him to override the statutory limits in certain circumstances.

Less noticed and commented on were the DTA's provisions dealing with detention. The first way in which the DTA reshaped detention policies was by purporting to strip the federal courts of their jurisdiction over Guantánamo Bay. The DTA stated that "no court, justice, or judge shall have jurisdiction to hear or consider . . . an application for a writ of habeas corpus filed by or on behalf of an alien detained by the Department of Defense at Guantanamo Bay."[11] This language sought to overturn the Supreme Court's ruling in *Rasul v. Bush* that the federal habeas statute extended to Guantánamo. But it did not settle the matter once and for all. As we will soon see, the provision spawned more litigation—over whether the jurisdiction strip applied to lawsuits filed prior to the DTA's enactment, and also whether habeas corpus rights at Guantánamo were guaranteed by the Constitution itself, in which case the jurisdiction-stripping provision might be unconstitutional.

The removal of jurisdiction, if upheld, would have reduced the role of litigation and court decisions in detention matters. But Congress was unwilling to completely remove judges from the detention process. Although the DTA attempted to cut off one litigation pathway, it substituted another pathway in its place. Scholars have documented many instances in which Congress has aided and abetted the turn to courts in the policy-making process.[12] That this occurred on a key matter of national security policy in wartime—and with the president's own party in control of Congress—is further evidence of the strength of this phenomenon. Prior to passage of the DTA, reviews of CSRT determinations occurred entirely within the executive branch. Rather than continue with this system, Congress elected to introduce judicial review of CSRT decisions. The DC Circuit Court of Appeals would review "any final decision" in which a CSRT concluded that a detainee was an enemy combatant.

As for the scope of that review, the DTA was unclear. It declared that review would be limited to two questions. First, the court would decide whether a CSRT decision "was consistent with the standards and procedures specified by the Secretary of Defense for Combatant Status Review Tribunals."[13] This sounded like the review would be heavily circumscribed, focused only on ensuring that the proper procedures had been followed. But second—and more ambiguously—the act also stated that the court would consider the following: "to the extent the Constitution and laws of the United States are applicable, whether the use of such standards and procedures to make the determination is consistent with the Constitution and laws of the United States."[14] These phrases arguably augured a somewhat more expansive role for judicial review. Litigation regarding the appropriate scope of review began shortly after the DTA's enactment.

This was not all the DTA had to say regarding the administrative review mechanisms established by the executive branch in 2004. The legislation mandated that Congress receive a report outlining the procedures for both CSRTs and ARBs. It also briefly addressed the use of evidence obtained through coercion in these proceedings, permitting CSRTs and ARBs to consider this sort of evidence if it had "probative value." This piece of the law was controversial, but some Democrats who reluctantly supported its inclusion used the new judicial review process for cover. Asked about the coercion provision in an interview,

Senator Carl Levin (D-MI) insisted that DC Circuit judges reviewing CSRT determinations could be trusted to discount this kind of evidence: "I don't think courts will allow coerced evidence in any proceeding."[15]

The passage of the DTA was an important moment in interbranch relations in the war on terror. For the first time since 2001, Congress passed a law dealing with military operations. And the DTA was far more detailed than the AUMF, offering clearer support for the detention of enemy combatants and shaping the process surrounding the use of that policy tool. In doing so, the DTA further constricted the sphere of presidential authority over detention policies. But the DTA was also notable for what it did *not* do. It offered no clarity on the fundamental question of who could be designated an enemy combatant and detained. It left ARBs and CSRTs in place with no adjustments. It offered only vague guidance for DC Circuit judges now charged with reviewing enemy combatant classifications. On a variety of issues related to detention, Congress was content to punt to executive branch officials and federal judges.

## CONGRESS AND THE COURTS CONTINUE THEIR COLLOQUY

As legislative debate over what became the DTA was unfolding, the habeas litigation moved forward. The pair of DC District Court cases decided in early 2005—*Khalid v. Bush* and *In re Guantánamo Detainee Cases*—had been consolidated before the DC Circuit Court of Appeals. Oral argument in the case, now called *Boumediene v. Bush*, occurred in September 2005.[16] But before the court could rule, the litigation was delayed by developments in Congress and the Supreme Court. The passage of the DTA was the first intervening event: the statutory language removing habeas corpus jurisdiction over Guantánamo Bay put the status of ongoing detention litigation into doubt. Then, in June 2006, the Supreme Court decided *Hamdan v. Rumsfeld*, a case challenging the legality of military commissions—the special tribunals created by executive order shortly after 9/11 to prosecute certain detainees for committing war crimes. Although the *Hamdan* litigation did not directly concern detention policy, it had important implications for it once the DTA became law.

The *Hamdan* lawsuit was brought on behalf of a Guantánamo detainee named Salim Hamdan, one of the first individuals to be charged in a military commission (see chapter 4). Hamdan argued that the commission system was illegal, and in late 2004 the DC District Court agreed. That decision was reversed by the DC Circuit in the summer of 2005, and the Supreme Court agreed to hear the case in November of that year. The Detainee Treatment Act's jurisdiction-stripping provisions added a new question to the case: could Hamdan's legal challenge even be entertained? In a 5–3 ruling, the Court held that the DTA did not prevent it from deciding the case.[17] The Court then ruled that the Bush administration's version of military commissions was unlawful. These holdings had significant consequences for detention at Guantánamo Bay. The Court interpreted the DTA's removal of jurisdiction as applying only to future lawsuits, not lawsuits already filed at the time of the DTA's enactment, meaning that scores of habeas corpus petitions filed after the *Rasul* decision but before the DTA could move forward. And with military commissions at least temporarily off the table, detention would be an attractive alternative.

This state of affairs was short-lived. Congress quickly resumed its volley with the Court, responding to the *Hamdan* ruling by passing another statute: the 2006 Military Commissions Act (MCA).[18] Signed into law less than four months after *Hamdan*, the MCA was primarily concerned with establishing a reformed system of military commissions. But it had something to say about detention as well. For the second time, Congress responded to a Supreme Court decision by revoking habeas jurisdiction over Guantánamo Bay. And this time the text of the legislation made it abundantly clear that the jurisdiction-stripping provisions applied to all lawsuits, pending and future. Republican lawmakers had argued that the litigation unleashed by *Rasul* would have deleterious consequences for the military's warfighting efforts.[19] Now, with the MCA, Congress appeared to have realized its objective: no more legal challenges from Guantánamo Bay.

This was not the end of the matter, though. Congress's unambiguous removal of statutory habeas jurisdiction merely replaced the statutory question with the underlying constitutional question: did the Constitution itself extend habeas corpus rights to Guantánamo Bay? In both *Rasul* and *Hamdan*, the Supreme Court grounded its rulings in statutory interpretation. By twice holding that laws passed by Congress allowed legal challenges to proceed, the Court avoided addressing the other argument advanced by Guantánamo detainees: that the Suspension Clause in Article I, Section 9, of the Constitution provided another source of habeas rights for individuals held at Guantánamo Bay. The Suspension Clause reads: "The Privilege of the Writ of Habeas Corpus shall not be suspended, unless when in Cases of Rebellion or Invasion the public

Safety may require it."[20] Whether this privilege extended to noncitizen wartime detainees at Guantánamo remained an open question, and it took two more years of litigation to provide an answer.

Amid this persistent legal uncertainty, the Bush administration continued to calibrate its detention operations. The transfer of new detainees to Guantánamo had already slowed to a crawl after the Supreme Court's first set of detention decisions in 2004. In May 2006—one month before the Court decided *Hamdan v. Rumsfeld*—President Bush spoke publicly about closing Guantánamo. The prospect had been raised repeatedly in internal executive branch discussions, but now it became the stated position of the administration. Bush announced his desire to "close the camp and put the prisoners on trial."[21] But even as the administration seemed to be pivoting away from the prolonged military detention option at Guantánamo, the detainee population in Afghanistan continued to climb. The Bagram detention facility—initially intended to function as a temporary screening area, not a long-term detention camp—kept expanding. By early 2006, the United States was detaining over five hundred individuals there. Untouched by lawsuits and court rulings, Bagram was an attractive place to house detainees. And with human rights groups and the media largely fixated on Guantánamo, detention overseas received scant attention.[22]

This lack of attention was perplexing, since the situation for detainees held at Bagram was indisputably worse than the situation for detainees held at Guantánamo Bay. After all, even if Congress succeeded in denying Guantánamo detainees habeas corpus hearings, detainees could still avail themselves of two review mechanisms: the CSRT process, which after the DTA now included at least a limited review by an Article III court, and an ARB assessing their prospective dangerousness. Bagram was a different story: there were review bodies called enemy combatant review boards (ECRBs), but these offered detainees significantly fewer protections. Unlike Guantánamo detainees, Bagram detainees did not have access to representatives to help them challenge their enemy combatant designations. In fact, the detainees themselves were not even involved in the ECRB process. Moreover, unlike CSRTs—which allowed detainees and their representatives to see summaries of classified evidence—ECRBs could utilize secret evidence without a detainee's knowledge.[23] Bagram also featured less transparency than Guantánamo Bay. In early 2006, litigation under the Freedom of Information Act (FOIA) yielded a district court order for the executive branch to release the names of Guantánamo detainees.[24] Rather than appeal, DOD complied.[25] FOIA litigation also generated disclosures about CSRT proceedings.[26] These developments were limited to Guantánamo Bay.

In spite of all this, Guantánamo did receive a new group of detainees in September 2006. President Bush announced the transfer of fourteen high-value detainees—including 9/11 mastermind Khalid Sheikh Mohammed—from CIA custody to DOD custody at Guantánamo Bay. There had been internal executive branch debates about doing this in 2005, with Condoleezza Rice, now the secretary of state, leading the effort. For a while she was successfully opposed by Vice President Dick Cheney, who favored keeping the CIA program as secret as possible, and Secretary of Defense Rumsfeld, who did not relish the idea of his department assuming responsibility for these detainees.[27] But the Supreme Court's *Hamdan* decision gave Rice the upper hand.[28]

President Bush's speech announcing the detainee transfer made clear that the *Hamdan* decision and the threat of additional litigation was a key factor in the move.[29] To see why, it is necessary to briefly examine part of the majority opinion in *Hamdan v. Rumsfeld*.[30] In a long and convoluted opinion, the *Hamdan* majority had concluded over the Bush administration's objection that a portion of the Geneva Conventions known as Common Article 3 applied to the war with al-Qaeda. In addition to barring torture, Common Article 3 includes more capacious language prohibiting "outrages upon personal dignity, in particular humiliating and degrading treatment."[31] As President Bush noted, this vague passage might be construed by judges to prohibit aspects of the CIA program. Bush said: "Some believe our military and intelligence personnel involved in capturing and questioning terrorists could now be at risk of prosecution under the War Crimes Act simply for doing their jobs in a thorough and professional way." He implored Congress to clarify matters in legislation so that the CIA's detention and interrogation program could continue, but in the meantime he announced its suspension.[32] Once again, a judicial decision cast a long shadow over detention policies. *Hamdan*'s direct effects on detention were significant, but so too were its more indirect ripple effects—and the prospect of more litigation to come.

## THE JUDICIARY'S SHADOW GROWS

The interbranch colloquy over detention policies did not end with Congress's enactment of the MCA in October 2006. On the heels of this legislative development the DC Circuit finally decided the consolidated Guantánamo detention case, *Boumediene v. Bush. Boumediene* had been put on hold during the lengthy DTA-*Hamdan*-MCA sequence described above.[33] The ruling came down in February 2007—more than a year and a half after it was first argued, and more than two years after DC District Court judges Leon and Green issued their divergent rulings. After another round of briefs and oral argument following the MCA's passage, the DC Circuit panel voted 2–1 to dismiss the habeas petitions for lack of jurisdiction.

Writing for himself and Judge David Sentelle, Judge A. Raymond Randolph held that the Constitution's Suspension Clause did not apply at Guantánamo Bay. Therefore, Congress was free to revoke statutory habeas jurisdiction without formally suspending the writ of habeas corpus. Judge Randolph's treatment of the issue began with a foray into the history of the writ's reach. Canvassing British history, he could find no clear example of the writ of habeas corpus being extended to "aliens beyond the Crown's dominions." Randolph concluded that the writ at the time of the Constitution's enactment would not have reached "aliens without presence or property within the United States."[34] The detainees at Guantánamo Bay fell into that category. Randolph also cited *Eisentrager* as foreclosing the possibility that noncitizens "without presence or property" in the United States possessed constitutional rights. Access to the writ, due process under the Fifth Amendment, other provisions of the Bill of Rights—none of these applied extraterritorially to noncitizens, the majority held. As for the detainees' argument that American control over Guantánamo was functionally equivalent to sovereignty, Randolph maintained that sovereignty determinations were exclusively the prerogative of the elected branches. And the Guantánamo lease agreement stated that "ultimate sovereignty" would remain with Cuba. For these reasons, the majority concluded that the habeas petitions had to be dismissed.

In her dissenting opinion, Judge Judith Rogers took issue with the majority's construction of the Suspension Clause and alleged that it had misread the Supreme Court's *Rasul* decision.[35] Finding a "paucity of direct precedent" on the reach of the Suspension Clause, she highlighted some historical examples and portions of the *Rasul* opinion that appeared to offer a broader understanding of the writ. Though *Rasul* was a statutory decision, Judge Rogers thought the Court's analysis was applicable to the constitutional question as well. Concluding that the writ ran to Guantánamo as a matter of constitutional law, Rogers argued that the MCA's removal of jurisdiction violated the

Constitution. Congress needed either to formally suspend habeas corpus or to provide an "adequate alternative," and in her view it had done neither.

Judge Rogers delved into the details of detention policy to make her point. She insisted that the review scheme created by the elected branches—CSRTs followed by review in the DC Circuit—was an insufficient substitute for habeas review. In her view, the existing review mechanisms created "a series of hurdles while saddling each Guantanamo detainee with an assortment of handicaps that make the obstacles insurmountable."[36] She was troubled by the presumption in favor of the government's enemy combatant classifications, the detainees' lack of access to lawyers, and the government's ability to use classified information or information obtained through coercion. She also worried that military officials might be susceptible to "command influence" when making decisions, expressing instead her preference for independent, impartial judges. And although Congress had integrated DC Circuit review into the CSRT process, Judge Rogers thought the scope of review granted to the DC Circuit was too limited. The Rogers dissent in *Boumediene* revealed continued deep divisions within the judiciary on the underlying legal issues surrounding detention policies at Guantánamo Bay. Rather than providing clarity, the MCA's removal of jurisdiction merely altered the legal questions at the heart of the litigation. Judges were forced from the statutory plane to the constitutional plane, but the disagreements on display in previous cases persisted.

Having lost in the DC Circuit, lawyers for the Guantánamo detainees appealed to the Supreme Court. In April 2007, the Court voted against hearing the case.[37] The denial of certiorari produced a rare written dissent from Justices Stephen Breyer, Ruth Bader Ginsburg, and David Souter, who believed the case demanded the Court's "immediate attention."[38] Noting that the detainees had been in custody for more than five years without judicial review, the dissenters thought the detainees deserved to know as soon as possible whether or not they were entitled to habeas corpus. Deciding the case would reduce the legal uncertainty surrounding Guantánamo's status. The Court was just one vote shy of the four necessary to grant certiorari. Despite siding with Guantánamo detainees in *Rasul* and *Hamdan*, Justices John Paul Stevens and Anthony Kennedy demurred, and they too took the unusual step of explaining their position in writing. In their view, the Court ought to stay its hand until "the exhaustion of available remedies." In other words, detainees should first avail themselves of the review procedures in the DTA. Stevens and Kennedy did qualify their stance, however: if the DTA process resulted in unreasonable delay or "some other and ongoing injury," they might reverse themselves.

As it turned out, the reversal happened quickly. Two and a half months after declining the case, the Court suddenly added *Boumediene v. Bush* to its docket. Justices Stevens and Kennedy changed their votes. They did so without explanation, but many observers surmised that heightened criticism of the CSRT process accounted for the shift.[39] When lawyers for the detainees asked the Court to reconsider its denial of review, they cited disparaging public statements from a military intelligence officer who worked on CSRTs. The officer, Stephen Abraham, suggested that senior military officials made it known that they favored swift CSRT rulings upholding detentions. He also expressed uneasiness with the quality of evidence used in CSRTs.[40]

The Court's about-face unsettled the detention policy landscape once again. In April 2007, it looked as if Guantánamo detentions would be subject to the DTA review process of CSRTs followed by DC Circuit review. But by June of that same year, it seemed quite possible that the highest court in the country would invalidate that entire scheme. In the face of this uncertainty, the elected branches appeared stuck. The executive branch remained internally divided over the issue. Rumsfeld's replacement at DOD, Robert Gates, favored closing Guantánamo. One of Gates's first moves as secretary of defense was to reject a proposal that would have updated and expanded facilities at Guantánamo.[41] Those who wished to keep Guantánamo open included Vice President Cheney, Attorney General Alberto Gonzales, and other administration lawyers who feared that closing the facility might create even more legal headaches for the administration.

As internal executive branch debates continued, Congress—now controlled by Democrats, following the 2006 midterm elections—discussed legislation that would have authorized the closure of Guantánamo and the transfer of detainees to US soil. Opponents of closure in Congress and in the executive branch expressed concern that the move would generate even more litigation and might result in courts granting the detainees additional rights.[42] The Democratic Congress also attempted to restore statutory habeas corpus jurisdiction over Guantánamo Bay.[43] Both legislative efforts failed. With a major Supreme Court ruling now on the horizon, the status quo at Guantánamo persisted. Very few new detainees were brought to the facility, and movement out of the facility continued. By January 2008, the Bush administration had released nearly five hundred detainees, bringing the population at Guantánamo under three hundred. Meanwhile, the population at the Bagram detention complex in Afghanistan—which had held fewer than one hundred detainees in 2004—was now more than double that.[44]

As inertia prevailed in the elected branches, the judiciary remained an active player. In July 2007—just one month after the Supreme Court agreed to hear *Boumediene*—the DC Circuit Court of Appeals issued its first-ever decision in a CSRT appeal under the DTA. *Bismullah v. Gates* concerned eight Guantánamo detainees whose enemy combatant designations were upheld by CSRTs. Before the DC Circuit could get to the merits, it had to rule on a procedural matter: how much information should the court have access to when reviewing CSRT determinations?[45] A unanimous panel rejected the government's argument that it ought to confine itself to the evidence presented in the CSRT proceedings. Instead, the DC Circuit demanded access to any additional relevant information in the government's possession. The panel also sided with the detainees on a second procedural issue, ruling that their lawyers enjoyed a presumption in favor of access to classified information.

The holdings in *Bismullah I* were rooted in a broad interpretation of the DTA's review provisions. The DTA instructed the DC Circuit to evaluate whether the "standards and procedures" for CSRTs had been followed—language that arguably described a more limited form of review than the one ordered by the *Bismullah I* panel. When the government asked the panel to reconsider, citing the burdens it would face, the panel unanimously denied the request in *Bismullah II*.[46] The government argued that it would have enormous difficulty producing the amount of information the court had demanded, because it had not retained all of the information when it conducted CSRT hearings years earlier. Why didn't the executive branch hold on to the information? There was a simple answer: it had no way of knowing it would later need it. CSRTs were established in July 2004, but it wasn't until a year and a half later that Congress created DC Circuit review of CSRT decisions. By that time CSRTs for hundreds of detainees had already been completed. Bush administration officials could not have known to prepare for judicial review that did not yet exist.

The *Bismullah II* panel was sympathetic to the government's plight but unwilling to budge. The judges reiterated their view that, under the terms of the DTA, they would need to see all of the government's information on each detainee, not just the information introduced in CSRT proceedings. Otherwise, the court could not be sure that no exculpatory evidence was left out and that the preponderance-of-the-evidence standard was met. If the government could not produce all of this preexisting information, the panel suggested another way forward: the Bush administration could arrange for a new round of CSRT hearings, this time retaining all of the information collected during the process. The panel wrote, "In summary, the record on review must include all the Government Information. . . . If the Government did not preserve that entire body of information with respect to a particular petitioner, then it will have either to reassemble the Government Information it did collect or to convene a new CSRT, taking care this time to retain all the Government Information."[47]

Running a new round of CSRTs would be a massive undertaking. The Bush administration elected to continue litigating the matter instead.[48] In February 2008, the full DC Circuit declined to rehear the case.[49] The vote was 5–5, one vote short of the majority required to trigger en banc review. In an unusual turn of events, the denial produced five written opinions signaling deep divisions among the judges regarding the proper contours of review under the DTA. The most noteworthy of the five opinions in *Bismullah III* was Judge A. Raymond Randolph's dissent from the denial, joined by Judges David Sentelle, Brett Kavanaugh, and Karen LeCraft Henderson. Citing affidavits from national security officials arguing that the *Bismullah* decisions would severely hinder their work, the dissent declared that the prior panel decisions were disastrous and would threaten national security.

In response to Randolph's blistering dissent, Judge Douglas Ginsburg—the author of *Bismullah I* and *II*—reiterated his position. Because CSRT officials were tasked with picking and choosing which pieces of information were relevant and worth forwarding for use in a CSRT proceeding, Ginsburg reasoned that it would be impossible to conduct meaningful judicial review without access to the information that CSRT officials chose *not* to pass along. Ginsburg also argued that CSRTs, unlike criminal proceedings or administrative agency proceedings, were not "open and adversarial" but rather "closed and accusatorial."[50] Detainees did not have lawyers, had only limited access to evidence against them, and would not be able confront witnesses. And instead of "an independent decisionmaker," CSRT members were "employed and chosen by the detainee's accuser."[51] All of these factors supported the prior panel rulings, according to Judge Ginsburg.

On the surface, *Bismullah III* was a dispute about how broadly or narrowly to interpret the judicial review provisions in the Detainee Treatment Act. But at its core were more fundamental disagreements over the proper role of the courts in detention matters. Those disagreements had been playing out for several years now across all three levels of the judiciary. But an additional factor influenced the DC Circuit's decision to deny rehearing in the *Bismullah* case: the Supreme Court's calendar. Oral argument in *Boumediene v. Bush* had already taken place, and some DC Circuit judges expressed concern that rehearing *Bismullah* might cause the Supreme Court to delay a decision in *Boumediene*.[52]

The concern was understandable. The two lines of litigation were closely linked. After all, if the Supreme Court found in *Boumediene* that the constitutional writ of habeas corpus extended to Guantánamo Bay, it would then have to decide whether the DTA review process represented an adequate substitute for habeas corpus review. And the fate of the *Bismullah* litigation might seriously impact the Court's calculation on that latter point, because the issue at the heart of *Bismullah* was how robust judicial review pursuant to the DTA should be. As Linda Greenhouse noted, there was a paradoxical relationship between the two cases: if the Supreme Court agreed to hear *Bismullah* and sided with the detainees (and the DC Circuit panel decisions) in favor of searching judicial review, it could actually undercut the detainees' argument in *Boumediene* that CSRTs and DC Circuit review under the DTA were an inadequate substitute for habeas corpus. On the other hand, if the Court sided with the government in *Bismullah* by limiting the scope of DTA review, it would weaken the government's argument in *Boumediene* that CSRTs and DTA review provided a sufficient replacement for habeas review.[53]

## THE SUPREME COURT DECIDES *BOUMEDIENE V. BUSH*

The Supreme Court declined to hear *Bismullah*, and on June 12, 2008, the Court handed down its decision in *Boumediene v. Bush*.[54] In a 5–4 ruling, the Court held that noncitizen detainees at Guantánamo Bay were entitled to habeas corpus hearings under the US Constitution absent formal suspension of the writ, which had not occurred. The Court also held that the existing DTA review scheme for detentions was an insufficient substitute for habeas review. Justice Kennedy wrote the majority opinion, joined by Justices Stevens, Ginsburg, Souter, and Breyer. The first part of Kennedy's opinion focused on the history and significance of the writ of habeas corpus. According to Kennedy, habeas corpus was a crucial component of the constitutional framework. He cast it first and foremost as a safeguard for the separation of powers: by requiring the executive to justify deprivations of liberty before a judge, habeas corpus served as a check on executive power.

The majority opinion scanned history for parallels to the current situation at Guantánamo Bay. Declaring that there were no obvious answers regarding the writ's precise reach, Kennedy pivoted to Guantánamo. Though the lease agreement with Cuba clearly stated that Cuba retained formal sovereignty, Kennedy asserted that the United States' "objective degree of control" there was so comprehensive that it amounted to de facto sovereignty over the territory.[55] He laid out three factors to be considered when determining the Suspension Clause's reach. The factors, which Kennedy claimed were derived from the *Eisentrager* decision, were: (1) the citizenship and status of a detainee, including the process that culminated in the status determination; (2) the "nature of the sites" of a detainee's initial capture and subsequent confinement; and (3) any "practical obstacles" to allowing a detainee access to the writ.[56] The opinion addressed these in turn, applying each to the situation at Guantánamo.

On the first point, the majority contrasted the Guantánamo detainees to the *Eisentrager* petitioners who were denied access to habeas review. Whereas the *Eisentrager* petitioners did not deny that they were combatants and received a military commission trial replete with "rigorous adversarial process," Kennedy noted that many Guantánamo detainees disputed their enemy combatant designations and enjoyed a "far more limited" process to challenge those designations.[57] The second factor also weighed in favor of Guantánamo detainees: Kennedy stated that the United States' control over the German prison in *Eisentrager* was temporary and not "absolute," while "in every practical sense Guantanamo is not abroad; it is within the constant jurisdiction of the United States."[58] And on the third factor, the majority found no insurmountable obstacle to extending the writ to Guantánamo Bay. Acknowledging that the move might impose some costs on the government, the Court doubted that it would significantly disrupt operations at the detention facility.

Having established that the Suspension Clause applied, the majority was unwilling to treat the MCA's jurisdiction-stripping provisions as a formal suspension of the writ. This teed up the next critical question: had the elected branches crafted an acceptable substitute for habeas corpus? Kennedy's opinion conceded that the Court would typically decline to answer this question until the DTA review process played out in full. But the majority made an exception:

the "gravity" of the case—both its implications for the separation of powers and the fact that the detainees had been held for more than six years now—called for resolution by the Supreme Court. Examining the existing review mechanisms—CSRTs and review by the DC Circuit under the DTA—the majority ruled that they were an unsatisfactory replacement for habeas corpus. Congress must have intended for the existing process to contain fewer protections for detainees than a habeas proceeding, Kennedy observed, or else "there would have been no, or very little, purpose for enacting the DTA."[59] Kennedy zeroed in on one fatal flaw: "We see no way to construe the statute to allow what is also constitutionally required in this context: an opportunity for the detainee to present relevant exculpatory evidence that was not made part of the record in the earlier proceedings."[60] Moreover, due to the length of their detentions, the petitioners should not be required to exhaust all other remedies first: "The costs of delay can no longer be borne by those who are held in custody. The detainees in these cases are entitled to a prompt habeas corpus hearing."[61]

The decision produced a pair of vigorous dissenting opinions, both of which were signed by all four dissenting justices. Two of the dissenters, Chief Justice John Roberts and Justice Samuel Alito, had joined the Court after the first round of detention litigation in 2004. The others were Justices Antonin Scalia and Clarence Thomas, both of whom had expressed profound disagreement with the Court's two prior decisions concerning Guantánamo detainees (*Rasul* and *Hamdan*). The first *Boumediene* dissent, written by Justice Scalia, took issue with the extension of the Suspension Clause to Guantánamo Bay, and the second dissent, written by Chief Justice Roberts, disputed the finding that the existing review process was inadequate. Scalia's dissent quickly established the depth and intensity of the disagreement in *Boumediene*. Scalia did not mince words, predicting that the ruling "will almost certainly cause more Americans to be killed."[62] In support of this inflammatory charge, Scalia cited reports of Guantánamo detainees who were released and later reengaged in the ongoing conflict. If military officials and other members of the executive branch had trouble figuring out which detainees posed a danger to national security, Scalia wondered, shouldn't judges be even more reluctant to involve themselves in such decisions? What Scalia did not point out here, but might have, was that the pressure of litigation had already contributed to releases from Guantánamo. According to Scalia, the majority was recklessly overturning wartime policy decisions made by the elected branches. The dissent ended with a series of predictions: that judges would soon extend habeas rights even further, in order to supervise detentions in other locations (like the Bagram prison in Afghanistan); that judges would soon announce the application of other constitutional provisions at Guantánamo Bay; and that "the Nation will live to regret what the Court has done today."[63]

Chief Justice Roberts's dissent, though more temperate in tone, also included sharp objections to the Court's decision. His dissent began with a stark claim: "Today the Court strikes down as inadequate the most generous set of procedural protections ever afforded aliens detained by this country as enemy combatants."[64] Roberts lamented the majority's willingness to undo the work of Congress and the executive branch, which had spent considerable time developing the set of review procedures the Court was now invalidating. Later in his opinion, he turned to the likely consequences of the ruling. Roberts correctly foresaw that, far from settling or clarifying matters of detention law and policy, *Boumediene* would add to the muddle and generate more litigation. The majority erased one review scheme and instituted an alternative, which Roberts referred to as "a set of shapeless procedures to be defined by federal courts at some future date."[65] The chief justice returned to this theme several times throughout his dissenting opinion. In his view, the judicial branch was effectively replacing the legislative and executive branches as the lead actor in detention policy, and in doing so it was substituting a new and undefined process for a far clearer one that already existed. Exhibiting a keen understanding of the forces and attributes of adversarial legalism, Roberts recognized that a possible unintended consequence of the ruling was that detainees might have to wait even longer for their day in court. Roberts suggested that if the majority was concerned with the length of detentions, wiping away the DTA review process was misguided: "There is no reason to suppose that review according to procedures the Federal Judiciary will design, case by case, will proceed any faster than the DTA process petitioners disdained."[66] In fact, Roberts predicted that it would be slower, since habeas review would require detainees to start in federal district court and work their way up to the DC Circuit Courts of Appeals. He contrasted this to the DTA system, which had detainees go straight from a CSRT to the DC Circuit.

Roberts also maintained that the majority's lack of detail regarding the precise contours of habeas review in this context would generate additional rounds of litigation. He correctly anticipated that the rules and procedures would emerge from a long, drawn-out process involving scores of lawsuits, district court rulings, and appeals. And because the AUMF was so vague and neither the DTA nor the MCA addressed detention in a detailed manner, judges would be working with little clear statutory law at their disposal.[67] As Roberts noted, the majority opinion did almost nothing to ameliorate this situation. For example, the majority opinion advised that judges need not intervene immediately to review each new detention at Guantánamo, but left unclear how long a detention could occur before habeas rights kicked in. The majority also acknowledged that adjustments to traditional habeas review might be necessary given the sensitive national security considerations at play, but it offered no specific guidance as to what those adjustments might be.

Roberts thought the Court's ruling was particularly problematic in light of the *Hamdi* decision. The plurality opinion in *Hamdi* had included suggestions for how review of detentions might unfold. Among these suggestions were evidentiary rules that favored the government and the use of military tribunals in lieu of regular courts. As Roberts noted, the description in *Hamdi* sounded a lot like CSRTs, which had been crafted by the Bush administration in the immediate wake of that ruling. Congress had then gone even further in the DTA, creating a review process for CSRT decisions in an Article III court. And *Hamdi* concerned an American citizen held on US soil. Surely a noncitizen detainee at Guantánamo Bay did not have more rights than a citizen detainee held inside the United States, Roberts reasoned. He thought the majority's objections to CSRTs and DC Circuit review under the DTA were unconvincing. In particular, he singled out the majority's central complaint—that a detainee would not be able to make use of exculpatory evidence discovered after his CSRT hearing. Insisting that it was a hypothetical concern for the time being, Roberts mentioned the possibility of holding a new CSRT if fresh evidence came to light. He also pointed to ARBs as providing another level of review that could incorporate additional evidence and factor it into potential release decisions. In concluding his opinion, the Chief Justice announced that he could not discern who the winners were under the Court's ruling. But he doubted that it was the detainees, who he said faced the prospect of more litigation, uncertainty, and delay. Roberts continued in this vein: "Not the rule of law, unless by that is meant the rule of lawyers, who will now arguably have a greater role than military and intelligence officials in shaping policy for alien enemy combatants. And certainly not the American people, who today lose a bit more control over the conduct of this Nation's foreign policy to unelected, politically unaccountable judges."[68]

Taken together, the Scalia and Roberts dissenting opinions put forth a series of criticisms and dire warnings about the future of detention policy. Though all nine justices clearly understood that the ruling would give courts a greater role in detention matters, they were profoundly divided over the likely costs and benefits of this development. As the remainder of this chapter and the next one will make clear, both sides got some things right and some things wrong. The majority's extension of the Suspension Clause to Guantánamo Bay gave detainees their day in federal court, and that move led to a number of releases from the detention facility. But the downsides of adversarial legalism were also readily apparent following the ruling. As Chief Justice Roberts predicted, it would take several more years of litigation to clarify detention law and policy.

## THE IMMEDIATE AFTERMATH OF *BOUMEDIENE*

The *Boumediene* decision again undercut one of the Bush administration's original reasons for using Guantánamo Bay to house detainees: keeping the detainees in a place where US courts would not get involved. Now, every detainee held there would be guaranteed an opportunity to challenge his detention before a federal judge in a habeas corpus proceeding. And because *Boumediene* located this guarantee in the Constitution itself, the ruling offered a degree of staying power that previous court decisions grounded in statutory interpretation did not. Barring the enactment of a constitutional amendment, a formal suspension of habeas corpus by Congress, or a future reversal by the Supreme Court, judicial involvement at Guantánamo Bay was here to stay.[69]

Once again, lawyers for the detainees filed scores of habeas petitions in the DC District Court. The litigation proceeded slowly at first, as the district court wrestled with various procedural issues. The *Boumediene* Court had punted almost every detail regarding how to handle these lawsuits to the lower courts. There was uncertainty about all kinds of things, including the standard of proof, how to manage classified information, and how secretive the proceedings ought to be. There were also logistical problems to be sorted out, like finding enough DOJ lawyers to litigate all the cases on behalf of the government and giving intelligence agencies enough time to gather information on the various detainees suing for their release.[70]

The *Boumediene* ruling also generated some momentum for those inside the executive branch who favored emptying Guantánamo of its 270 remaining detainees. Secretary of Defense Gates and Secretary of State Rice, the leading proponents of closure, saw an opportunity to use the Court decision to their advantage. Their plan, which included bringing some Guantánamo detainees to facilities inside the United States, might be more palatable now that detainees would be entitled to habeas corpus hearings whether they were kept at Guantánamo or held on American soil. As Bush's final months as president wound down, the Defense and State Departments worked on plans for emptying the facility.[71] In mid-2008 Gates testified to Congress that closing Guantánamo would likely mean continuing to detain somewhere in the range of eighty individuals indefinitely—individuals deemed too dangerous to release but who could not be charged and convicted of a crime. Gates estimated that another group of about eighty detainees could be prosecuted for war crimes.[72] The remaining detainees could be transferred out of Guantánamo, but finding nations that were willing and able to take them required painstaking diplomatic efforts.[73]

The Bush administration's discussions of a last-ditch effort at closure were influenced not only by the *Boumediene* decision, but by other litigation concerns as well. Administration lawyers remained preoccupied with the question of what additional rights, if any, detainees would receive if they were held on US soil instead of at Guantánamo Bay. Other considerations were also in play: Gates has reported that the proposal to bring some detainees to the United States met with opposition from White House staff who worried the move could harm the Republican Party's electoral prospects.[74] In the end, with the 2008 presidential election fast approaching, President Bush sided with those inside his administration who opposed closing Guantánamo. A combination of political, legal, and practical arguments against closure ultimately proved persuasive.

Of particular concern to DOJ and Department of Homeland Security (DHS) officials was the possibility that Guantánamo detainees who won their habeas challenges might receive a court-ordered release into the United States.[75] They had good reason to fear such an outcome: in October 2008, a DC District Court judge did exactly that. The case involved a group of seventeen Chinese Muslims, known as Uighurs, who were captured in Afghanistan in 2001. The US government initially alleged that the Uighur detainees had spent time at a terrorist training camp and could therefore be detained as enemy combatants. But as the pressure of litigation increased—one of the Uighurs, a man named Parhat, had already won his CSRT appeal in the DC Circuit—the government changed its position, concluding that it could no longer sustain the Uighurs' classification as enemy combatants.[76] But where would they be sent? Repatriating them to China would place them in serious danger of persecution for their religious beliefs. Albania had already accepted a handful of Uighurs who had been detained at Guantánamo, but no nation had expressed a willingness to take the remaining seventeen. When they sued, Judge Ricardo Urbina ordered their release into the United States. The government appealed and won a stay of Urbina's order in the DC Circuit Court, but the threat of more rulings in this vein remained.[77] And they might become even more likely if the detainees were already inside the United States, as the Guantánamo closure plan proposed.

The ruling on the Uighurs was significant. But it is important to note that it was *not* a judicial repudiation of an enemy combatant classification, since the government had already conceded that the Uighurs were not enemy combatants. The first such repudiation came in late November 2008, in the litigation involving the six *Boumediene* plaintiffs. District Court Judge Richard Leon—the same judge who in 2005 issued a strongly progovernment ruling in *Khalid v. Bush*—found that the evidence did not support the detention of five of the six men.[78] Leon went further and urged the government not to appeal since the men had already been detained for several years. In December, with his administration on its way out the door, President Bush announced that three of these detainees would be sent to Bosnia. Observers were quick to point out that these were the first Guantánamo releases made pursuant to a court order.[79] But as this chapter and the prior chapter make clear, that observation substantially understates the impact of litigation and court decisions on detention policies. The steady drumbeat of lawsuits and court rulings contributed to the enactment of significant policy reforms and the release of scores of Guantánamo detainees.

## CONCLUSION

By the end of George W. Bush's presidency in January 2009, detention policies had undergone a remarkable evolution. On a core national security issue, and with a war still very much in progress, presidential unilateralism rapidly gave way to an extended interbranch tug-of-war in which neither the courts nor Congress was merely willing to defer to executive authority. The existence of internal divisions within the executive branch only exacerbated this state of affairs. Litigation and court decisions played a central role in the institutional back-and-forth. In anticipation of and response to lawsuits and judicial intervention, Congress and the executive branch erected multiple layers of review for Guantánamo detainees—first through ARBs and CSRTs, and later through judicial review of CSRT determinations in the DC Circuit Court of Appeals. When the Supreme Court found this system was constitutionally flawed, Guantánamo detainees received the right to challenge their detentions in habeas corpus proceedings. Henceforth, detention decisions at Guantánamo Bay—whether to bring newly captured individuals to the facility and whether to continue detaining those already there—would be made against this backdrop.

The consequences for Guantánamo detainees were mixed. On one hand, as Chief Justice Roberts pointed out in his *Boumediene* dissent, some detainees might have to wait years to have their habeas lawsuits definitively resolved by judges. In the meantime, they would remain in a state of limbo. On the other hand, noncitizen suspected terrorists held outside sovereign US territory were receiving an unprecedented degree of due process. And the existence of multiple review mechanisms and the looming threat of litigation created ongoing pressure to release many of the detainees. By the end of its tenure, the Bush administration released approximately five hundred Guantánamo detainees. It is difficult to imagine the administration doing so in the absence of litigation and the policy changes it produced. Yet even as the population at Guantánamo dwindled, the population at the Bagram detention facility in Afghanistan kept ticking upward. That facility, unlike Guantánamo, remained beyond the reach of the federal judiciary.

President Bush's decision to keep Guantánamo open meant that the question of what to do with the detention camp and its occupants would be passed off to his successor. The two candidates for president in 2008—Republican John McCain and Democrat Barack Obama—campaigned in favor of closing Guantánamo. But Bush administration officials made a prescient prediction: shutting down Guantánamo would be extremely hard. Secretary of Defense Robert Gates, asked to remain in his post by president-elect Barack Obama, warned the Obama transition team that emptying the facility would be more difficult than they imagined.[80] One outgoing Bush administration official put it in especially vivid terms: "The new president will gnash his teeth and beat his head against the wall when he realizes how complicated it is to close Guantánamo."[81] They were right: Guantánamo remains open to this day, more than a decade after President Obama formally vowed to close it in his first year as president. The next chapter will help explain why.

# 3. Detention Policy in a Post-*Boumediene* World (2009–2017)

President Barack Obama entered office determined to fundamentally alter—or perhaps even do away with—the detention policies he inherited. As we have seen, those policies had already undergone a series of modifications after their inception in 2001. Lawsuits and court decisions—and the interbranch back-and-forth they helped enliven—led to policy changes that offered detainees held at Guantánamo and inside the United States greater protections and enhanced opportunities to challenge their detentions. Presidential discretion was circumscribed, as detention decisions were subject to multiple checks and robust oversight. One result of these developments was a reduction in the number of detainees held at Guantánamo Bay and a corresponding increase in the number of detainees held in Afghanistan—a trend that continued into the Obama administration.

One of Barack Obama's first acts as president was an executive order declaring that the detention facility at Guantánamo Bay would be closed within a year.[1] But the order did not specify how this would occur, and it soon became clear that the goal would be extremely difficult to achieve.[2] A task force composed of national security officials from relevant agencies reviewed each of the 242 ongoing detentions at Guantánamo Bay to determine whether a detainee should be prosecuted, released or transferred to another country, or kept in indefinite detention.[3] President Obama and some of his advisors expected the last category to be tiny or nonexistent, but the task force put the number at four dozen. These were individuals who could not be prosecuted due to insufficient admissible evidence tying them to a specific crime, but who were also deemed too dangerous to release.[4] The task force's conclusions meant that closing Guantánamo would be more challenging than anticipated.

This chapter traces the development of detention policies from the beginning of the Obama presidency to the end of it. Although the Obama administration was able to reduce the population at Guantánamo and scale back the use of detention as a policy tool in the war on terror, it ultimately did away with neither. Moreover, as I note toward the end of this chapter, President Obama's successor, Donald Trump, has had similar trouble fulfilling campaign promises on these issues. Where Obama sought to close Guantánamo and limit or do away with detention, Trump pushed for the opposite. He announced his desire to increase the population at Guantánamo and reestablish prolonged military detention as a policy option. But like Obama, Trump has so far failed to realize his objectives. Detention policy has become highly insulated from direct presidential control.

Although the big picture has not fundamentally changed, detention policies have continued to evolve in important ways since 2009. As with so much policy development in the United States, the devil has been in the details—and litigation and court decisions have been a driving factor. One little-noticed but significant set of detention policy changes affected US detention operations in Afghanistan. After the Supreme Court's June 2008 *Boumediene* ruling, detainees held in US custody in Afghanistan seized on the decision and filed lawsuits claiming that they should enjoy the same rights as Guantánamo detainees. A district court judge agreed, and the Obama administration instituted reforms giving detainees held in Afghanistan more protections and a greater ability to challenge their confinement. Though the US Court of Appeals for the District of Columbia Circuit ultimately reversed the ruling on appeal, litigation had once again helped generate important policy changes.

Detention operations at Guantánamo Bay were also shaped by ongoing litigation. A steady stream of lawsuits and release orders from district court judges ramped up the pressure to move detainees out of the facility. These detainee transfer efforts faced complications, including an unstable environment in Yemen (home to many of the remaining Guantánamo detainees), statutory restrictions on transfers imposed by Congress, and a more progovernment approach to habeas lawsuits in the DC Circuit Court of Appeals. But these obstacles did not prevent further winnowing of the Guantánamo population under President Obama. The Obama administration implemented a revamped version of administrative review boards (ARBs) known as periodic review boards (PRBs) that were more favorable to detainees. And through sustained diplomatic efforts, the administration successfully convinced other countries to accept many of the detainees who were cleared for transfer by PRBs. Entrepreneurial lawyering on a range of issues related to Guantánamo continued, creating another source of momentum for additional reductions in the detainee population. By the end of the Obama administration, the population at Guantánamo fell all the way to forty-one. The number currently sits at forty, and despite President Trump's promises to the contrary, no new detainees have been brought to Guantánamo Bay since 2008.[5]

The detention policy reforms described above benefited many suspected enemy belligerents being held by the United States. But adversarial legalism continued to create unintended consequences and perverse incentives. As the detention option—fraught with legal challenges and multiple layers of review and oversight—became increasingly inefficient, other alternatives became more appealing for policy makers. In what is almost certainly not a coincidence, the past several years have seen increases in targeted killings via drone and detentions by proxy, where the United States passes off detention responsibilities to other nations. These and other alternative policy options come with costs and benefits of their own, which will be explored later in this chapter.

## THE CASE OF ALI AL-MARRI

President Obama faced a number of vexing questions related to detention. Upon entering office, one of the first to reach his desk concerned the detention of a man named Ali al-Marri. Al-Marri was a lawful resident (but not a citizen) of the United States who was taken into custody in Illinois shortly after 9/11, held as a material witness for a brief period, and then charged with credit card fraud and other relatively minor offenses. But after evidence of al-Marri's relationship to al-Qaeda surfaced, the Bush administration dropped the criminal charges and designated him an enemy combatant.[6] Al-Marri sued, and a Fourth Circuit panel eventually ruled his detention unlawful.[7] The government appealed, and an en banc rehearing produced a split ruling: al-Marri could be detained as an enemy combatant, but was entitled to more due process.[8] The Supreme Court granted certiorari in December 2008, and a brief from the Obama administration was due within its first couple of months in office.[9]

The *al-Marri* litigation bore a close resemblance to the *Padilla* litigation from a few years earlier. Like al-Marri, Jose Padilla was taken into custody on US soil and detained by the military. The only major difference was that Padilla was a citizen and al-Marri was a lawful resident. Despite the similarities, the outcome in *al-Marri* was uncertain because the *Padilla* litigation never produced a Supreme Court ruling on the legality of Padilla's detention.[10] After the Supreme Court ruled in 2004 that Padilla had filed his lawsuit in the wrong court, the Fourth Circuit upheld his detention.[11] This was directly at odds with a Second Circuit ruling in 2003 finding Padilla's detention to be unlawful.[12] But shortly after the Fourth Circuit decision, the Bush administration transferred Jose Padilla to civilian custody and brought criminal charges against him. Many observers suspected that the sudden shift marked an effort to avoid a negative outcome in the Supreme Court, which had already agreed to hear the case. In a highly unusual move, the Fourth Circuit initially denied the government's motion requesting to transfer Padilla from military to civilian custody. Circuit judge Michael Luttig wrote a blistering opinion accusing the government of a cynical attempt to dodge Supreme Court review.[13] The Supreme Court reversed, allowing the custody transfer to proceed and revoking its grant of certiorari on the grounds that the case was moot.[14]

Confronted with this uncertain legal landscape—and with the due date for the government's brief in *al-Marri* fast approaching—the Obama administration had to make a decision. In February 2009, it elected to do what the Bush administration did with Padilla: move al-Marri into the criminal justice system, where he was charged with a crime and prosecuted in an Article III court.[15] Ali al-Marri was convicted of material support for terrorism and sentenced to fifteen years in prison. After factoring in time already spent in custody, al-Marri was incarcerated for six more years and then released to his native Qatar in January 2015.[16] Jose Padilla remains in prison today, having been convicted in federal court of material support for terrorism and other offenses.[17]

## DETENTION OPERATIONS IN AFGHANISTAN AND AT GUANTÁNAMO BAY

Just as the litigation calendar forced the new administration to sort out the al-Marri situation, so too did it compel the Obama administration to quickly develop positions on other detention matters. This was a common theme in the first few months of the new administration: with litigation in progress on an array of national security issues, the administration faced a series of deadlines for articulating its legal and policy positions. This frustrated President Obama, whom journalist Daniel Klaidman quotes as uttering the following: "It's another one of these damn litigation decisions they want to talk about, and I'm tired of it. I'm tired of being jammed this way."[18] In the same vein, an aide to Attorney General Eric Holder, Amy Jeffress, related that "the legal process drove the policy process."[19]

The time pressures imposed by litigation made significant policy change more difficult. Before the new administration could study all of the legal and policy issues in depth, it was compelled to take official positions in court. The safest course was to hew closely to the preexisting positions of the prior administration, which the Obama administration largely did.[20] One area of continuity concerned detention operations in Afghanistan. Following the *Boumediene* decision extending habeas corpus rights to Guantánamo Bay, a group of detainees held by the US military in Afghanistan at the Bagram detention facility sought to capitalize on the ruling.[21] DC District Court judge John Bates required the Obama administration to weigh in on the lawsuit by February 20, 2009—just one month after Obama's inauguration. The Department of Justice (DOJ) announced that it would adhere to the existing view that habeas rights did not apply at Bagram.

Soon after, the Obama administration had to articulate its views on detention at Guantánamo Bay. The habeas corpus lawsuits unleashed by the *Boumediene* ruling were moving forward, and the DC District Court wanted to know whether the change in administrations meant a change in the government's interpretation of its detention authority. In mid-March, in a case called *Hamlily v. Obama*, DOJ submitted a brief indicating that the answer was mostly no.[22] The brief outlined a position that became known as the "March 13 Standard" (named for the date it was introduced). The March 13 Standard largely embraced the Bush administration's understanding of its power to detain enemy fighters. Obama's DOJ agreed that the 2001 Authorization for Use of Military Force (AUMF) authorized indefinite military detention of individuals who fell within its ambit. The March 13 Standard said that "individuals who provide substantial support to al-Qaida forces in other parts of the world may properly be deemed part of al-Qaida itself. Such activities may also constitute the type of substantial support that . . . is sufficient to justify detention."[23] This was only a slight modification of the Bush administration position, which held that mere "support"—as opposed to "substantial support"—was sufficient to warrant detention.

The Obama administration made three other relatively minor alterations. In a symbolic break with its predecessor, it discontinued the use of the term "enemy combatant," opting instead for terms such as "enemy forces" or "belligerents." The other two changes concerned the legal framework and not the substance of detention policies: DOJ stopped citing Article II of the Constitution as a source of detention authority, relying exclusively on the AUMF instead, and it explicitly stated that international law could play a role in determining the precise scope of that detention authority.[24] The March 13 Standard would be applied broadly, covering existing detentions at Guantánamo and Bagram as well as any future detention operations. Importantly, it would also spill over into the realm of targeted killing: since the primary legal basis for drone strikes against al-Qaeda and associated terrorist organizations was the AUMF, the Obama administration's interpretation of that statute in the context of detention litigation would shape executive branch deliberations about who could and could not be targeted in lethal operations.[25]

As Charlie Savage's remarkable account of the Obama administration's internal decision-making shows, legal considerations completely penetrated the executive branch from the very beginning of Obama's tenure. Even in the absence of litigation deadlines, the Obama administration repeatedly conducted extensive internal debates about legal issues raised by various aspects of the war. A cadre of lawyers from agencies concerned with national security matters met regularly and often got the first crack at questions regarding the war's conduct.[26] Savage quotes one administration official expressing shock at "how central the discussion of legal questions seemed to be to every facet of policymaking."[27] Tom Donilon, Obama's deputy national security advisor and later his national security advisor, seconded that observation, suggesting that nearly every single wartime issue to come before the administration had legal considerations attached to it.[28] Savage calls this way of doing things "government by lawyer," and he highlights a trade-off that it created: on the positive side, more deliberation; on the negative side, a slower process for making important decisions.[29] Legalization and its effects not only were playing out in the courts, but were being mirrored within the executive branch as well.

## LITIGATION GOES TO AFGHANISTAN

In April 2009, the DC District Court rejected the Obama administration's argument that habeas rights did not extend to detainees at the Bagram detention facility in Afghanistan. The case, *Al Maqaleh v. Gates*, involved four detainees held by the US military at Bagram, each of whom was captured outside of Afghanistan but brought there to be detained.[30] Judge John Bates issued a lengthy opinion finding that three of the four plaintiffs—the three who were not Afghan citizens—were entitled to habeas corpus hearings in federal court.

Though the ruling was eventually overturned on appeal, it spurred policy changes in the military's detention operations in Afghanistan.

According to Judge Bates, the three non-Afghans in *Al Maqaleh* were in a situation fundamentally akin to the Guantánamo detainees in *Boumediene*. None of the petitioners were US citizens and all had been captured abroad. Judge Bates placed special emphasis on the location of capture: like the *Boumediene* plaintiffs, who were picked up in various countries and brought to Cuba, the *Al Maqaleh* plaintiffs were taken into custody elsewhere and then brought to Afghanistan. This fact allowed Bates to limit the reach of his ruling, since most of the detainees at Bagram were captured inside Afghanistan. The *Al Maqaleh* petitioners, on the other hand, were moved to Afghanistan by choice, which in Bates's words "resurrect[ed] the same specter of limitless Executive power the Supreme Court sought to guard against in *Boumediene*—the concern that the Executive could move detainees physically beyond the reach of the Constitution and detain them indefinitely."[31] Bates also focused on the current location of the detentions, arguing that the US military's "near-total operational control" at Bagram was comparable to US control at Guantánamo Bay.[32]

Bates then turned to another pillar of the *Boumediene* decision: the question of process. Here, he noted that the Guantánamo Combatant Status Review Tribunal (CSRT) process featured greater protections for detainees than the status reviews at Bagram. He pointed out that unlawful enemy combatant review boards (UECRBs)—the Bagram analogue to CSRTs—did not provide detainees with personal representatives, did not allow detainees to appear in person, did not permit detainees to see the evidence against them, and did not include an appeals process. If the Detainee Treatment Act process—CSRTs plus review in the DC Circuit—was an inadequate substitute for habeas corpus at Guantánamo, Bates concluded that the same was true of the more skeletal UECRBs. And Bates could find no "practical obstacles" to extending the writ's reach to Bagram. Although the facility was located in an active war zone, he insisted that any difficulties could be mitigated with a bit of flexibility from the judiciary. Because Bates accepted the US government's argument that habeas litigation brought by Afghans might create tension with the government of Afghanistan, he dismissed the Afghan citizen's petition. But the other three men won.

At the end of his opinion, Judge Bates indicated that the outcome of the case might have been different if Bagram detainees received more protections.

The Obama administration decided to appeal the *Al Maqaleh* ruling, but it also accepted Judge Bates's suggestion and strengthened review procedures at Bagram.[33] Again, a court ruling and the specter of ongoing litigation were key drivers of policy change. Shortly before submitting its brief in the *Al Maqaleh* appeal, the Obama administration announced that it would institute enhanced review mechanisms for detainees held in Afghanistan. A Department of Defense (DOD) official confirmed the motivation behind the change: "We want to be able to go into court and say we have good review procedures."[34]

UECRBs, now renamed detainee review boards (DRBs), received a serious overhaul.[35] Henceforth, new detainees would be entitled to an initial DRB hearing within sixty days of their capture. For the first time, detainees in Afghanistan began receiving formal opportunities to learn about the allegations against them and to challenge them. The new DRB system provided detainees with personal representatives to assist them. The representative, a military official, was assigned to a detainee no more than thirty days after the detainee's arrival at Bagram. The official would meet repeatedly with the detainee, explain the contours of the review process, summarize the basis for the individual's detention, and help the detainee mount a challenge. This included gathering information and tracking down witnesses who could testify at the DRB hearing in defense of the detainee.[36] Personal representatives appeared alongside detainees at DRB hearings, helping detainees make statements and answer questions. And although detainees could be excluded from parts of the hearing involving classified evidence, their representatives could not.[37]

The provision of personal representatives was arguably the most important reform, but other policy changes were similarly favorable to detainees. One such change was the creation of an exclusionary rule categorically prohibiting the use of evidence obtained via torture or other cruel, inhuman, or degrading treatment. Judge advocates came to play a larger role in the proceedings; instead of military intelligence analysts gathering the information for status reviews, military lawyers would now do so. There was also greater transparency: any individual with access to the Bagram facility—including members of human rights organizations, such as the International Committee of the Red Cross (ICRC)—could attend DRB hearings. And the new review boards were more thorough than their predecessors: the average length of a DRB proceeding was more than an hour and a half, up from just forty minutes per hearing before the changes were made. With these new procedures in place—and with the somewhat more restrictive March 13 Standard for detention authority now operative—approximately one-third of the detainees who went before DRBs were recommended for transfer or release instead of continued detention.[38]

In May 2010, a DC Circuit panel unanimously reversed the district court ruling in *Al Maqaleh.*[39] It declined to consider the new review procedures, taking issue instead with other elements of Judge Bates's application of *Boumediene.* But despite the DC Circuit's ruling in *Al Maqaleh*, the new review procedures were already in place. By late 2009, the United States had finished constructing a new detention facility in Afghanistan. Conditions of confinement were significantly better at the new facility, and detention operations became more transparent.[40] In early 2010, responding to litigation by the ACLU under the Freedom of Information Act (FOIA), the Obama administration released the names of detainees held in US custody at Bagram.[41] Litigation had again resulted in significant policy changes—this time, changes favorable to noncitizens detained an ocean away in a spot where active hostilities were ongoing. It was an outcome few could have imagined in late 2001, when George W. Bush first ordered the detention of enemy fighters.

## MEANWHILE, AT GUANTÁNAMO . . .

In May 2009 President Obama delivered a major national security policy speech at the National Archives. In the speech he laid out a path to closing Guantánamo Bay. First, his administration would prosecute as many of the remaining detainees as possible, either in civilian courts or in reformed military commissions. Others would be released, either in response to court rulings or because the executive branch determined that they could be safely resettled elsewhere. Finally, Obama outlined what he called "the toughest single issue that we will face": the group of detainees who could not be prosecuted but who were too dangerous to let go. He called for establishing a "legitimate legal framework" to deal with these detainees, and vowed to partner with Congress to create one.[42]

In the meantime, the DC District Court continued to grapple with habeas lawsuits from Guantánamo. Early on, detainees amassed an impressive winning percentage: twenty-six of the first thirty-one detainees to challenge their detentions in the wake of *Boumediene* won their cases.[43] This presented the Obama administration with two options: appeal the rulings or release the victorious detainees. Although President Obama was committed to emptying Guantánamo, the release option was complicated. His administration had to find places willing to accept the detainees. And when rumors swirled that some detainees might soon be brought to the United States, Congress made the task even harder by enacting the first of several restrictions on transferring detainees out of Guantánamo.[44] In the fall of 2009, a Congress controlled by President Obama's own party enacted a ban on releasing detainees inside the United States (though it permitted transfers to the US for prosecution). Congress also demanded that the executive branch notify lawmakers whenever it chose to move a detainee out of Guantánamo.[45] In light of these restrictions, the Obama administration had to find other nations willing to accept detainees. Those detainees who had their enemy combatant classifications overturned would now have to be released somewhere other than the United States.[46] So too would other detainees who remained classified as enemy fighters, but who had undergone parole-style reviews concluding they were no longer too dangerous to leave Guantánamo. Those detainees could be transferred subject to security measures meant to guard against their return to the battlefield, such as travel restrictions or monitoring.

Detainee resettlement became a complex and protracted diplomatic exercise. The situation was particularly acute for detainees from Yemen, who by 2009 constituted approximately 40 percent of the remaining Guantánamo population. Even as many of these Yemeni detainees were ordered released by judges or recommended for transfer by parole-style review boards, most remained stuck at Guantánamo for years because their home country was deemed too unstable to resettle them and other countries were unwilling to take them.[47] But there were exceptions, driven by litigation: in December 2009, the Obama administration repatriated six Yemenis after concluding they were likely to win their habeas lawsuits.[48] The mere threat or anticipation of losses in pending or future litigation cast a shadow over executive branch decisions about whether to transfer detainees. The report issued by Obama's detainee task force made this clear, noting that officials considered "the evidence against the detainees, and the government's ability to successfully defend the lawfulness of their detentions in court."[49] The Yemeni repatriations were soon brought to a halt, however, following a failed attempt to bring down an airplane over Detroit, Michigan, on Christmas Day 2009. The terrorist, Umar Farouk Abdulmutallab, had spent time training with Al-Qaeda in the Arabian Peninsula (AQAP), an influential al-Qaeda offshoot headquartered in Yemen. The Obama administration responded by stopping all detainee transfers to Yemen.[50]

President Obama's one-year deadline for closing the detention facility at Guantánamo Bay came and went without much fanfare. For a while it looked as if Congress and President Obama might reach a deal that would close Guantánamo and bring the remaining detainees to US soil for prosecution or continued detention. Republican senator Lindsey Graham (SC) was a key player in these negotiations: he supported closing Guantánamo in exchange for legislation that would explicitly authorize detention and make military commissions the preferred venue for prosecuting terrorist suspects.[51] But bringing detainees to the United States was a difficult sell. It presented a NIMBY ("not in my back yard") problem of epic proportions: members of Congress and their constituents were not enthusiastic about suspected terrorists being housed in their communities. The proposal also met with opposition from civil liberties groups, who viewed a statute explicitly authorizing detention without trial inside the United States as normalizing a policy they abhorred.[52] Despite vowing to work with Congress on detainee issues, President Obama seemed content to let the legislative efforts peter out. Lawmakers from both parties criticized the White House for its lack of engagement on detention matters.[53] An Obama administration official confirmed that an all-out push for closure was, at least for the time being, not in the cards: "Closing Guantánamo is good, but fighting to close Guantánamo is O.K."[54]

Congress soon made closure more unlikely by enacting a new and more stringent set of Guantánamo transfer restrictions. A provision in the National Defense Authorization Act (NDAA) for 2011 blocked the transfer of Guantánamo detainees to US soil for any reason, including prosecution. It also extended a ban on spending money to build or equip a facility in the United States to hold Guantánamo detainees. And the statute regulated transfers to other countries, adding to the preexisting notification requirement a provision demanding that the secretary of defense formally approve all detainee transfers.[55] Though this provision received less attention, it turned out to be quite significant: by making the secretary of defense personally accountable for approving each detainee transfer, it injected a degree of risk aversion into the process. Congress was motivated in large part by the release of recidivism statistics indicating that approximately one-quarter of the individuals released from Guantánamo were either suspected of or confirmed as having reengaged in the conflict.[56] President Obama objected to the transfer restrictions in a signing statement but elected not to veto the bill.[57]

The NDAA 2011 was a clear indication that the politics of detention policy had changed in a short period of time. Early in his second term President

Bush openly discussed his desire to close Guantánamo, and his administration repeatedly debated whether and how to do so. Democrats in Congress had long criticized the Bush administration for its policies at Guantánamo. Both candidates for president in 2008 supported closure. Now, just a couple of years later, a Congress controlled by Democrats enacted statutory restrictions that would make emptying Guantánamo much more difficult. One reason for the shift was the reaction to the attempted Christmas Day terror attack. When the Obama administration used the civilian criminal justice system to handle the would-be attacker, Republicans pounced, accusing the administration of failing to treat the conflict as a war. The criticism was not particularly principled—the Bush administration had subjected terrorist plotters such as Zacarias Moussaoui and Richard Reid to civilian custody and criminal prosecution rather than military detention or trial by military commission with little to no pushback—but it was politically effective.[58]

Another episode that contributed to the enactment of the new transfer restrictions was the prosecution of Ahmed Khalfan Ghailani, a Guantánamo detainee brought to the United States for a civilian trial. In November 2009, Ghailani was convicted of one charge and sentenced to life in prison, but his acquittal on almost three hundred other charges received much of the attention.[59] Republicans seized on the acquittals as further confirmation of the follies of using a law-enforcement approach to combating terrorism. The Ghailani prosecution dovetailed with another significant development: the Obama administration's decision to prosecute Khalid Sheikh Mohammed (KSM) and a handful of other 9/11 conspirators held at Guantánamo in an Article III court in New York. When Republicans and some Democrats raised the prospect of similar acquittals in that case and New York City officials expressed concerns about security and the cost of the trial, support for the move crumbled.[60] These events led Congress to enact the stricter transfer limits in NDAA 2011, banning transfers to the United States even for the purposes of prosecution. KSM and the other 9/11 plotters were kept in the military commission system. Ghailani remains the only Guantánamo detainee ever brought to the United States for trial.

## DEFERENCE ON THE DC CIRCUIT

Around this time the tide began to turn in the courts as well.[61] As we have seen, in the initial flurry of habeas lawsuits after *Boumediene*, DC District Court judges were highly receptive to detainees' claims. These early rulings generated momentum for transfers—for detainees who won their cases, but also for detainees who could reasonably be *expected* to win their cases. As Savage reports, these prodetainee decisions "created pressure inside the bureaucracy" to speed up releases. They also provided political cover for the Obama administration to continue trimming the population at Guantánamo Bay: administration officials could point to courts as the reason for the reductions, insulating themselves somewhat from Republican charges that the administration was weak on national security.[62] Though the District Court's jurisprudence ostensibly aided the Obama administration with its closure goal, the administration chose to appeal some of the prodetainee rulings. And in those appeals, the DC Circuit Court of Appeals was far more deferential to the government.

If the District Court was moving in step with the White House's preferences, why did the Obama administration opt for appeals? One reason was the ongoing instability in Yemen. Fearing that released Yemenis could not be safely managed by the Yemeni government, the Obama administration felt pressure to defend the continued detention of even some of the most low-level of these detainees. As Savage has noted, this required adopting a broad interpretation of the government's detention authority.[63] And the DC Circuit embraced that expansive interpretation. Representative of the DC Circuit's more deferential posture toward the government was its decision in *Al-Adahi v. Obama*, the first case in which it reversed a release order from the court below.[64] A unanimous panel held that the District Court had erred in its treatment of the evidence against the detainee.[65] District Court judge Gladys Kessler had found that no single piece of evidence, considered by itself, proved that Al-Adahi was "more likely than not" part of al-Qaeda, and ordered his release on those grounds. The DC Circuit panel thought this was preposterous: Al-Adahi had traveled to Afghanistan, lived with a close associate of Osama bin Laden, met bin Laden in person, stayed at an al-Qaeda guesthouse and later was present at an al-Qaeda training camp, and remained in Afghanistan after the American invasion. Those pieces of evidence needed to be viewed as a whole, according to the DC Circuit, which ruled that the government had shown by a preponderance of the evidence that Al-Adahi was part of al-Qaeda and could be lawfully detained.[66]

The DC Circuit Court handed down a series of similarly deferential decisions in 2010 and 2011. One that received lots of attention came in a case called *Latif v. Obama*, decided in the fall of 2011.[67] A divided panel reversed a ruling in favor of the detainee, holding that the government's evidence was entitled to a "presumption of regularity." This provoked a vigorous dissent from Judge David Tatel, accusing the majority of gutting the Supreme Court's *Boumediene* decision.[68] With a presumption in favor of the government's evidence, Tatel argued that detainees would not receive meaningful judicial review. That judges on the DC District Court and the DC Circuit Court of Appeals could disagree so vehemently regarding the meaning and application of *Boumediene* showed that the Supreme Court had done little to clear up the legal uncertainty surrounding detention. The Supreme Court's repeated denials of certiorari after *Boumediene* effectively gave the DC Circuit the final judicial word on detention.[69] Critics labeled the DC Circuit a rubber stamp for the government and called for the Supreme Court to reenter the fray.[70] Linda Greenhouse highlighted remarks by DC Circuit judges that were openly critical of the *Boumediene* decision: one had written of the Supreme Court's "airy suppositions . . . caus[ing] great difficulty for the Executive and the courts," and another likened the *Boumediene* majority to Tom and Daisy in *The Great Gatsby*, calling them "careless people, who smashed things up" and "let other people clean up the mess they made." Greenhouse urged the Supreme Court to reassert itself lest it keep being "dissed."[71]

Critics of the DC Circuit's deferential posture thought *Boumediene* was being hollowed out and deprived of real-world impact. But in downplaying the effect of the Supreme Court's *Boumediene* decision, critics missed the broader, more indirect effects of lawsuits and judicial intervention. They overlooked the detention policy changes in Afghanistan. They failed to recognize that many releases from Guantánamo Bay under Presidents Bush and Obama were driven by the presence of CSRTs, the Detainee Treatment Act, and the persistent threat of litigation. Those who believed the Supreme Court's intervention lacked real impact also did not appreciate the prospective consequences of all this: moving forward, detention became increasingly unappealing as a policy tool.

As Benjamin Wittes has explained, the judiciary's foray into detention matters created unintended consequences. It had the effect of elevating other policy options. At least two of these alternatives were less desirable from the perspective of would-be detainees: targeted killing by drone or Special Forces raid, or detention in the custody of other nations where conditions of confinement would be markedly worse than in US military custody.[72] The Obama administration's increasing reliance on drone strikes resulted in greater numbers of dead terrorist suspects and a decline in the number captured and detained.[73] Klaidman has put this increase in stark terms: "By his third year in office, Obama had approved the killings of twice as many suspected terrorists as had ever been imprisoned at Guantánamo Bay."[74] Multiple explanations are put forth for the jump in drone strikes, including continued improvements in drone technology, President Obama's preference for a "light footprint" abroad involving minimal use of ground troops, and concerns about violating the sovereignty of other nations. But the increase is also likely attributable at least in part to developments in detention policy. In the words of one CIA official, "It's a lot simpler and easier for a sniper to shoot or to use a Predator to launch a lawful attack than to detain and interrogate prisoners. Once they're dead, then Human Rights Watch or Amnesty International doesn't bring a habeas [corpus] case for them."[75] The top Republican on the Senate Intelligence Committee, Senator Saxby Chambliss (GA), made a similar observation: "[The Obama administration's] policy is to take out high-value targets, versus capturing high-value targets. They are not going to advertise that, but that's what they are doing."[76]

The challenges associated with defending detentions in court—in terms of time and resources, and also the attention and criticism it begot—had become great. Prospective calculations about the costs of detentions inevitably shaped front-end decisions about whether to capture and detain individuals in the first place.[77] Those who were captured were increasingly kept in the custody of other countries. According to Congressman Mike Rogers, "The tangled mess of legal and policy issues surrounding detention right now makes it very difficult, if not impossible, to gain complete access for questioning. This forces us to work through the host country, which is not always optimal for a number of reasons."[78] As with drone strikes, detention by proxy meant that the US government might be forgoing valuable intelligence. The chief downside for detainees was the poor conditions in which they were held. The Bosaso prison in Somalia is one example: the United States turned over several Somalis to Somali government custody, and they were imprisoned at a facility with no running water and massive overcrowding.[79] Conditions at Guantánamo Bay or in American military custody in Afghanistan were far better than conditions at Bosaso.

These two scenarios—death by targeted killing or confinement in countries with poor human rights records—are clearly suboptimal from the perspective of suspected enemy fighters, who might otherwise be captured and detained by the United States. They also create costs for the government, including the potential loss of valuable intelligence and higher numbers of civilian casualties. Moreover, without a credible detention option, the United States faces the prospect of letting dangerous individuals go free. This policy alternative surfaced at a congressional hearing in mid-2011, during an exchange between the head of the Joint Special Operations Command (JSOC), Admiral William McRaven, and Senator Lindsey Graham (R-SC).[80] Graham pressed McRaven on the following question: what would the military do if it captured a suspected terrorist in a place like Yemen or Somalia, where the United States did not have its own facility for detaining that individual? This was a tricky situation, because the Afghan government had since restricted bringing non-Afghans to Bagram and the Obama administration was opposed to bringing new detainees to Guantánamo. Admiral McRaven hemmed and hawed for a bit in response to Graham's question, then mentioned the possibility of temporary detention on a military ship followed by either commencing criminal prosecution in the United States or handing the person over to a third party. Graham followed up: what if there was insufficient admissible evidence to prosecute the person, and no other nation was willing to assume custody? McRaven replied, "Sir . . . if we can't do either one of those, then we'll release that individual and that becomes the—the unenviable option, but it is an option."[81]

## CONGRESS AND THE EXECUTIVE BRANCH CLASH

Admiral McRaven's testimony vividly illustrated the real-world impact of the uncertainty swirling around detention law and policy. While a variety of legal issues were being adjudicated in a back-and-forth between trial judges and appellate panels in the DC Circuit, the other two branches continued to reshape detention policies. In March 2011 President Obama issued an executive order creating his own version of parole-style review boards for Guantánamo detainees called periodic review boards (PRBs).[82] Like ARBs, their predecessors established in 2004, PRBs are tasked with weighing a detainee's prospective dangerousness. Specifically, PRBs evaluate whether "continued detention of particular individuals held at Guantánamo remains necessary to protect against a continuing significant threat to the security of the United States."[83] If not, PRBs may recommend transfer subject to security measures. Where ARBs were more informal and were administered by the military, PRBs are more rule-bound and are staffed by officials from several different executive branch agencies. PRBs comprise representatives from DOJ, DOD, the Department of Homeland Security (DHS), the State Department, the Joint Chiefs of Staff (JCS), and the Office of the Director of National Intelligence (ODNI). Detainees undergoing PRB hearings are given a representative to assist them and receive greater access to classified information than the ARB system offered. Once again, detention policy evolved in a favorable direction for detainees. But it took a long time to get PRBs up and running. From 2011 to 2013—when the first PRBs got underway—the Guantánamo population hovered around 170.[84] No new detainees came in, but few departed.

President Obama's policy against bringing new detainees to Guantánamo received its toughest test in April 2011, when the United States captured a Somali terrorist named Ahmed Abdulkadir Warsame.[85] Warsame was a leading member of the Somali terrorist organization known as al-Shabab and had links to AQAP. After his capture Warsame was transferred to a US ship, where he was held by the military and interrogated. His confinement aboard the ship lasted more than two months, during which time the Obama administration engaged in an extended internal debate about what to do with him.[86] Some in the administration pushed for a civilian trial in the United States, while others leaned toward trial by military commission.[87] Transferring a high-level terrorist like Warsame to Somalia was off the table due to its instability, and long-term military detention without charges was a nonstarter given Obama's opposition to it. The administration eventually settled on the civilian trial approach.[88] When Warsame's military interrogation concluded, a "clean team" of FBI officials informed Warsame of his Miranda rights and interrogated him anew, after which he was flown to the United States for prosecution in federal court. This so-called hybrid model became the Obama administration's preferred method of dealing with a handful of high-level terrorists captured outside of Afghanistan: short-term military detention and interrogation aboard a ship, followed by transfer to law enforcement custody and a civilian trial inside the United States.[89]

The emerging hybrid approach worked well on Warsame: he was convicted, and in the process he cooperated with the government and provided lots of useful information.[90] But the new approach faced a test from a Republican-controlled Congress in late 2011, when Republican lawmakers began pushing to make military detention and prosecution in military commissions mandatory for those with links to al-Qaeda. Short of the votes required to do this, Republicans and some Democrats reached a compromise: the military approach would be the default option for new captures, but the executive branch could waive it if it deemed a law enforcement or hybrid approach to be in the interest of national security.[91] These provisions were part of the National Defense Authorization Act for 2012 (NDAA 2012). Controversially, the military custody provisions would even apply to noncitizen al-Qaeda suspects captured on American soil. NDAA 2012 contained another important passage that explicitly authorized detention of enemy fighters—something the 2001 AUMF had not expressly done.[92] In NDAA 2012 Congress effectively ratified the March 13 Standard, authorizing the detention of any individual "who was part of or substantially supported al-Qaeda, the Taliban, or associated forces that are engaged in hostilities against the United States or its coalition partners, including any person who has committed a belligerent act or has directly supported such hostilities in aid of such enemy forces."[93]

Congress had finally offered explicit support for detention and a more specific definition of who could be detained. It largely ratified the results of the back-and-forth between the courts and the executive branch. But it was something that NDAA 2012 did *not* say that received the most attention. The statute's detention provisions did not make clear whether they would apply to American citizens taken into custody on American soil.[94] That remained an open legal question, since Jose Padilla's case produced a circuit court split that the Supreme Court never resolved. Rather than answer it, Congress punted. Consistent with the work of Mark Graber and others who have highlighted legislators' tendency to dodge difficult questions and pass them off to judges, Congress was content to let the courts decide the issue if and when a situation like Padilla's arose again.[95] Senate Democrat Carl Levin summed it up this way: "We make clear that whatever the law is, it is unaffected by this language in our bill."[96]

The interbranch tug-of-war over detention policies persisted. When President Obama reluctantly signed the bill into law, he vowed to interpret the military custody provisions with a "maximum measure of flexibility."[97] He made good on this promise in February 2012, issuing sweeping waivers to the military custody provisions.[98] The order, called Presidential Policy Directive 14 (PPD-14), eschewed case-by-case waivers and instead excluded entire categories of detainees from the mandatory military custody provisions. As Charlie Savage writes, "The waivers were so all-encompassing that Obama had effectively gutted the new law: no real mandate, as a practical matter, existed."[99] The Guantánamo transfer restrictions—extended in the NDAAs for 2012 and 2013—proved more effective as a constraint: not a single detainee departed Guantánamo in the fifteen-month period between January 2011 and April 2012.[100] Transfer efforts stagnated so much that the State Department office dedicated to doing diplomatic outreach for detainee resettlement was closed.[101] In the spring of 2013, Guantánamo detainees staged a widespread hunger strike to draw attention to their ongoing confinement and the lack of detainee releases.[102]

One reason for the slowdown in transfers was the steady drumbeat of reports that roughly 25 percent of the 600-plus detainees released from Guantánamo were either confirmed as or suspected of returning to the battlefield.[103] Obama administration officials were quick to note that the lion's share of the transfers had occurred during the Bush administration and that recidivism rates for those transfers were considerably higher than the rates for Obama's transfers. But with Republicans trumpeting these statistics and opposing further releases—and with the secretary of defense now statutorily responsible for signing off on each individual transfer—risk aversion prevailed in the executive branch at this time.[104] Contributing to the delay was the sluggish implementation of PRBs.[105] The 2009 detainee task force had viewed all of the evidence against each detainee when making its recommendations, but some members of the administration now wanted evidence obtained through torture or coercion to be kept out of PRB hearings.[106] Over objections from DOD and CIA, the arrangement that emerged ensured that evidence deemed to be tainted would be withheld unless it was helpful to a detainee.[107]

Meanwhile, the Obama administration was confronted with a different detention policy issue: how to handle the detainees being held by the United States in Afghanistan as the United States wound down its involvement there. By early 2012, the population at the Bagram detention facility exceeded three thousand. Most of these detainees were Afghan citizens, captured in Afghanistan and suspected of having ties to the Taliban. They would soon be turned over to Afghanistan government custody. But there was a group of about fifty detainees—individuals captured outside of Afghanistan and suspected of having links to al-Qaeda—over whom the United States was hesitant to relinquish control.[108] Negotiations regarding their status carried on into 2013.[109] The Afghan government eventually assumed full control over all of the detainees at Bagram, and while it agreed to prosecute some of the detainees the United States thought should not be released, it released many others it claimed could be neither charged nor detained.[110] The United States retained custody of a small group of non-Afghan detainees through the end of 2014, at which point all but one of those detainees were either handed over to Afghan custody or the custody of another nation. One detainee with direct links to an attack on Americans was flown to the United States for a civilian trial and was convicted.[111]

## A FINAL PUSH TO CLOSE GUANTÁNAMO

As the United States unwound its detention operations in Afghanistan, the Obama administration also revived efforts to close Guantánamo. In a May 2013 speech, President Obama vowed to begin transitioning away from a "perpetual wartime footing" in combating terrorism.[112] This would include ending wartime detention. Citing the high cost of keeping Guantánamo open and its negative effects on the United States' reputation abroad, Obama called on Congress to lift the transfer restrictions it had imposed. He also announced the appointment of a pair of envoys—one at the State Department, one at the Department of Defense—who would oversee efforts to transfer detainees to other countries. And he declared an end to a blanket moratorium on transfers to Yemen. Obama was not clear about what should happen to detainees who could not be prosecuted but were deemed too dangerous to release, but the address signaled a renewed commitment to moving as many detainees as possible out of Guantánamo Bay.

Progress on this front was slow but noticeable. Two Algerian detainees were sent home in the summer of 2013, and there was a flurry of transfers in December.[113] Civilian administration officials committed to shuttering Guantánamo rejected a request from the military for money to renovate the facilities there.[114] President Obama signed into law the NDAA for 2014, which included small changes to the detainee transfer restrictions, making transfers to other nations easier. Instead of having to certify that each of a number of transfer conditions were met or waived, the secretary of defense would simply have to confirm that all of the conditions had been taken into account before approving a transfer. Another important milestone came in January 2014: a Yemeni man became the first detainee to have his status changed by a PRB. The detainee, previously designated for continued detention, was now recommended for transfer.[115] And in February 2014, a court ruling added to the ongoing litigation pressures at Guantánamo. The DC Circuit held that detainees could use habeas corpus proceedings to challenge their conditions of confinement at the detention facility.[116] The case, *Aamer v. Obama*, concerned the detainee hunger strike at Guantánamo, which had resulted in the use of force-feeding procedures that some argued were painful and inhumane. Though the government ultimately won the lawsuit on the merits, DOD modified some of its force-feeding procedures while the litigation was unfolding.[117]

By the middle of 2014, there was also significant internal executive branch pressure on the issue of Guantánamo. The White House was pushing Secretary of Defense Chuck Hagel to speed up his approvals of detainee transfers. National Security Advisor Susan Rice sent Hagel a memo asking for regular updates and instructing him that the risk of a detainee returning to the battlefield must be balanced against the harms resulting from Guantánamo remaining open. The State Department, troubled by Guantánamo's impact on relations with other countries, also pressed for expedited transfers. But Hagel was cross-pressured, as the military expressed concerns that released detainees might rejoin the fight and threaten American troops.[118] In an interview with a reporter, Hagel explained that his reluctance stemmed in part from Congress's requirement that he sign off on transfers: "My name is going on that document. That's a big responsibility. . . . What I'm doing is, I am taking my time. I owe that to the American people, to ensure that any decision I make is, in my mind, responsible."[119] Under continued pressure on this issue and others, Hagel submitted his resignation. Before departing, however, he signed off on several transfer agreements, and his successor Ashton Carter proved more amenable to the White House's position.[120]

Starting in late 2014 and continuing through the remainder of President Obama's time in office, transfers out of Guantánamo Bay picked up speed. Administration officials ramped up diplomatic efforts to resettle detainees recommended for transfer, and PRBs moved more detainees into that category.[121] Litigation continued despite the DC Circuit's generally deferential posture in habeas corpus appeals. The *Aamer* decision spawned lawsuits that created additional momentum for transfers.[122] Entrepreneurial lawyering persisted, as counsel for detainees tried out a variety of novel legal strategies. Detainees from Afghanistan seized on President Obama's public statements that major combat operations there were over, arguing that their detentions were therefore no longer valid.[123] Judges rejected that argument.[124] Other lawyers cited their clients' health problems as grounds for release.[125] Those claims also met with judicial resistance, though at least one detainee who made this argument was released shortly after losing his case.[126] Another lawsuit challenged the constitutionality of Congress's transfer restrictions but was dismissed for lack of standing.[127] In yet another case the DC District Court sided with detainees who sued to halt groin searches—a decision reversed on appeal by the DC Circuit.[128]

As President Obama's second term drew to a close, his administration initiated a full-court press to resettle as many Guantánamo detainees as possible. Many of the transfers in Obama's final year in office were lower-level Yemenis sent to places such as Oman, Saudi Arabia, and the United Arab Emirates.[129] By the time Obama left office in January 2017, just 41 detainees remained at Guantánamo. This was down from the 242 detainees he inherited from the Bush administration, but short of his goal of completely emptying the facility. And his successor, Donald J. Trump, had promised to bring new detainees to the facility and halt the transfers of existing detainees. Would Trump's election mean a new lease on life for Guantánamo and for long-term military detention as a wartime policy tool? Or would the status quo on detention policy prevail?

## DETENTION POLICY IN THE TRUMP ADMINISTRATION

Shortly after Donald Trump won the 2016 presidential election, ACLU executive director Anthony Romero fretted that the Obama administration's continuation of many of the Bush administration's legal positions and policies meant handing President Trump "a fully loaded weapon."[130] But Trump's hardline rhetoric on Guantánamo notwithstanding, his administration's approach to detention has closely resembled his predecessor's. After years of litigation, judicial intervention, and interbranch interaction, detention policies are to a great degree insulated from direct presidential control. At Guantánamo, there has been almost no change whatsoever under Trump: no new detainees have been brought to the facility, and only one detainee has left—Ahmed al-Darbi, who was repatriated to Saudi Arabia pursuant to a military commission plea deal.[131]

Early on in the Trump administration, there were internal debates about whether to bring ISIS captives to Guantánamo. US military operations against ISIS—the terrorist organization formerly known as al-Qaeda in Iraq—began under President Obama in 2014, and the Obama administration's approach to ISIS detainees had generally been to hold them in military custody briefly, if at all, relying instead on others to handle them.[132] Reporting shortly after Trump's inauguration indicated that the new administration was considering using Guantánamo Bay to house ISIS fighters, but that has not happened. A key reason for this is the threat of litigation: as careerists in the executive branch warned, ISIS detainees at Guantánamo would be able to challenge their detentions in court, and it is not clear whether judges would find ISIS to be within the ambit of existing detention statutes. The executive has statutory authority to detain "associated forces" of al-Qaeda, but ISIS and al-Qaeda formally split from one another years ago. A court ruling finding ISIS to lie beyond the reach of the 2001 AUMF and 2012 NDAA would not only imperil detentions of ISIS fighters, but also might undermine ongoing military operations abroad against ISIS, including targeted killings by drone.[133]

The Trump administration's approach to detainees is substantially similar to its predecessor's. The Obama administration's preference for criminal prosecution in the United States or detention by proxy has largely continued under President Trump. For example, in the summer of 2017 an al-Qaeda recruiter named Ali Damache was flown to the United States for a civilian prosecution.[134] A few months later, a suspect in the Benghazi embassy attack, Mustafa al-Imam, was captured and brought to the United States for a criminal trial.[135] These moves were consistent with the Obama administration's use of Article III courts to handle a number of terrorist suspects captured on its watch. And there is evidence that the other prong of the Obama approach—relying on other nations to handle detainees—is also being utilized by the Trump administration.[136]

There is at least one possible exception to the apparent convergence between Obama and Trump on detention matters: for over a year, the US military detained an American citizen, Abdulrahman Ahmad Alsheikh, who was captured on the battlefield in Syria. For eight years under President Obama, no citizen was held in prolonged military detention. However, a brief look at the episode suggests that the deviation was the result of unusual circumstances rather than a conscious policy shift by the Trump administration. Alsheikh, a dual citizen of Saudi Arabia and the United States, came into US custody via Syrian rebel forces in September 2017 and was detained in American military custody inside Iraq. DOD officials expressed a desire to hand him off to DOJ for prosecution, but reports indicate that DOJ believed it lacked sufficient admissible evidence to undertake a successful prosecution.[137] The Iraqi government did not want to assume custody of Alsheikh, and turning him over to the brutal Assad regime in Syria was a nonstarter. Thus, the use of the military detention option seemed more like a last resort, adopted reluctantly and in response to the specific facts of the situation, than it did a deliberate policy decision.

Regardless of the exact motivations behind the move, a lawsuit quickly followed. Within weeks of Alsheikh's capture, the ACLU filed a habeas corpus petition on his behalf. The government refused to disclose Alsheikh's name at this time, identifying him only as John Doe. The government asked the DC District Court to dismiss the lawsuit, *Doe v. Mattis*, on the grounds that the ACLU could not serve as Doe's next friend since it had no relationship with him and did not even know whether he wished to sue. Judge Tanya Chutkan disagreed, ruling that Doe was entitled to unmonitored conversations with an attorney. She then went further: the Trump administration was discussing sending him to Saudi Arabia, but Judge Chutkan ordered the government not to transfer Doe without additional legal proceedings.[138] When the government informed Doe that it wished to transfer him to Saudi Arabia, Doe objected. Judge Chutkan sided with Doe, blocking the transfer. The DC Circuit upheld that decision by a 2–1 vote in May 2018, ruling that the government would first have to prove that Doe was an enemy combatant before it could transfer him to Saudi custody.[139]

Rather than continue to litigate the matter, the Trump administration ultimately elected to release Alsheikh in Bahrain in the fall of 2018.[140] Alsheikh's passport was revoked, but he retained his US citizenship. The legal complications caused by the prolonged detention of an American citizen had a profound impact on DOD officials, several of whom stated that their department would be highly reluctant to repeat the episode in the future. They maintained that unless DOD was assured that prosecution would eventually ensue, it would oppose taking custody of citizen detainees like Alsheikh. Alsheikh's lawyer, Jonathan Hafetz, celebrated the effects of the litigation: "A resounding message is that the government is going to think long and hard before it tries to detain an American citizen without charges again—and it should."[141] Again, litigation and court decisions had a decisive impact on the government's detention policies. And as Hafetz recognized, the consequences would not merely be retrospective. They would loom over policy makers confronted with similar situations in the future.

## CONCLUSION

In a 2014 op-ed in the *New York Times*, a law professor who has represented Guantánamo detainees in litigation, Ramzi Kassem, wrote that "Guantánamo remains at its core a lawless place."[142] A more recent op-ed by two Yale Law School students leveled a similar critique, labeling the detention site a place of "enduring injustice."[143] For critics like these, it seems that indefinite detention of suspected enemy fighters in the current armed conflict is illegitimate—and that no amount of procedural protections or review mechanisms short of a full civilian trial can undo that fact. But whatever one's view of the underlying morality or fairness of US detention policies, charges of lawlessness are difficult to reconcile with the past two decades of policy development. As this chapter demonstrates, legal challenges and checks on presidential authority did not end with the 2008 Supreme Court decision in *Boumediene v. Bush*. The evolution of detention policies has continued down similar pathways over the past decade, resulting in policies shaped by ongoing litigation, court decisions, and the ordinary push-and-pull of what Richard Neustadt called "separated institutions sharing powers."[144]

In the roughly ten-year period explored in this chapter, all three branches of the federal government exerted significant influence over detention policies. Numerous decisions by the DC District Court and the DC Circuit Court of Appeals—and the ever-present prospect of additional lawsuits on related issues—led to policy changes at Guantánamo and in Afghanistan. Litigation, already profoundly important at Guantánamo Bay, traversed half the globe and generated reforms to detainee policies in an active theater of war. And it contributed to more reductions in the detainee population at Guantánamo Bay. Congress again injected itself into the policy muddle as well, explicitly authorizing detention for the first time and levying restrictions on transfers from Guantánamo Bay, among other things. And President Obama, despite being hemmed in considerably by the accumulated actions of the judiciary and the legislature, managed to make some policy adjustments, including replacing ARBs with PRBs and significantly limiting the use of military detention as a wartime policy tool.

The election of Donald Trump, a political outsider whose campaign rhetoric exhibited no discernible concern for checks and balances or the rights of suspected terrorists, posed an especially hard test for one of the core arguments advanced here in this book: that lawsuits and court rulings—and the separation of powers tug-of-war they have helped engender—have produced enemy combatant policies that are largely insulated from presidential control. But the first term of the Trump presidency offers additional support for this claim. Contrary to his campaign promise to increase the number of individuals held at Guantánamo Bay, the Trump administration has brought exactly zero new detainees to the facility. And it has mostly eschewed the use of prolonged detention abroad as well, opting instead to retain the Obama administration's preferences for pursuing civilian prosecutions in the United States or passing the buck to other nations whenever possible.

The policy developments explored in these three chapters on detention have yielded a complex array of costs and benefits. As detentions have become increasingly difficult for the government to sustain, other policy options—including proxy detention, targeted killing, civilian prosecution, and acceptance of some potentially dangerous individuals walking free—have become more commonplace. These policy tools have numerous downsides for both the government and terrorist suspects that lawyers and judges have not comprehensively examined. For example, drone strikes deprive suspected terrorists of not only their liberty but their lives, make it more difficult for the United States to collect important intelligence, and may result in collateral damage that takes innocent lives and hurts the American cause abroad. Allowing other countries to shoulder the responsibility for handling detainees is liable to similar objections: detainees may be worse off in the custody of others, and the United States may have more trouble obtaining intelligence. It is also possible that the interests of other nations will not align with US security interests, leading to the release of dangerous individuals. Moreover, even when the United States does temporarily assume custody of terrorist suspects, it may elect to free them rather than go through the trouble of detaining them. Or it may seek to prosecute them in civilian trials, which entails costs of its own. There is, however, another alternative: prosecution in special military tribunals called military commissions. That is the subject of the next three chapters.

# 4. "Kangaroo Courts?" The Troubled Beginnings of Military Commissions (2001–2005)

The decision after 9/11 to create military commissions to prosecute enemy fighters for war crimes was a clear example of presidential unilateralism. With little debate, President George W. Bush signed a closely held executive order announcing the creation of military commissions in November 2001. Ever since then, however, legal and policy developments surrounding military commissions have been the product of extended litigation and interbranch interaction, not presidential dictates. From the initial implementation of Bush's executive order to the ongoing struggle to prosecute 9/11 mastermind Khalid Sheikh Mohammed and others held at Guantánamo Bay, military commissions have become increasingly independent of presidential control and more protective of defendants. Because of these reforms, the commission system today is a far cry from the one first envisioned by the Bush administration.

Even before the Supreme Court ruling in 2006 that invalidated the Bush administration's system of military commissions, military commissions were reenvisioned and reformed by the executive branch in ways that circumscribed presidential discretion and took into account legal considerations. One crucial piece of the story is the extent to which the executive branch was internally divided over the structure, scope, and rules of the commissions. Different bureaucratic actors—possessing diverse perspectives, interests, and professional norms—battled with one another from the beginning, and these internecine struggles resulted in significant policy shifts from the 2001 baseline. Perhaps the most important players in these scuffles were judge advocates general (JAGs)—military lawyers who were circumvented initially, but who helped shape the rules for commissions during the implementation phase. JAGs have a strong professional code of conduct that prizes a strict commitment to the rule of law. And they found allies in the Bush administration, including officials at the State Department and the Department of Justice (DOJ), whose motivations were different but whose policy preferences aligned with the JAGs.

Executive branch actors who supported reforms were aided by the separation of powers. The actions of other institutions, whether real or merely anticipated, bolstered their position. In response to congressional criticism of the

White House's unilateral decision to use military commissions and concerns that they would be "kangaroo courts" lacking sufficient protections for the accused, the Department of Defense (DOD)—the agency tasked with developing implementing regulations for commissions—vowed to consider the views of legislators. Reform proponents in the executive branch were able to use the specter of litigation to their advantage. At multiple junctures, they cited ongoing lawsuits and the threat of judicial resistance as a reason to make changes to the military commission system. Litigation combined with the nonunitary character of the executive branch and the separation of powers to spur policy changes that made military commissions friendlier to defendants and less amenable to presidential control than most observers expected them to be. All of this occurred before the Supreme Court's intervention in 2006—an important reminder that the role of lawsuits and courts in policy evolution often exists independent of the highest court in the land.

The developments described above—military commissions featuring additional protections for the accused and more walled off from the whims of the White House—may sound salutary. But the chief drawbacks of adversarial legalism were also evident, and remain evident to this day: its tendency to create legal uncertainty, an enormous amount of delay, and unintended consequences. By the summer of 2006—almost five years after President Bush issued his executive order—not a single military commission proceeding had been completed. The slow pace of litigation challenging the commission system and the legal uncertainty it stirred up contributed greatly to the sluggishness. Instead of receiving a speedy military trial and a defined sentence, many detainees were kept in limbo. Military commissions became a less appealing option for the government to use against terrorist suspects. It is far from clear that this is a good outcome for either party.

## THE EXECUTIVE ORDER CREATING MILITARY COMMISSIONS

Two months removed from the events of September 11, with the US military response underway, President Bush signed an executive order establishing military commissions to prosecute captured enemy belligerents for war crimes.[1] The idea to use military commissions was first floated by executive branch lawyers in the immediate wake of the 9/11 attacks.[2] They were reminded of

Franklin Delano Roosevelt's decision to employ military commissions in World War II, including an episode involving several Nazi saboteurs—a move that the Supreme Court unanimously upheld in a controversial case called *Ex parte Quirin.*[3] The Office of Legal Counsel (OLC) produced a memo, signed by Deputy Assistant Attorney General Patrick Philbin, arguing that President Bush had legal authority under existing legislation and Article II of the Constitution to establish a system of military commissions to prosecute terrorist suspects for war crimes.[4] Advocates of military commissions saw them as a valuable tool for efficiently incapacitating enemy fighters who violated the laws of war. These individuals could be prosecuted outside the more cumbersome civilian justice system, replete with its many protections for defendants.[5]

At first, it looked as if the process of creating military commissions would include a wide range of voices. JAGs began working on a plan, believing they would be put in charge of the new system.[6] White House Counsel Alberto Gonzales formed a working group including lawyers from several agencies to study various options for prosecuting war criminals. But some members of the Bush administration thought the process was moving too slowly.[7] A small group of White House and DOD officials took the reins, and reservations expressed by JAGs and members of the working group were shunted aside.[8] JAGs were afraid that if commissions were insufficiently protective of defendants, it would give adversaries an excuse to subject American troops to similar treatment. And JAGs also worried about pushback from allies and potential legal challenges in US courts.[9] The State Department warned of negative diplomatic consequences, arguing that other countries might balk at cooperating with the United States if the commission system was perceived as unfair. DOJ's assurances that it could successfully prosecute terrorists in Article III courts likewise went unheeded. So too did concerns that relying on a relatively obscure and often-criticized World War II–era precedent was an inadequate legal foundation upon which to build a system of military commissions.[10]

Only a few administration officials saw the final draft of the executive order before President Bush signed it. Written by Vice President Dick Cheney's legal counsel David Addington, according to Barton Gellman and Jo Becker the document "changed hands four times." Neither National Security Advisor Condoleezza Rice nor Secretary of State Colin Powell laid eyes on the document before it was released to the public.[11] Attorney General John Ashcroft was largely cut out of the process as well, and his complaints about the lack of DOJ involvement in administering the commission system were ignored.[12]

OLC took the position that DOD ought to oversee the new military commission system, since it was to be understood primarily as a military institution rather than a law enforcement body.[13]

Modeled after FDR's order creating a military commission to try the Nazi saboteurs, Bush's order was short on specifics.[14] It began by citing relevant legal authorities in support of the move—a combination of constitutional power under Article II and statutory authorization from the 2001 AUMF and an older law called the Uniform Code of Military Justice (UCMJ)—a decades-old statute regulating various elements of the American military justice system. The next section of the order laid out a series of "findings" justifying the decision to use military commissions, including an assertion that the rules and procedures used in ordinary civilian trials were "not practicable" in military commissions.[15] The order also contained language delineating the scope of the commission system. It would be used to try noncitizens who fell into one of three categories: members of al-Qaeda; those who "engaged in, aided or abetted, or conspired to commit, acts of international terrorism, or acts in preparation therefor [*sic*]"; or those who "knowingly harbored" any person who met either of these two criteria.[16]

The executive order left a host of questions unanswered. For example, one provision stated that individuals could be "tried for any and all offenses triable by military commission" without specifying what those offenses were. Many policy details were delegated to the secretary of defense. Section 4 of the order empowered the secretary to issue "orders and regulations" on a multitude of issues, including what qualifications commission lawyers would have to possess, where the commissions would take place, and how the commissions would be composed. The text of the executive order did address a few baseline procedural matters—defendants were to receive a "full and fair trial," for instance, and it would take a two-thirds vote to convict and sentence a defendant—but the main thrust was to punt a number of key decisions to DOD.[17] The rules and procedures for military commissions would emerge months later in a set of regulations.

The November order creating military commissions was a unilateral presidential act. Few individuals outside of the White House were involved in the process of drafting the document, and Congress was circumvented entirely. This irked many lawmakers. Representative John Conyers Jr. (D-MI) criticized the order for resting on the "thinnest of legal precedents."[18] Senator Patrick Leahy (D-VT) called for legislation guaranteeing, among other things, a presumption of innocence for commission defendants and Supreme Court review of commission verdicts.[19] Senator Arlen Specter (R-PA) expressed reservations about the Bush administration's decision to bypass Congress and called for hearings on the issue. Lawmakers listened to Bush administration officials as well as experts who supported and opposed the plan, and legislative proposals began to circulate on Capitol Hill.[20] Administration officials, led by Secretary of Defense Donald Rumsfeld, promised to consider Congress's concerns during the process of writing implementing regulations for the commission system. That assurance, combined with President Bush's extraordinary popularity following the terrorist attacks, helped convince Congress to remain on the sidelines.[21]

## THE PENTAGON ISSUES MILITARY COMMISSION ORDER NO. 1

The rule-writing process for military commissions took time. More than one hundred drafts of the regulations bounced back and forth among the various entities involved.[22] On March 21, 2002, a sixteen-page document called Military Commission Order No. 1 (MCO No. 1) emerged.[23] MCO No. 1 filled in many of the blanks in President Bush's November executive order. It established the basic structure and composition of military commissions: commissions would be composed of between three and seven members and one or two alternates, and those individuals would be chosen by the "appointing authority"—either the secretary of defense, or an official designated by the secretary. The appointing authority would select commissioned officers in the US military deemed "competent to perform the duties involved," and members of the commission could be removed only by the appointing authority "for good cause." The appointing authority would designate one commission member the "presiding officer," charged with overseeing the proceedings. The presiding officer was the only commission member required to have legal training: he or she had to be a lawyer in the armed forces. The presiding officer's responsibilities included ruling on the admissibility of evidence, closing the proceedings or excluding the defendant if necessary to protect classified information, and ensuring "the expeditious conduct of the trial."

MCO No. 1 also established rules for prosecutors and defendants. Prosecutors would have to submit charges for approval by the appointing authority.

Defendants wishing to hire civilian attorneys to supplement their representation by military lawyers were permitted to do so. MCO No. 1 also contained a section delineating "procedures accorded the accused." The awkward phrase reflected a conscious decision by administration officials to avoid using the word "rights" in the context of military commissions.[24] In fact, the only mention of "rights" appeared in section 10 of the order, which began, "This order is not intended to create any right, benefit, or privilege, substantive or procedural, enforceable by any party, against the United States." Granting defendants "procedures" rather than rights was a strategic calculation by Bush administration lawyers, who believed the judiciary was less likely to intervene if commissions looked more like a military operation than an ordinary court.[25]

Among the protections defendants received was a guarantee that they were innocent until proven guilty beyond a reasonable doubt. Axiomatic in civilian courts, the presumption of innocence was not part of President Bush's initial order. In the period between Bush's November order and MCO No. 1, there had been serious debate about whether to include it. But JAGs protested the potential omission during the rule-writing phase, and their view prevailed.[26] As Dawn Johnsen has noted, this was not the only example of regulations being tempered in response to pressure from inside and outside the executive branch.[27] MCO No. 1 made death sentences contingent on a unanimous vote by a seven-member panel (the equivalent of a jury in the civilian justice system), even though Bush's November order merely stated that a two-thirds vote would be required for conviction and sentencing.[28] Other defendant-friendly features of MCO No. 1 included the provision allowing the accused to hire civilian counsel and the creation of an appeals mechanism—a review panel of three military officers who would review a verdict and make a recommendation to the secretary of defense, with final disposition left up to the president.[29]

The nonunitary character of the executive branch was clearly on display during the interagency process of writing rules for military commissions. Unlike the drafting of President Bush's November order, which in highly unusual fashion circumvented key actors in favor of a process centralized in the White House, MCO No. 1 was the product of months of deliberation among a variety of stakeholders. DOJ and the State Department had seats at the table, from which they aired their respective concerns about defending the commission system in court and incurring diplomatic fallout. Both departments feared negative repercussions if military commissions were slanted too far in favor of the government.[30] Secretary of Defense Donald Rumsfeld also pushed back against hawkish White House lawyers during this period.[31] He convened a bipartisan group of legal experts from outside government to consult with DOD lawyers during the rule-writing stage.[32] Conscious of the criticism of Bush's initial order, Rumsfeld later wrote that he desired "a process considerably more protective of the rights of the accused than any previous military commission in our nation's history."[33] Perhaps most importantly, the involvement of the chairman of the Joint Chiefs of Staff (JCS) ensured that uniformed members of the military, including JAGs, could exercise some sway over the content of the implementing regulations.

These internal divisions between the White House and key departments resulted in rules and procedures for military commissions that were more protective of defendants than President Bush's November order suggested they would be. The episode embodies insights in leading work on bureaucracy and executive branch decision-making. As James Q. Wilson has shown, the bureaucracy comprises a vast array of agencies, each of which has its own perspective, culture, and mission.[34] Rebecca Ingber has observed that there is "enormous diversity of actors and processes within the executive branch that overlap, collide and collaborate to formulate executive decisions."[35] And, as Jack Goldsmith's work has demonstrated, layers of bureaucracy—and, in particular, lawyers inside those layers of bureaucracy—have multiplied in recent decades, increasing the amount of deliberation and vetting that precedes virtually every major wartime decision made by the executive branch.[36] What must be added to this is the recognition that internal executive branch divisions intersect with the separation of powers, such that actors in other institutions may capitalize on the dissension to bolster their position.

Those who argue that the contemporary wartime presidency is imperial might point to the November 2001 executive order as evidence for their claim. But as the foregoing analysis shows, that order settled very little about the form and substance of military commissions. The policy details emerged not by presidential fiat, but in a series of regulations published after an extended period of deliberation inside the executive branch. The discussion featured an array of officials from different agencies, and it was shaped by bureaucratic imperatives and external pressures—including threats of congressional and judicial intervention. That the policy-making process played out this way just months after the 9/11 attack is striking. On a core national security issue, the White House was at least partly constrained from the beginning. Soon, litigation and institutional interactions would lead to more limits on presidential discretion and policy changes that made commissions more favorable to the accused.

## GETTING COMMISSIONS UP AND RUNNING

One of the Bush administration's main arguments for using military commissions was their supposed ability to swiftly and effectively incapacitate terrorists.[37] By creating a separate justice system unencumbered by some of the rules present in civilian courts, the Bush administration hoped to prevent lengthy appeals and guarantee that no dangerous individuals could walk free on legal technicalities. It also wished to pursue aggressive intelligence-gathering efforts without jeopardizing the ability to win convictions. Streamlined procedures in military commissions would give the administration flexibility in dealing with terrorist suspects and preclude messy, protracted litigation. It was the same line of thinking that undergirded the administration's detention policies at Guantánamo: hold detainees beyond the reach of federal courts and preserve maximum flexibility over their treatment and disposition. But none of the central assumptions about military commissions—that they would be quick, effective, and immune to judicial intervention—turned out to be correct. Viewed alongside the World War II Nazi saboteur episode, which took just over one month to move from FDR's initial order to convictions, the post-9/11 experience provides a stunning contrast.

The implementation process for military commissions was slow-moving and rocky from the very beginning, frustrating top administration officials. When President Bush and Secretary Rumsfeld expressed their desire for a quicker pace, however, they were warned by lawyers that their entreaties could constitute "improper command influence" over the commission system.[38] One reason for the delay was that additional regulations continued to trickle out in 2003 and early 2004. Some of these dealt with personnel matters: Military Commission Order No. 2, signed by Rumsfeld in June 2003, made Deputy Secretary of Defense Paul Wolfowitz the first appointing authority for commissions.[39] Wolfowitz was replaced as appointing authority by retired General John Altenburg Jr. in March 2004.[40] Other regulations came in the form of military commission instructions (MCIs) issued by DOD general counsel William Haynes. MCIs were more granular than MCOs, fleshing out substantive details unaddressed by MCO No. 1. A batch of MCIs issued in April 2003 spelled out what crimes were "triable by military commission," the precise qualifications required of civilian defense lawyers, and various "administrative procedures" for the conduct of trials.[41] The question of what crimes were "triable by military commission" was a particularly thorny one and was the leading cause of the delays.[42] (The issue would resurface several years later in a series of legal challenges to the commissions, as discussed in chapter 6.) Other MCIs published in 2003 and 2004 laid out the responsibilities of the prosecution, the defense, and the appellate review panel.[43]

Rule-writing and staffing issues were not the only reasons for the delays. Commission prosecutors needed to gather evidence for prospective cases, which took a tremendous amount of effort.[44] The Office of Military Commissions (OMC) prosecution team took a long time to announce the first set of formal charges. In fact, even the prior step—designating individuals eligible for trial by military commission—took longer than expected, as it became clear early on that the government lacked crucial information about many Guantánamo detainees. Finally, on July 3, 2003, DOD announced President Bush's finding that six detainees met the criteria for a military commission trial.[45] But it would take another year for four of these six individuals to be charged. Two of them, Feroz Abbasi and Moazzam Begg, both British citizens, were never charged and were released in January 2005 after the British government protested the use of military commissions to try its citizens.[46] Of the remaining four, three of them—Salim Hamdan, Ibrahim al Qosi, and Ali al Bahlul—were charged with the offense of conspiracy to commit war crimes. The other individual, an Australian named David Hicks, was also charged with conspiracy but faced additional charges for attempted murder and aiding the enemy.[47] The charges against Hamdan, Qosi, and Bahlul were announced shortly after the Supreme Court ruling in *Rasul v. Bush* finding that statutory habeas corpus rights extended to Guantánamo Bay (Hicks was charged before the case was decided). Undeterred by the Court's determination that the judiciary could entertain lawsuits from Guantánamo detainees, the Bush administration soon announced that several more individuals were eligible for a commission trial.[48]

It was clear even before the first commission proceedings got underway that the system would be aggressively attacked by defense counsel. Uniformed military lawyers tasked with representing terrorist suspects did not hesitate to criticize the commissions and civilian leadership, including the commander in chief himself.[49] As Joshua Dratel, a civilian defense attorney at Guantánamo, has observed, the fact that commissions had a "global audience" composed of not only academics and the media but also foreign nations and international nongovernmental organizations (NGOs) "created an atmosphere conducive to pressuring the military commissions apparatus by appeals to those audiences" and "provided the lawyers available outlets for their message on a daily basis."[50] Defense counsel took advantage of these opportunities. They did not confine their challenges to the specific facts of their clients' cases, but also mounted a broader attack on the commission system as a whole. For example, the lawyer for David Hicks, Major Michael Mori, derided the commissions as "kangaroo courts" and declared, "It offends my understanding of what justice is that's been ingrained in me by the Marine Corps and by my legal training."[51] Alleging that the system concentrated too much power in the executive branch and lacked insulation from politics, Mori labeled the entire scheme "unfair" and said it was incapable of providing a "full and fair trial."[52] Military counsel for Ali al Bahlul, Lieutenant Commander Philip Sundel, made similar arguments, claiming "concerns about virtually every aspect of the military commission process" and arguing that the system lacked the "checks and balances" necessary to ensure a "fair, impartial, and independent process."[53] As Sundel later related, "They expected us to stay within the box they designed for us—accept the rules, accept the process and just fight on the facts. That was never going to happen."[54]

The first round of pretrial proceedings finally commenced in summer 2004, and they got off to a very shaky start. Defense attorneys doggedly challenged the process, structure, and composition of the commission system. For example, when the presiding officer, army colonel Pete Brownback, began ruling on legal motions during pretrial hearings, defense counsel protested that the text of President Bush's November 2001 order made the entire military commission panel "the triers of both fact and law."[55] Defense counsel for Salim Hamdan sought to have Brownback and several commission panelists removed for lacking impartiality.[56] Pretrial proceedings for Ali al Bahlul were the most troubled of all. They were thrown into disarray immediately when Bahlul asked to represent himself.[57] Later, when Bahlul began to deliver what appeared to be a confession of guilt, he was interrupted by Brownback, who warned the commission panel not to take such statements as evidence. Brownback's admonition was baffling, since commission rules did not include protections against self-incrimination and Bahlul's remarks were voluntary. Bahlul did not resume his confession after the interruption. And the

Bahlul proceedings were also marred by disputes over translation, with Arabic-speaking reporters in attendance repeatedly questioning Arabic renderings provided by the military commission interpreter.[58]

The opening round of pretrial proceedings in military commissions was anything but a formality. Defense attorneys made good on their promise to assault head-on the basic legitimacy of the new commission system, calling the entire enterprise into question. Members of the prosecution team worried that the inauspicious beginning would generate negative media coverage and exacerbate existing criticism of the commission system at home and abroad.[59] With the internal challenges from defense lawyers now in progress, opponents of military commissions turned to another avenue of attack: the federal courts. Adversarial legalism, already unfolding in a series of lawsuits challenging detention policies, was about to begin reshaping military commissions too.

## LITIGATION SPURS REFORMS

In April 2004, a few months prior to the pretrial proceedings described above, Salim Hamdan's military defense lawyer, Lieutenant Commander Charles Swift, opened a second front against the military commission system. Teaming up with a like-minded ally outside of government, law professor Neal Katyal, Swift filed a lawsuit in federal district court in Seattle, Washington.[60] Katyal was the coauthor of an important law review article in 2002 contending that the military commissions set up by the Bush administration were unlawful.[61] Katyal and Swift expanded on these arguments in the lawsuit, maintaining that the current version of military commissions violated statutes, the Geneva Conventions, and the Constitution. The decision to file the lawsuit in Seattle, where Swift had established residency, was a strategic move. An appeal would go to the US Court of Appeals for the Ninth Circuit, known for its liberal bent, thereby increasing Hamdan's chances of winning.[62] But the attempt to shop for a hospitable forum failed. District Judge Robert Lasnik granted the government's request for a stay pending the Supreme Court's decisions in the detention cases.[63] After the Supreme Court decided those cases in June 2004, legal challenges from Guantánamo detainees were directed to the District of Columbia. The military commission case brought by Swift and Katyal, *Hamdan v. Rumsfeld*, was moved to the DC District Court.

Judge James Robertson issued his ruling on November 8, 2004.[64] In a sweeping forty-page opinion, Judge Robertson sided with Hamdan, finding two main legal flaws with the military commission system. First, Judge Robertson found that they violated the Geneva Conventions. Article 21 of the UCMJ contained a phrase contemplating the use of military commissions to try "offenders or offenses that by statute or by the law of war may be tried by military commissions."[65] According to Robertson, the term "law of war" included the Third Geneva Convention, which deals with the treatment of captured individuals. He was unwilling to defer to President Bush's finding that the Third Geneva Convention did not apply to the conflict with al-Qaeda.[66] Because Hamdan was captured in Afghanistan—he had worked there as a driver for Osama bin Laden—and Afghanistan was a party to the Geneva Convention, it was applicable. For support, Judge Robertson cited an amicus brief from a group of retired generals and admirals making an argument to this effect.

Having established the applicability of the Third Geneva Convention, Robertson turned to its text. He zeroed in on Article 5, which states that a detainee whose status is uncertain ought to be treated as a lawful combatant entitled to "prisoner of war" (POW) status "until such time as their status has been determined by a competent tribunal."[67] President Bush had designated Hamdan an unlawful enemy combatant, not a lawful combatant entitled to POW status. The presidential finding declared that Hamdan was a member of al-Qaeda involved in acts of international terrorism against the United States, making him an unlawful combatant triable by military commission. While Judge Robertson did not deny that members of al-Qaeda engaged in terrorism could be classified as such, he found the process for arriving at Hamdan's classification to be deficient. Status determinations were to be made by "a competent tribunal." Rejecting the government's argument that the presidential determination should receive "extraordinary deference," Robertson matter-of-factly wrote, "The President is not a 'tribunal.'"[68] For additional support, Robertson pointed to US Army Regulation 190-8, which tracked the Geneva Convention language. And he was unwilling to accept combatant status review tribunal (CSRT) proceedings as a substitute, since CSRTs—created after the Supreme Court's 2004 rulings in the detention cases—were designed to review only an enemy combatant designation, not a detainee's status under the Geneva Conventions as a lawful or unlawful combatant.

Judge Robertson made another significant move with respect to the Geneva Conventions. A separate portion of the Geneva Conventions called Common Article 3 establishes baseline guarantees for any individual who takes part in "armed conflict not of an international character occurring in the territory of one of the High Contracting Parties."[69] Those protections, which are not limited to lawful combatants, include the prohibition of "torture" and other "outrages upon human dignity, in particular, humiliating and degrading treatment," as well as a rule against the "passing of sentences . . . without previous judgment pronounced by a regularly constituted court affording all the judicial guarantees which are recognized as indispensable by civilized peoples." A determination that Common Article 3 applied to the war on terror would raise the following question: did the military commissions created by the Bush administration qualify as "regularly constituted court[s]" offering "judicial guarantees . . . recognized as indispensable by civilized peoples?" If not, even an individual properly classified by a "competent tribunal" as an unlawful combatant might not be triable by military commission.

In what looked like a small victory for the government, Judge Robertson stopped short of holding this. But on closer inspection, his treatment of the Common Article 3 question contained an important rebuke to the administration. The Bush administration's position was that Common Article 3 did not cover the conflict with al-Qaeda, because its key phrase—"armed conflict not of an international character"—solely referred to local conflicts like civil wars, not a global conflict like the war on terror.[70] Judge Robertson rejected that interpretation, finding that Common Article 3 applied to the conflict. But he declined to decide whether the current version of military commissions violated its terms. That judicial dodge was largely inconsequential in the case at hand, because the next part of his opinion found that the commissions violated the UCMJ. But Robertson's interpretation of Common Article 3 was nonetheless significant, because its provisions banning "torture" and "humiliating and degrading treatment" had potential consequences for the administration's detention and interrogation policies.

Confronting the legality of military commissions head-on, Judge Robertson held that the commissions violated statutory limits imposed by Congress. First, though, he offered some noteworthy praise for the commission system. "In most respects," Robertson wrote, "the procedures established for the Military Commission at Guantanamo under the President's order define a trial forum that looks appropriate and even reassuring when seen through the lens of American jurisprudence."[71] He ticked off several elements of MCO No. 1 in support of this claim—further evidence that the interagency rule-writing process yielded more moderate policy outcomes than many observers have appreciated. But there was one big problem with the rules, according to Judge Robertson: commission defendants could in some cases be excluded from their own trials and prevented from seeing classified evidence. He held that this conflicted with the UCMJ.

Article 36 of the UCMJ authorized the president to prescribe "procedures" and "modes of proof" for courts-martial and military commissions. But the UCMJ also contained provisions stating that defendants in court-martial proceedings must be present at their trial and able to view the government's evidence against them. The Bush administration argued for a flexible reading of the UCMJ that would allow military commission rules to diverge from the rules for courts-martial when necessary. But while Judge Robertson intimated that a compelling showing of a "need" for deviations might receive judicial acquiescence, he rejected the administration's "blanket finding" that certain rules were "not practicable" in military commissions. Pointing out that the military regularly handles classified information in court-martial proceedings without denying defendants access to it, Robertson held that the government had to make a specific, convincing showing that a military commission required different procedures. Because the government had not done so, Hamdan's military commission was unlawful under the UCMJ, and the president's authority under Article II of the Constitution did not permit him to override those legislative restrictions. Robertson ordered that commission proceedings against Hamdan cease until the two legal flaws he identified were fixed: Hamdan was found by a "competent tribunal" not to be entitled to POW status and the commission rules in MCO No. 1 were altered to prevent exclusion from his trial and allow him access to classified evidence.

By 2004, federal judges had already surprised many observers by pushing back against the executive branch in detention litigation. Now, in the first lawsuit challenging military commissions, a federal district court judge once again refused to defer to the Bush administration in a major national security case. In fact, the DC District Court did exactly the opposite, carefully probing the government's arguments and assertions and repeatedly rejecting them. Back at Guantánamo Bay, military commission proceedings that were halted after the troubled preliminary hearings had just resumed. But Jess Bravin reports that as Presiding Officer Brownback waded through more pretrial motions, a theatrical scene unfolded. A marine bailiff approached Brownback with a note informing him of Judge Robertson's ruling, and Brownback abruptly announced without explanation that the commission was in recess and left the room. He returned shortly thereafter and declared the recess "indefinite," at which point Neal Katyal—who was present at the commission hearings—reportedly uttered the words, "We won."[72]

Judge Robertson's decision in *Hamdan v. Rumsfeld* initially met with defiance on the part of some in the OMC, who suggested ignoring it.[73] Some Bush administration officials floated the idea of only narrowly complying with the ruling: halt Salim Hamdan's commission but continue with others, in hopes that another judge might issue a different ruling. But the appointing authority for commissions, General Altenburg, chose a different course. Insisting that it was foolish to challenge a federal judge, and worried that scattered, inconsistent court decisions would further muddy the waters for military commissions, Altenburg brought all commission proceedings to a stop. Hamdan and the other commission defendants would continue to be held as wartime detainees. Like other detainees designated as enemy combatants, they could no longer be sure if or when their next day in court—or in commission—would arrive.

The district court decision shook up the status quo, giving proponents of reforming military commissions leverage. Coming on the heels of rocky pretrial proceedings, the *Hamdan* ruling prompted debate within the Bush administration about revising or even revoking the November 2001 order that created the commissions.[74] The State Department used the moment to advocate for a more robust review process for commission decisions and a rule explicitly prohibiting the use of evidence obtained through torture.[75] The court ruling also generated discussion within OMC's prosecution office, where officials worried about the potential for additional legal challenges. An internal report cautioned that having "non-lawyers [on military commission panels] deciding what the law is" was "inefficient, and prone to appellate attack." The leading recommendation in the report was to seek legislation from Congress bringing military commissions more in line with courts-martial and explicitly authorizing their use. Proponents of this approach thought this would shore up the administration's ability to defend the system in court. The report predicted that otherwise, commissions would continue to be susceptible to judicial invalidation.[76]

After debating these issues, the Bush administration elected not to make any changes at this time. Instead, the administration appealed Judge Robertson's ruling and defended the existing commission system before the DC Circuit Court of Appeals. Military commission proceedings remained at a standstill for months pending the decision. In July 2005, the DC Circuit reversed the district court ruling.[77] A unanimous three-judge panel issued an opinion diametrically opposed to District Judge Robertson's. Circuit Judge A. Raymond Randolph wrote the DC Circuit's opinion, joined by Judge Stephen Williams and future Supreme Court appointee Judge John Roberts. Before highlighting the differences between the two rulings, however, it is worth noting one area of overlap: like the DC District Court, the DC Circuit Court declined the government's invitation to dismiss the case and instead decided it on the merits. This was not a foregone conclusion, since the government argued that judges ought to wait until commission proceedings were completed before weighing in. Had judges wished to sidestep a sensitive wartime case in the early years of the war, they had a way to do so. That they chose not to take it is yet another indication of the judiciary's increasingly interventionist posture in the national security realm since 9/11.

Unlike the DC District Court, though, the DC Circuit's ruling was hospitable to the government. One key distinction between the DC Circuit and District Judge Robertson's approach concerned their views of the statutory landscape. The DC Circuit construed the UCMJ as conferring some degree of congressional support for military commissions, but unlike the district court, the DC Circuit focused on another, more recent statute as well: the 2001 AUMF. It interpreted the AUMF's "all necessary and appropriate force" language to include the creation of military commissions. By finding that Congress had implicitly authorized the commissions, the DC Circuit did not have to address the Bush administration's claim that Article II of the Constitution gave the president independent constitutional authority to convene military commissions.

Another key difference was the DC Circuit's treatment of the Geneva Conventions, which diverged sharply from the district court's approach. The DC Circuit found them to be unenforceable in the courts: if a treaty was being violated, the avenue for redress was diplomacy, not litigation. The DC Circuit also held that even if the Geneva Conventions were judicially enforceable, they did not apply to the conflict with al-Qaeda. Circuit Judge Randolph's opinion counseled deference to the executive branch's interpretation of the Geneva Conventions. This was the only point on which the DC Circuit panel was not unanimous: Judge Stephen Williams appended a concurring opinion agreeing with the lower court's judgment that Common Article 3—which applies to "conflict not of an international character"—covered the war with al-Qaeda.[78] Because Judge Williams thought the Geneva Conventions were judicially unenforceable, though, his analysis of Common Article 3 stopped there. The panel unanimously endorsed President Bush's determination that Hamdan was not a lawful combatant entitled to POW status under Geneva's terms.

The DC Circuit Court also departed from Judge Robertson's reading of the UCMJ. Robertson had interpreted the UCMJ to mean that military commissions must adhere to the rules used in courts-martial except in cases of necessity. The DC Circuit adopted a different understanding: under its view, only the select few passages of the UCMJ that explicitly mentioned military commissions were applicable. As a result, the vast majority of the UCMJ's rules and procedures applied exclusively to courts-martial, not military commissions. According to the DC Circuit, the rules and procedures for the Bush administration's version of military commissions did not violate the limited restrictions on military commissions in the UCMJ.

The panel had to confront one final argument. According to Hamdan's lawyers, army regulations dictated that Hamdan was entitled to a status review by a "competent tribunal." Although the DC Circuit had already rejected the argument that the "competent tribunal" language in the Geneva Conventions entitled Hamdan to a status review, US Army Regulation 190-8 included a line stating that individuals taken into military custody would receive Geneva Convention protections "until some other legal status is determined by competent authority." Hamdan's lawyers claimed that "competent authority" was the legal equivalent of "competent tribunal." But the distinction in terminology did not matter to the DC Circuit, which found that the president was a "competent authority" and the military commission itself was a "competent tribunal." The army regulation was satisfied either way.

The DC Circuit Court's decision in *Hamdan v. Rumsfeld* was by most measures a resounding victory for the Bush administration. Unlike the district court opinion, which was almost entirely devoid of deferential language, the circuit court repeatedly counseled judicial deference to the executive branch. And on the underlying question—whether Hamdan's military commission was lawful and could move forward—the Bush administration won. Still, the DC Circuit decision provided further evidence that judicial involvement in the war was here to stay. Moreover, although the DC Circuit found that the executive possessed broad statutory authority to prosecute the war, it declined to endorse the Bush administration's expansive construction of the president's powers under Article II of the Constitution. Those who feared that the Bush administration's legal positions marked the return of an imperial presidency ought to have been mollified at least somewhat by the DC Circuit's reasoning in *Hamdan*, even if the outcome itself was disappointing.

As soon as the decision came down, the Bush administration announced the resumption of military commission proceedings.[79] But just weeks after the DC Circuit ruling, a new development cast doubt on the future of the commissions. Military officials with reservations about the commission system leaked internal emails from 2004 that revealed considerable dissension among OMC prosecution staff regarding the basic fairness of the system. Some expressed concern that commissions were being engineered to guarantee convictions. Critiques from OMC's defense attorneys were to be expected, but complaints from prosecutors were more jarring. Although a DOD inspector general review uncovered no wrongdoing, the public airing of discord within the ranks of the prosecution team added force to existing criticisms of the commission system.[80]

Shortly after the email leak the Bush administration modified the rules for commissions. The revisions to MCO No. 1, enacted on August 31, 2005, made two changes.[81] One modification made the presiding officer the sole authority on questions of law and entrusted factual decisions to the rest of the panel, expressly excluding the presiding officer. The previously unclear division of labor had caused problems during the first set of pretrial proceedings. Now, the presiding officer would operate more like a judge and the rest of the panel more like a jury. But as Jess Bravin notes, the rule change had questionable legal underpinnings, since President Bush's initial executive order appeared to make the entire military commission the trier of "fact and law."[82] The second change dealt with the issue of excluding the accused from their own trial—something the district court had seized upon in finding the commissions illegal. The revision involved a minor change in wording that was nevertheless potentially significant: instead of saying commission defendants "may be present to the extent consistent with the need to protect classified information," the updated version replaced the word "may" with "shall." Though this still allowed exclusion in some circumstances, the change created a stronger presumption in favor of openness.[83]

These alterations may have been driven in part by a desire to make commissions run more smoothly. But another motivation lurked behind the changes: the ongoing specter of litigation. Just as the ever-present threat of lawsuits and judicial resistance shaped detention policies, the rules for military commissions were adapted in response to litigation pressures. With the possibility of

Supreme Court review in *Hamdan* looming, the Bush administration hoped to either stave off review entirely or increase its chances of winning the case.[84] The Supreme Court's willingness in 2004 to hear a trio of detention cases and extend habeas corpus rights to detainees held at Guantánamo Bay made the threat of judicial intervention a very real prospect. After the Supreme Court granted Hamdan's petition for certiorari, policy makers made another regulatory modification. In March 2006, DOD issued MCI No. 10, barring the use of evidence obtained through torture in military commissions.[85] The move was mostly symbolic according to the Bush White House, which categorically denied engaging in torture.[86] But DOJ pushed for the new rule anyway, demanding that it be codified prior to oral argument in the *Hamdan* litigation. Despite objections from some White House lawyers and DOD officials, DOJ—tasked with arguing *Hamdan*—got its way.[87] Again, internal executive branch advocates for reform utilized the presence of litigation and the threat of an adverse court decision to help drive a change in commission rules.

## CONCLUSION

In November 2001, President Bush signed an executive order establishing a system of military commissions to prosecute individuals suspected of committing war crimes. This was a clear instance of unilateral presidential action: only a small circle of executive branch officials reviewed the policy document before it was published in the Federal Register. Bush's move lent credence to the arguments of observers who feared the return of an imperial presidency. But those alarmed by Bush's use of executive power to create military commissions ought to have been comforted by the developments that followed. It took months to hammer out the first set of regulations and years for the first commission proceedings to get underway. Instead of the brisk, progovernment process anticipated by critics, implementation was slow and uneven. Furthermore, the detailed rules and policy changes that emerged in the wake of Bush's order were favorable to military commission defendants, not the US government.

Even in the very early stages of the war on terror, traditional features of policy making in the United States were clearly on display. Diverse viewpoints within the executive branch gave rise to bureaucratic struggles that in some cases generated policy outcomes not preferred by the White House. And individuals inside the executive branch whose policy preferences diverged from those of the White House were able to use the American system of "separated institutions sharing powers" to their advantage. This was especially true with respect to the courts: on multiple occasions, the ongoing threat of judicial review provided a powerful tool for those who supported making military commissions more protective of defendants and less susceptible to top-down presidential control. In this way, litigation exerted an influence over the law and policy surrounding military commissions even before the Supreme Court entered the fray.

The benefits and drawbacks of adversarial legalism were apparent in the early years of military commissions. Federal judges were open to entertaining the claims of a noncitizen terrorist suspect held outside the United States at Guantánamo Bay. A district court judge even ruled in Salim Hamdan's favor, in what appeared to many to be a break with a World War II–era precedent—not to mention a long-standing norm of judicial deference in wartime. That norm had already been unsettled by Supreme Court decisions in the detention cases. Just months after those rulings came down, a district court judge followed a similar path. The positive attributes of adversarial legalism were on display: the judiciary was open to an unpopular defendant and responsive to novel legal claims, and the litigation had a concrete impact, giving rise to legal and policy developments that checked presidential power and protected commission defendants.

The drawbacks of adversarial legalism were also readily apparent. Conflicting court rulings from the DC District Court and the DC Circuit Court of Appeals enhanced legal uncertainty surrounding the commission system. So too did repeated alterations to the rules and regulations for commissions, at least some of which were undertaken in anticipation of or in response to court rulings. Legal uncertainty contributed to the remarkable amount of delay that plagued the system, as commission proceedings stopped and started. Shortly after the 9/11 terrorist attack, the belief that commissions would be quick and effective was widespread within the upper ranks of the Bush administration. That sentiment filtered down to some of the personnel chosen to staff the new commission system. Asked by a military lawyer contemplating whether to accept a position in the commission system how long the appointment would last, OMC's first chief prosecutor, Colonel Fred Borch, estimated that commissions would wind down completely by 2006.[88] But by 2006, not a single trial had taken place.

In a clear example of adversarial legalism's tendency to cause unintended or perverse consequences, the delays and uncertainty—and the prodefendant reforms litigation helped generate—made military commissions a less attractive option for policy makers. This mirrored developments in the area of detention policy. As military commissions became subject to more legal obstacles and greater protections for the accused, they became a less desirable policy tool for removing suspected terrorists from the battlefield. Some number of captives—it is impossible to say precisely how many—who might otherwise have gotten an opportunity to defend themselves in a military commission trial instead remained in indefinite detention, held by the military as enemy combatants and not charged with any crimes. Also, the ineffectiveness of military commissions may have contributed to the Bush administration's decision to release scores of detainees from Guantánamo Bay. The consequences of litigation and judicial involvement were complicated, and its broader effects may have been suboptimal for at least some suspected enemy fighters and the US government.

As the Bush administration waited for the Supreme Court to decide *Hamdan v. Rumsfeld*, Salim Hamdan's military commission proceedings were halted again. After some debate, the Bush administration chose to continue pretrial proceedings for other commission defendants.[89] On January 11, 2006—more than a year after news of Judge Robertson's district court ruling rippled through the Guantánamo courtroom—military commission hearings finally resumed.[90] The proceedings inched forward for the next few months, but they were soon discontinued once again. This time, it was the Supreme Court of the United States that caused the stoppage.

# 5. The Supreme Court Intervenes: Military Commissions, Version 2.0 (2006–2008)

By the time the Supreme Court heard *Hamdan v. Rumsfeld*, the military commission system had already undergone a number of changes from President Bush's initial executive order. Among the most important of these developments were the creation of an appellate review body staffed by military officials, a higher bar for imposing the death penalty, a stronger presumption that commission defendants would not be excluded from their trials, and an explicit prohibition on the use of evidence obtained through torture. But these modifications were not enough to save the commission system from judicial invalidation. In June 2006, the Supreme Court ruled it illegal. The *Hamdan* litigation had already helped spur changes to military commissions, and the Supreme Court's decision generated momentum for additional reforms. The interbranch tug-of-war over military commissions continued in the wake of the Court's intervention.

One major consequence of the Supreme Court ruling was congressional action. In the fall of 2006, Congress passed the Military Commissions Act (MCA). The MCA explicitly authorized the use of military commissions, but only after making several alterations to them. Lawmakers who favored reform—including, most notably, a cadre of influential Republicans led by Senator Lindsey Graham (R-SC)—were able to use the Supreme Court decision and the prospect of more litigation to their advantage. Reformers in Congress also benefited from the presence of like-minded allies in the executive branch, including military lawyers who had repeatedly expressed concerns that commissions failed to meet preexisting legal standards. The separation of powers created opportunities for cross-institutional alliances to form, producing additional pressure for policy changes. Bureaucratic actors, legislators, and judges whose preferences for change aligned proved to be a powerful force for limiting presidential discretion and reforming military commissions.

The statute that emerged was no rubber stamp for the Bush administration. The MCA was a detailed piece of legislation that made numerous alterations to the military commission system. These alterations included evidentiary rules making it more difficult for the government to use hearsay or evidence obtained via coercion, a significantly stronger presumption in favor of open trials with defendants present throughout them, and the creation of a new court to review commission decisions. Once again, military commissions evolved in ways that favored the accused and constrained the White House. The changes were caused by a combination of litigation and the interbranch push-and-pull generated by the separation of powers. But Congress's involvement did not put an end to the legal challenges. Lawsuits and legal uncertainty continued to hover over the commission system even as it finally yielded its first convictions in 2007 and 2008. And the looming change of presidential administrations only enhanced the uncertainty surrounding the future of military commissions.

## THE SUPREME COURT INTERVENES

The legal team for Salim Hamdan did its best to frame their appeal in *Hamdan v. Rumsfeld* as a challenge to excessively broad assertions of executive power.[1] Their side was aided by a staggering number of amicus briefs from legal advocacy groups such as the ACLU and the Center for Constitutional Rights, academics with backgrounds in law and military history, and retired military officers. When petitioning the Supreme Court to hear their appeal, Hamdan's lawyer Neal Katyal sharply criticized the US Court of Appeals for the District of Columbia Circuit decision upholding the Bush administration's version of military commissions for being unduly deferential to presidential authority. According to Katyal, "No decision, by any court, in the wake of the Sept. 11, 2001, attacks has gone this far."[2]

In the lower courts the *Hamdan* litigation had featured a welter of legal arguments involving various sources of domestic and international law. But the legal landscape was even more cluttered by the time the Supreme Court took the case. In between the Court's grant of certiorari in November 2005 and oral argument in March 2006, Congress passed the Detainee Treatment Act (DTA).[3] Though the law's primary focus was the detention and interrogation of enemy combatants, the DTA contained a section establishing a limited form of judicial review of military commission decisions in the DC Circuit Court of Appeals, with the possibility of Supreme Court review after that. But even as the DTA added judicial oversight to the commission system, it simultaneously pared back the jurisdiction of federal courts over habeas corpus challenges from Guantánamo Bay. According to the government, the DTA's jurisdiction-stripping language meant that Salim Hamdan's lawsuit must be dismissed. He could avail himself of the DTA's review scheme for military commission decisions once his military commission trial was completed.

It was no coincidence that the DTA was enacted shortly after the Supreme Court agreed to hear the *Hamdan* case. Litigation affected the policy-making process: legislators had the lawsuit in mind when they wrote the jurisdiction-stripping provisions and established DC Circuit review of commission decisions.[4] The DTA was also a response to the Supreme Court ruling in *Rasul v. Bush*, which held that detainees at Guantánamo Bay were entitled by statute to seek writs of habeas corpus in US courts. The DTA appeared to override that decision by amending the federal habeas corpus statute. Congress stated that aside from the DC Circuit review process outlined in the DTA, "no court, justice, or judge shall have jurisdiction to consider . . . an application for a writ of habeas corpus filed by or on behalf of an alien detained by the Department of Defense at Guantánamo Bay, Cuba."[5] The Supreme Court would have to decide whether that language removed its ability to decide the *Hamdan* case.

Oral argument in *Hamdan v. Rumsfeld* took place in March 2006.[6] Both sides claimed that precedent supported their positions. Hamdan's lawyer, Neal Katyal, asked the Court to fulfill its time-honored role of enforcing limits on the executive. He repeatedly instructed the justices to avoid issuing a "blank check" to the president—a reference to Justice Sandra Day O'Connor's plurality opinion in the 2004 *Hamdi* case, which declared that "a state of war is not a blank check for the President."[7] Katyal omitted the second half of O'Connor's sentence "when it comes to the rights of the nation's citizens"—presumably because Salim Hamdan was not a citizen. Solicitor General Paul Clement, arguing on behalf of the government, insisted that a wide berth for executive authority over military commissions dated all the way back to the American founding. Clement's presentation to the Court largely steered clear of the Bush administration's most aggressive interpretations of presidential power under Article II of the Constitution; instead, Clement placed most of his emphasis on statutes and court precedents.[8]

The Supreme Court handed down its ruling on June 29, 2006, the final day of its term.[9] The Court voted 5–3 in favor of Salim Hamdan (Chief Justice John Roberts recused himself, having been a member of the DC Circuit panel in *Hamdan*). With multiple concurrences and dissents, the opinions totaled nearly 180 pages. Justice John Paul Stevens's majority opinion took up 70 of those pages. Given the extraordinary significance of the case for the future of military commissions—and given the complexity of the legal issues involved—it is necessary to unpack the opinions at some length. The majority opinion by Justice Stevens was joined in full by Justices Stephen Breyer, David Souter, and Ruth Bader Ginsburg, and joined in large part by Justice Anthony Kennedy, who objected to a small but important portion of Stevens's opinion.

The majority addressed the jurisdictional issue first, finding that the DTA did not prevent the Court from deciding the case. It construed the jurisdiction-stripping provision narrowly, holding that it did not apply to cases already pending in federal court at the time of the DTA's enactment. This interpretation allowed the Court to sidestep for the time being the underlying question of whether the Constitution itself guaranteed Guantánamo detainees such as Hamdan access to the courts. In dissent, Justice Antonin Scalia—joined by Justices Clarence Thomas and Samuel Alito—harshly criticized the majority's interpretation of the DTA, claiming that the law "unambiguously" removed the Court's power to consider Hamdan's challenge.[10] And the dissenters believed there was another reason for the Court to avoid reaching the merits: in their view, the Court ought to wait until the military commission process played out before weighing in. They pointed to the newly created DC Circuit review process for commission decisions as a main reason for abstention.

On the merits, the central question was this: did the current iteration of military commissions conform to legal standards set forth in statutes, treaties, the laws of war, and the US Constitution? For the majority, the answer was no. Justice Stevens wrote that while a combination of the Uniform Code of Military Justice (UCMJ), Authorization for Use of Military Force (AUMF), and DTA conferred "a general Presidential authority to convene military commissions," no statute specifically authorized departures from the requirements imposed by the UCMJ and the Geneva Conventions.[11] Like the DC District Court did in 2004, the majority read Article 36 of the UCMJ as imposing limits on the extent to which rules and procedures for military commissions could diverge from those used in courts-martial. And it followed the district court too in holding that the Bush administration had failed to demonstrate that courts-martial rules were impracticable in commissions. The majority was unwilling to defer to vague claims of military necessity to justify the deviations.

The Supreme Court majority also ruled that the commissions violated Common Article 3 of the Geneva Conventions. The DC Circuit panel below had held that the Conventions were unenforceable in court, but Justice

Stevens's opinion cleverly sidestepped that issue by finding that Congress had incorporated the laws of war—including the Geneva Conventions—into the UCMJ. This made it unnecessary to decide whether the Geneva Conventions were by themselves judicially enforceable.[12] Next, the majority held that Common Article 3—which applied to "armed conflict not of an international character"—covered the conflict with al-Qaeda and its associates. The majority then concluded that the current system of military commissions conflicted with Common Article 3, which forbids "the passing of sentences and the carrying out of executions without previous judgment pronounced by a regularly constituted court affording all the judicial guarantees which are recognized as indispensable by civilized peoples."[13] Justice Stevens explained that the term "regularly constituted court" meant a court-martial, unless the government could demonstrate its impracticability. Because the government had not done so, the military commissions violated Common Article 3's requirements. The majority's holding regarding the applicability of Common Article 3 had consequences for more than just military commissions. It had spillover effects, placing the future of the CIA's detention and interrogation program in legal jeopardy (for more on this, see chapter 2).

Two parts of Justice Stevens's opinion failed to garner Justice Kennedy's vote. First, Kennedy was unwilling to hold that Common Article 3's language about "judicial guarantees . . . recognized as indispensable by civilized peoples" had been violated. The four-justice plurality argued that customary international law gave defendants a right to be present at their trial and see the evidence against them. Because the commission system did not afford defendants this guarantee, the plurality claimed it ran afoul of the "all judicial guarantees" clause. Kennedy thought it unnecessary to decide this, since the majority already agreed the UCMJ had been violated.

Second, and more importantly, Justice Kennedy declined to join the portion of Stevens's opinion that dealt with the validity of conspiracy charges in military commissions. Each of the first four detainees slated for trial by commission was charged with conspiracy, and for three of four it was the sole charge they faced.[14] The decision to make conspiracy an offense triable by military commission had been controversial among commission prosecutors, who feared that its status as a law-of-war offense triable by military commission was unclear.[15] The issue received a good deal of attention during oral argument. Article 21 of the UCMJ provided the following: "The provisions of this chapter conferring jurisdiction upon courts-martial do not deprive military commissions, provost courts, or other military tribunals of concurrent jurisdiction with respect to offenders or *offenses that by statute or by the law of war may be tried by military commissions*, provost courts, or other military tribunals."[16] The four-justice plurality concluded that conspiracy was not one of these offenses. Justice Stevens could find no statute making conspiracy a crime triable by military commission and could locate no "plain and unambiguous" precedent under the laws of war for charging conspiracy as a war crime. Hamdan's military commission was therefore unlawful on these grounds as well, in the eyes of the plurality. Believing it unnecessary to decide this question at this time, Justice Kennedy withheld his vote.

Justice Stevens's opinion was, like the DC District Court opinion by Judge James Robertson, almost entirely bereft of deferential language. His examination of the executive branch's actions and legal positions was thorough and unsparing. The majority proved to be comfortable second-guessing the Bush administration's judgments on a matter of national security. This provoked sharp objections from the dissenters, who assumed the DC Circuit Court's more deferential posture. Justice Thomas penned a dissent, joined by Justice Scalia in full and Justice Alito in large part, lambasting the majority's approach. The Court's opinion, Thomas wrote, "openly flouts our well-established duty to respect the Executive's judgment in matters of military operations and foreign affairs." He was incredulous that the Court felt qualified "to pass on the 'military necessity' . . . of the Commander in Chief's decision to employ a particular form of force against our enemies."[17] Justice Thomas argued that judges lacked the capacity to override the executive's judgment on such matters. Citing Article II of the Constitution and the 2001 AUMF, Thomas's dissent claimed that President Bush had ample authority to establish the present system of military commissions. It also rejected the majority's reading of the UCMJ. As for the Geneva Conventions, Thomas's dissent deferred to the Bush administration's interpretation of them as inapplicable to the war, and added that even if Common Article 3 did apply, its requirements were satisfied. Finally, the dissenters disagreed with the plurality's view that a conspiracy charge was not available in military commissions.

Two years after the Supreme Court decided *Rasul v. Bush* and *Hamdi v. Rumsfeld*, the *Hamdan* ruling offered another example of judicial assertiveness in wartime. Much of the commentary following the ruling treated it as momentous. Walter Dellinger, the former head of the Office of Legal Counsel (OLC) under President Bill Clinton, called the *Hamdan* ruling "simply the most important decision on presidential power and the rule of law ever. Ever."[18] *New York Times* Supreme Court correspondent Linda Greenhouse likened the case to the *Steel Seizure Case* and *U.S. v. Nixon*, in terms of both its magnitude and its constraining effects on executive power.[19] One law professor expressed "wonderment about the sweep of the decision."[20] Neal Katyal, law professor and counsel for Salim Hamdan, referred to the outcome as "a rare Supreme Court rebuke to the President during armed conflict."[21] Former associate White House counsel for President Bush Bradford Berenson summed up his view this way: "Nothing about the administration's solution [of using military commissions] was radical or even particularly aggressive. What is truly radical is the Supreme Court's willingness to bend to world opinion and undermine some of the most important foundations of American national security law in the middle of a war."[22] Whether one celebrated or lamented the outcome in *Hamdan*, there seemed to be a consensus that the Supreme Court had done something extremely consequential—and extremely unusual.

Like the detention litigation, the *Hamdan* litigation featured the hallmarks of adversarial legalism. Entrepreneurial lawyers—from the legal academy (Katyal) and from the military (Swift)—initiated the lawsuit and successfully moved it through the courts. They encountered judges who were open to innovative legal arguments, especially those that involved interpretations of ambiguous statutes or treaties. The litigation moved slowly—it took more than two years after the lawsuit was filed for the Supreme Court to finally resolve it—and it generated considerable legal uncertainty in the interim. Military commission proceedings repeatedly stopped and started under this cloud of uncertainty. Moreover, adversarial legalism made its presence felt outside of the courthouse as well. As we have seen, both in the preceding chapters on detention and in the *Hamdan* episode, court decisions by themselves are only part of the story. At numerous junctures, policy makers thought about future court battles and argued for policy changes that would increase the likelihood of favorable judicial outcomes. And even after courts rule, policy responses sometimes exceed the four corners of the decision. This was true in the realm of detention policy, and as we will soon see, in the realm of military commissions as well.

Events during the first five years of military commissions bore the characteristics of adversarial legalism. And law and policy around military commissions emerged from a back-and-forth between "separated institutions sharing powers." All three branches of government had a hand in the development of military commissions in the run-up to the Supreme Court's intervention. The system of commissions, originally conceived of as a centralized and efficient wartime tool for incapacitating unlawful enemy combatants, was buffeted by legal challenges and shaped by a variety of actors outside of the White House. Far from operating with impunity, President George W. Bush confronted a decentralized system of checks and balances that prevented him from implementing all the policies he desired. Viewed as a whole, the *Hamdan* episode provides more evidence that lawyers and judges have gone to war, that this development has added momentum to the ordinary push-and-pull of the separation of powers, and that the result is outcomes that are favorable to terrorist suspects and restrictive of presidential power. But the *Hamdan* ruling did not mark the end of military commissions. As it turned out, it was just another chapter in a long-running saga. Soon after the Supreme Court decision, military commissions were back up and running, courtesy of legislation passed by Congress.

## THE ELECTED BRANCHES RESPOND: THE MILITARY COMMISSIONS ACT OF 2006

The *Hamdan* decision brought the entire military commission system to yet another standstill and threw its future into doubt. But beneath the Supreme Court's declaration that the commission system was illegal lay a simple fact: Congress could pass a law curing the defects identified by the Court. In a brief but potent concurring opinion, Justice Breyer made this point explicit: "The Court's conclusion ultimately rests upon a single ground: Congress has not issued the Executive a 'blank check.' Indeed, Congress has denied the President the legislative authority to create military commissions of the kind at issue here. Nothing prevents the President from returning to seek the authority he believes necessary."[23] The White House wasted no time in accepting this invitation. The first legislative proposal came out of the vice president's office. It would have authorized the existing commission system with no changes.[24] But the Bush administration decided against the rubber-stamp approach and declined to send the draft proposal to Congress. Instead, the administration resolved to work with Congress on a more detailed piece of legislation. Had the Bush administration gone to the legislature with the first proposal, it almost certainly would not have passed. Congress was controlled by the president's party, but it was unwilling to defer to the commander in chief on this matter of national security policy. Senator Lindsey Graham—an influential member of the Senate Armed Services Committee who had served as a judge advocate during his time in the armed forces—led the charge. Like JAGs and their allies in the executive branch, Graham favored a reformed version of military commissions that would be more protective of the accused and more insulated from top-down direction by civilian leaders.

Reform proponents had advocated for these sorts of policy changes before, but now they had another card to play. As Congress began working on legislation, Graham made clear that he believed the *Hamdan* ruling necessitated significant engagement between Congress and the Bush White House. Using the ruling to his advantage, Graham stated, "The Supreme Court has set the rules of the road, and the Congress and the president can drive to the destination together."[25] Other members of his party followed suit. Senator John McCain (R-AZ) urged Congress to abide by "the guidelines laid down by the Supreme Court."[26] Senator Arlen Specter (R-PA) agreed: "We have to get the details as to what the administration thinks they can do. We've got to look at the Supreme Court decision. And we have to reconcile it. But it has to be Congress because it's our constitutional responsibility."[27] As debate in Congress and between Congress and the White House unfolded, reform-minded legislators used the Supreme Court decision—and the prospect of continued litigation—as leverage. Members of Congress from both parties stressed that any legislation would need to be written with an eye to surviving judicial scrutiny down the road. Again, the specter of litigation helped shape the policy-making process, bolstering the position of those who supported meaningful reforms to the military commission system.[28]

The warnings issued by Senator Graham and other lawmakers were not idle threats. When the Bush administration circulated the first draft of a bill, they objected.[29] The administration's proposal would have made very few adjustments to the existing system of commissions. Though it cleared the House Armed Services Committee in early September of 2006, the bill ran into opposition in the Senate.[30] Among its most vociferous critics were members of the president's own party. Senator John Warner (R-VA) justified his opposition to the administration's draft bill partly on the grounds that it would be unlikely to survive review by the courts. "It's got to be dealt with so that we do not face a future court challenge," Warner insisted.[31] Graham concurred: "I do not think we can afford to again cut legal corners that will result in federal court rejection of our work."[32] The senators also benefited from the presence of likeminded allies outside of Congress, including Colin Powell (no longer in government at this time) and a number of military lawyers. The lawmakers and their allies focused in particular on the part of the *Hamdan* ruling that applied Common Article 3 of the Geneva Conventions to the current conflict, arguing that whatever Congress passed would have to comply with Common Article 3 or else risk another round of repudiation in the courts.[33]

With these considerations now front and center, the Senate Armed Services Committee passed its own bill with greater protections for military commission defendants. After negotiations between lawmakers and the White House, a compromise emerged.[34] The statute, called the Military Commissions Act (MCA), passed both houses of Congress in late September and was signed into law shortly thereafter. The most significant change the MCA made was to increase transparency for commission defendants. Under the new rules, defendants could be excluded from their own trials only for two very narrow reasons—to protect the "physical safety" of those in the courtroom or to prevent "disruption of the proceedings." Defendants were also entitled to know about any classified evidence used against them.[35] The Bush White House had opposed these changes during the legislative process, but it lost on these points.

The MCA made other important modifications to the existing system of military commissions.[36] At the most basic level, the MCA unambiguously authorized the use of military commissions in the war on terror. This was significant: the lack of a clear statutory foundation had plagued the system in the courts from the beginning. At a more granular level, the statute changed a number of things. It replaced the "presiding officer" with an actual military judge and mandated that military commission panels—the equivalent of juries in the civilian justice system—consist of no fewer than five members (the previous minimum was three). The MCA also increased the size of panels in death penalty cases to twelve members (the previous number was seven). While convictions in capital cases and the imposition of death sentences still required unanimous votes and sentences of less than ten years still required a two-thirds vote, the MCA increased the threshold for sentences of more than ten years from two-thirds to three-quarters. The MCA also mandated that defendants be notified of the charges against them as soon as possible and allowed to defend themselves. In a key passage safeguarding the independence of the commission system, the MCA prohibited external "command influence" over the operations of the commission system and the personnel who staff it.

That language was meant to guarantee insulation from military and civilian higher-ups who might wish to meddle in the commission process.

The MCA was a longer and more prescriptive statute than many observers might have expected. The entire episode did not conform to the standard view of Congress as hesitant to involve itself in the details of national security policy. This was most obvious in the MCA's detailed treatment of evidentiary rules and procedures. One existing Department of Defense (DOD) rule for military commissions stated that evidence was admissible if it had "probative value to a reasonable person." The MCA codified this standard, but also included language giving military commission judges more authority to reject evidence. Under the new law, commission judges were instructed to exclude evidence if they found it to be "substantially outweighed by the danger of unfair prejudice, confusion of the issues, or misleading the commission" or "by considerations of undue delay, waste of time, or needless presentation of cumulative evidence." Hearsay remained admissible under the MCA, but the rules for introducing it were tightened to require greater disclosure to the defense. The MCA also revised the rules for evidence acquired through the use of coercion: in addition to codifying the existing ban on evidence obtained through torture, it also limited the admissibility of evidence obtained via coercive methods not rising to the legal definition of torture.

Another section of the MCA listed all of the offenses that could be tried in military commissions and described them in detail. This was a particularly important part of the law: as noted above, the inclusion of conspiracy in the initial version of commissions had created controversy among commission prosecutors, and now four justices on the Supreme Court were on record opposing its use. Some experts in military law were also convinced that conspiracy was not a recognized war crime and was therefore outside the jurisdiction of military commissions.[37] In spite of this, conspiracy was included in the MCA's litany of crimes triable by military commission. So too was the offense of providing material support for terrorism, which was liable to similar objections. The incorporation of these two offenses would provoke multiple legal challenges in the years to come.

The MCA ushered in one other crucial change: the creation of a new appellate court to replace the existing three-member body tasked with reviewing commission decisions. The court, called the Court of Military Commission Review (CMCR), would be staffed by military or civilian judges. (The existing review panel was solely staffed by members of the military and was required to have only one judge.) The CMCR would automatically review any guilty verdict issued by a military commission. After that, the DTA review process was left mostly undisturbed: CMCR rulings could be appealed to the DC Circuit Court of Appeals, with the possibility of Supreme Court review to follow. The MCA did make one slight adjustment to that process, permitting all commission judgments—not just those resulting in sentences greater than ten years—to be appealed to the DC Circuit. The MCA declared that its review scheme was to be the exclusive mechanism for legal challenges to the commission system. Habeas corpus lawsuits were no longer permitted under the MCA, which reenacted the DTA's removal of habeas jurisdiction over Guantánamo Bay and explicitly applied the removal to pending and future lawsuits. Despite the habeas strip, the review process created by Congress ensured that legal challenges would continue.

Even where little to no policy change occurred, the MCA was significant because it gave the commission system a more stable foundation. Before the MCA's enactment, rules for commissions emerged in a piecemeal fashion and were subject to revision by DOD at any time. Statutory codification of the structure and procedures endowed the commission system with more stability—and presumably more staying power. And although DOD retained the power to issue specific regulations pursuant to the statute, the MCA required that any modifications be reported to Congress prior to their implementation. Thus, one consequence of the legislation was to narrow considerably the executive branch's field of discretion. Moving forward, the basic form and functioning of military commissions could be changed only by an act of Congress.

The Military Commissions Act of 2006 was a comprehensive statute that made a host of important changes to the military commission system. Benjamin Wittes has called it the "most ambitious congressional effort to write the rules of the war on terrorism."[38] Although the legislation gave the Bush administration much of what it wanted, Congress's actions did not conform to the traditional understanding of the legislature's role in wartime national security policy. The Congress that passed the MCA did not settle for vague, broad-brush legislation. And it was not overly deferential to the White House: Congress got its way on the issues of classified evidence and exclusion of defendants from their trials, and the MCA also included several other modifications to the Bush administration's version of commissions. All of this occurred despite Congress being controlled by the president's own party. Congress joined the interbranch tug-of-war, and the result was a commission system more favorable to unlawful enemy combatants and less amenable to presidential control. Many opponents of the initial iteration of commissions remained skeptical of the reformed system, but some tempered their criticism. In the words of one leading scholarly critic, military commissions under the MCA were "considerably improved over those proposed in 2001."[39]

## MILITARY COMMISSIONS, VERSION 2.0

The MCA was signed into law in October 2006, but military commission proceedings did not resume right away. DOD and the Office of Military Commissions (OMC) needed time to adapt to the new rules. As Jess Bravin notes, the passage of the MCA "required the Pentagon to draft new manuals and procedures, sift the detainee population for new defendants, and revise old cases to fit the modified structure."[40] It was also necessary to construct the new CMCR from scratch.[41] And putting together prosecutions of Khalid Sheikh Mohammed and other high-value detainees—who were transferred from CIA prisons to Guantánamo Bay in September 2006, partly in response to the *Hamdan* ruling—would require an enormous amount of effort from OMC and various government agencies.[42]

The new Manual for Military Commissions (MMC) was published in January 2007. Lawyers from the Department of Justice (DOJ) and DOD—both civilian attorneys and JAGs—were the primary drafters of the document, though it was also reviewed by intelligence agency officials. In a clear nod to the Supreme Court decision in *Hamdan*, the introduction stated that the MMC was based on the Manual for Courts-Martial, and Secretary of Defense Robert Gates declared that the rules and procedures for courts-martial were followed "so far as I have considered practicable or consistent with military or intelligences activities."[43] More than two hundred pages long, the MMC went into detail on a variety of topics, including pretrial processes for discovery and depositions, sentencing guidelines, rules for introducing hearsay and classified evidence, and the handling of witnesses. One month after the MMC's publication, President Bush issued Executive Order 13425 restarting the reformed system of military commissions.[44]

Shortly after Bush issued his order, the commission system produced its first ever conviction. David Hicks avoided a trial, pleading guilty to material support for terrorism.[45] Under the old system, Hicks had been charged with other offenses, including conspiracy, aiding the enemy, and attempted murder. But when charges were refiled in the reformed commission system, the Convening Authority (the MCA's new title for the "Appointing Authority") authorized only the material support charge, apparently because she believed there was insufficient evidence to support the others.[46] Though Hicks faced the possibility of a life sentence, he wound up getting only seven years—with time spent in detention counted toward that number. He would spend just nine more months in custody, and under the terms of his plea agreement he could serve those nine months in Australia, his home country.[47] Hicks's brief sentence provoked comparisons to John Walker Lindh, an American citizen caught fighting alongside the Taliban. Lindh was prosecuted in federal court and received a twenty-year sentence, leading some to question whether military commissions were a more effective tool for incapacitating unlawful combatants than regular Article III courts.[48]

The brevity of Hicks's sentence notwithstanding, one might have thought military commissions were finally hitting their stride. They had been challenged in the courts and reformed while that litigation was ongoing. Now, following the Supreme Court ruling, military commissions were operating with the unambiguous support of Congress and the president under a detailed set of rules and procedures codified in legislation. And in March 2007, the system finally secured its first conviction. This chain of events raised questions: Had military commissions finally found their footing? Would they become a useful tool for combating terrorists and reducing the number of detainees held without charges at Guantánamo Bay? Would litigation challenging the commission system cease? The answer to all three of these questions turned out to be no.

Following the David Hicks plea agreement, the government moved forward with cases against two other detainees: Salim Hamdan and Omar Khadr. But in June 2007, those proceedings were brought to a sudden halt. Military commission judges in both cases ruled that the charges against the two men had to be dismissed for lack of jurisdiction, because neither Hamdan nor Khadr was properly designated an "unlawful enemy combatant." They had gone before combatant status review tribunals (CSRTs) and had their detentions as "enemy combatants" upheld, but according to the commission judges, this finding was insufficient to bring someone within the jurisdiction of military commissions.[49] The text of the MCA required that a commission defendant be an "unlawful enemy combatant." Until that determination was made, a military commission could not proceed. The rulings stirred up considerable legal uncertainty and had potentially enormous consequences for the future of the commission system: under the judges' reasoning, not a single Guantánamo detainee was duly classified as an unlawful enemy combatant. The episode provided fodder for both supporters and opponents of the commission system: for its backers, the rulings demonstrated the commission system's fairness and independence; for critics, it was just another indication that the system was poorly conceived and doomed to fail.[50]

The rulings unsettled Congress and the White House. On Capitol Hill, there were discussions about revising the MCA in response to the decisions. Other lawmakers capitalized on the turns of events and called for restoring habeas corpus rights at Guantánamo or closing the detention facility altogether.[51] The commission rulings and legislative debates spurred renewed discussions about the future of Guantánamo in the executive branch, where multiple officials including President Bush himself were already on record in support of closing the facility as soon as possible.[52] But rather than make more policy changes at this time, the Bush administration appealed the commission rulings to the CMCR. It was the first appeal to that new body; because it was not even up and running yet, this caused more delay.[53] In September 2007, a three-judge panel unanimously reversed the rulings of the commission judges.[54] Although the CMCR agreed that CSRT "enemy combatant" classifications were inadequate under the MCA, it held that the commission trial judges ought to have made their own independent determinations regarding the defendants' status. By refusing to allow prosecutors to present evidence of unlawful combatancy, the judges below had erred.

Legal challenges in the federal courts may have run their course for the time being, but legal challenges within the commission system were clearly alive and well. The CMCR appeal was not the only cause of delay, however. The commission system faced other troubles, including supplying enough defense lawyers for defendants and coordinating information from a variety of sources.[55] Evidence obtained through coercive interrogations posed an especially difficult problem. Defense lawyers argued that detainees subjected to harsh treatment and "enhanced interrogation techniques" (EITs) provided unreliable and unusable information.[56] Aware of the litigation risk this posed, OMC prosecution staff expended lots of effort tracking down as much untainted evidence as possible.[57] They had good reason to do so: in May 2008, Convening Authority Susan Crawford dismissed charges against Mohammed al-Qahtani, one of the six military commission defendants with direct links to the 9/11 plot.[58] Crawford confirmed in an interview that the cause of her dismissal was al-Qahtani's treatment, which in her view "met the legal definition of torture."[59] Commission proceedings for the rest of the 9/11 plotters continued to be rocky affairs. There were requests for self-representation and a blitz of legal motions in June 2008, followed by an about-face in November when the 9/11 defendants abruptly announced their desire to plead guilty. The change in tack generated legal confusion, because the rules for courts-martial prohibit guilty pleas in capital cases and the MCA was unclear on the point.[60] (The 9/11 defendants later changed their minds about pleading guilty, and the case remains mired in pretrial proceedings as of this writing.)

Despite these difficulties, the commission system was moving toward conducting its first trial. After the CMCR decision discussed above, the commission judge in Salim Hamdan's case reviewed the government's evidence and concluded that Hamdan met the definition of unlawful enemy combatant. Proceedings inched forward, with the defense team filing a flurry of legal motions.[61] In a remarkable turn of events, the former chief prosecutor for military commissions, Colonel Morris Davis, testified for the defense.[62] Davis had stepped down from his position in October 2007, citing ongoing disagreements with the legal advisor to the convening authority. According to Colonel Davis, the legal advisor, Brigadier General Thomas Hartmann, encroached on the prosecution's independence by urging Davis to quicken the pace of charging individuals, initiate more high-profile prosecutions that would capture the public's attention, and rely more heavily on classified evidence to secure convictions. After his resignation, Davis publicly aired his criticisms of the commission system, labeling it "rigged" in favor of the government. In April 2008, he testified in person before Hamdan's commission about Hartmann's alleged meddling. The commission judge, Captain Keith Allred, sided with the defense and removed Hartmann from the case.[63]

Developments in the Supreme Court slowed down Hamdan's commission proceedings. With the Court approaching a decision in *Boumediene v. Bush*—a detention case about Guantánamo detainees' access to federal courts under the Constitution—Judge Allred temporarily suspended commission proceedings. He wanted to wait for the Court's ruling, which he said "may well change the tenor or conduct of [Hamdan's] trial."[64] In June 2008, the Court ruled that detainees held at Guantánamo Bay have a right to habeas corpus review under the Suspension Clause of the Constitution and that the existing review scheme for detentions was an inadequate substitute for it (for more on this case, see chapter 2).[65] Although *Boumediene* did not directly address military commissions, it had two important ramifications for them. First, federal courts could again entertain legal challenges to commissions via habeas petitions. Second, the decision injected new legal uncertainty into the commission system. By confining its ruling to the reach of the Suspension Clause, the Supreme Court left unclear whether other constitutional provisions might also apply at Guantánamo.

Capitalizing on the *Boumediene* decision, Hamdan's lawyers again challenged the commission system in federal court. They adopted a broad interpretation of *Boumediene*, claiming that multiple constitutional provisions applied and were being violated, including the Ex Post Facto Clause, the Due Process Clause, and the Equal Protection Clause. They focused in particular on the government's ability to use hearsay evidence and evidence obtained via coercion. This time, District Judge James Robertson sided with the government, allowing Hamdan's commission to proceed.[66] According to Judge Robertson, the MCA had made "significant improvements," including tightening the rules for introducing evidence and enhancing the review process for commission decisions.[67] He concluded that in light of these reforms, the proper course for the judiciary was abstention until the reformed commission system was given a chance to work.

Judge Robertson's opinion in *Hamdan v. Gates* contrasted Hamdan's situation to the victorious petitioners in *Boumediene.* The *Boumediene* plaintiffs had received only administrative CSRT reviews of their enemy combatant status, he noted, while Hamdan was getting much more. The military commission system offered far greater protections than CSRTs: Hamdan had an attorney; he was charged with a crime and received notification of the charges against him; he had comparatively generous access to witnesses and exculpatory evidence; he benefited from a presumption of innocence; and he was entitled to a "fully adversarial trial."[68] Furthermore, after the trial's completion, Hamdan could avail himself of a multitiered posttrial review process, including eventual review by an Article III court. Judge Robertson concluded his opinion with a spirited defense of the new system's capacity to handle the legal issues raised by Hamdan's defense team: "Article III judges do not have a monopoly on justice, or on constitutional learning. A real judge is presiding over the pretrial proceedings in Hamdan's case and will preside over the trial. . . . If the Military Commission judge gets it wrong, his error may be corrected."[69]

As it turned out, parallel proceedings were occurring at Guantánamo before Judge Allred during the days leading up to Judge Robertson's ruling. The release of the rulings was nearly simultaneous. Judge Allred also rebuffed the arguments proffered by Hamdan's legal team.[70] Legal challenges inside and outside the commission system failed to stop Hamdan's trial, which commenced in late July. Hamdan faced two charges—conspiracy and material support—and pleaded not guilty to both offenses. In early August 2008, the commission returned a split verdict: it acquitted Hamdan of conspiracy but found him guilty of material support.[71] He was sentenced to five and half years; with credit for time spent in detention, Hamdan's confinement would last only five more months. The government had sought thirty years to life, so the sentence he received looked extraordinarily light. Some defenders of commissions put a positive spin on the partial acquittal, claiming it demonstrated the system's independence.[72] Hamdan's defense counsel, Charles Swift, offered a different take: "What happened—despite the system—is justice."[73] In November 2008 Hamdan was sent from Guantánamo to his native Yemen, where he completed the final month of his sentence.[74]

## CONCLUSION

As President Bush prepared to leave office, the military commission system had finally completed its first trial. It took almost seven years for this to happen. Bush issued the executive order creating commissions in November 2001, two months after the 9/11 terrorist attack, and only now was the system beginning to yield results. In the interim, the commission system experienced a series of reforms and an extraordinary amount of delay. Both the reforms and the delays are attributable in large part to litigation and judicial intervention, which gave actors in all three branches of government the opportunity to shape law and policy around military commissions. The reformed version of military commissions that emerged in 2006 reflected detailed input from a variety of players, including federal judges, members of Congress, and actors inside the executive branch whose views diverged from those of the White House. Litigation was a potent weapon for proponents of reform, who were able to use court decisions and the threat of additional lawsuits to move the policy-making process in their preferred direction. The outcome of these interbranch interactions was a revised system of military commissions more protective of defendants and further removed from White House control. The system showcased its independence in 2007 and 2008, as military commission judges and the convening authority made decisions that went against the government.

One might have thought that multiple years of legal challenges, culminating in a ruling by the Supreme Court and a congressional response, would have spelled an end to litigation and the institutional tug-of-war it helped energize. Moving forward, perhaps the military commission system, increasingly insulated from presidential control, would also be insulated from the forces of adversarial legalism. But this was not to be. The interbranch dialogue had not yet run its course, and there was much more litigation on the way.

Salim Hamdan's conviction was the second conviction secured by a military commission, and the first to occur after a trial. Shortly before Election Day in 2008, the commission system completed another trial: Ali Hamza al Bahlul, a leading propagandist for al-Qaeda, was found guilty of conspiracy, material support, and solicitation to commit war crimes. Bahlul, who declined to mount a defense despite pleading not guilty, received a life sentence.[75] But after Barack Obama's election victory, the future of military commissions seemed highly uncertain. As a senator and as a presidential candidate, Obama was very critical of the Bush administration's approach to combating terrorism. Reacting to Salim Hamdan's trial and conviction during the presidential campaign, Obama condemned the system's delays and claimed they stemmed from "dangerous flaws in the [Bush] administration's legal framework." He advocated using regular Article III courts or courts-martial instead.[76] Upon entering office, President Obama issued an order freezing military commissions in order to conduct a review of the system. Many of Obama's supporters assumed the review was a formality—an intermediate step on the way to bringing commissions to an end once and for all.[77] They were wrong.

# 6. Litigation without End: Military Commissions after *Hamdan* (2009–2017)

By the time Barack Obama took the presidential oath of office on January 20, 2009, military commissions had experienced significant changes since their inception shortly after 9/11. Despite these developments, reform efforts and legal challenges continued unabated during Obama's presidency. At President Obama's request, Congress enacted a series of amendments to the Military Commissions Act (MCA) in 2009. But these statutory changes did not put an end to litigation and judicial intervention. Lawsuits on a variety of issues related to the commission system persisted, perpetuating the legal uncertainty surrounding commissions and rendering them unable to perform their core function of giving suspected terrorists a trial and a defined prison sentence. This state of affairs continued into the Trump administration. And despite early indications that the Trump administration might make greater use of them, military commissions remain relegated to the margins of the ongoing war against al-Qaeda and its affiliates.

As a senator and a presidential candidate, Barack Obama was a leading critic of the military commission system. However, after his administration froze commission proceedings and conducted a review, he chose to pursue reforms but keep the system in place. Those reforms, enshrined in amendments to the MCA, included strengthening the ban on using evidence obtained through coercion, making it more difficult for the government to use hearsay evidence, and expanding the scope of review in the Court of Military Commission Review (CMCR) and the US Court of Appeals for the District of Columbia Circuit. The interbranch back-and-forth continued, and—like prior rounds of reform—the latest set of policy changes made it harder for the government to win and sustain convictions and deepened checks on the executive. As with the passage of the MCA in 2006, the specter of litigation provided reform proponents—which now, in 2009, included the White House itself—with a powerful justification for their cause. Adopting a broad interpretation of the Supreme Court's decision in *Boumediene v. Bush*, reformers were again able to frame additional changes to the commission system as a legal imperative rather than a mere policy choice. This helped combat congressional inertia and improved the prospects for statutory changes.

Even with another set of legislative reforms, however, litigation has persisted. Although the commission system produced a handful of guilty pleas in 2010 and 2011, the DC Circuit soon began reversing previous commission verdicts, generating widespread uncertainty about the future of military commissions. Much of the litigation centered on which offenses could and could not be tried in military commissions. The DC Circuit issued rulings that have narrowed the jurisdiction of military commissions, reducing their utility to the government and shrinking the number of terrorist suspects who can be prosecuted in them.

The results of persistent litigation and the policy changes it has helped spur have been a mixed bag. On the positive side, today's military commissions are fairer to defendants and more insulated from political influence and presidential control. Moreover, having been repeatedly vetted by all three branches of government, the current system of commissions can claim broader support and legitimacy than earlier iterations. On the other hand, though, lawsuits and court rulings have caused interminable delays, generated lots of legal uncertainty, and shrunk the universe of possible military commission cases. These developments have benefited neither the government nor the suspected enemy fighters it has captured. Instead of sending terrorist suspects through a military commission system significantly more favorable to them than ever before, the government has often had to choose between keeping them in indefinite detention—without charges and with less due process—or transferring them out of Guantánamo Bay altogether. In this way, adversarial legalism has produced unintended consequences that seemingly harm both parties. By invigorating the institutional tug-of-war generated by the separation of powers, litigation and judicial decisions have cabined presidential discretion over military commissions and made them more protective of defendants—but it has done so at a cost.

## PRESIDENT OBAMA RETAINS MILITARY COMMISSIONS, WITH REFORMS

Shortly after taking office, President Barack Obama announced a review of the military commission system and called for a four-month hiatus in its proceedings. After lengthy internal debate, Obama revealed that his administration would pursue alterations to the commissions but leave them in place.[1] Though Obama declared a preference for civilian trials in Article III courts "whenever feasible," he gave a reformed version of military commissions his seal of approval.[2] He called for congressional action and outlined a few regulatory changes that would be instituted immediately.[3] As the administration tweaked the regulations and engaged Congress, commission proceedings were held in abeyance through the summer of 2009. But even as the commission system itself lay dormant, it was battered by litigation in federal court. The episode involved Mohammed Jawad, one of the individuals whose commission proceedings were on hold.[4] Jawad was alleged to have lobbed a hand grenade at US forces in Afghanistan in 2002. His early commission proceedings were rocky for the government: one prosecutor resigned in protest because he felt Jawad was being mistreated, and military judge Colonel Stephen Henley suppressed confessions that Jawad made to interrogators after his capture. Judge Henley also seriously considered dismissing the charges against Jawad because of harsh treatment he experienced at Guantánamo Bay.

In July 2009 Jawad's military commission prosecution was on hold, but his lawsuit challenging his detention in federal court was not. The government's case for detaining Jawad as an enemy combatant relied heavily on the very same confessions commission judge Henley had thrown out. Now, in a habeas corpus challenge before US District Court for the District of Columbia judge Ellen Segal Huvelle, the Department of Justice (DOJ) acceded to Henley's ruling and stated that it would no longer use Jawad's confession. Without it, however, there was very little evidence upon which to sustain Jawad's detention. Labeling the government's presentation "riddled with holes," Judge Huvelle demanded that the government produce more information or let Jawad go.[5] The government quickly announced that it would stop holding Jawad as an enemy combatant, and the convening authority for military commissions dropped the charges against him.[6] Legal challenges playing out in two separate but interrelated channels had combined to undercut the government's case against Jawad, who was released from US custody in August 2009.[7]

Meanwhile, debates over revising the MCA were playing out on Capitol Hill. Congressional hearings continued throughout the summer. At one Senate hearing, Obama administration officials made an important claim: although the administration's position was that the full range of constitutional protections was not applicable to noncitizens held at Guantánamo Bay, it believed that some degree of due process was constitutionally required under the Supreme Court's *Boumediene* decision.[8] *Boumediene* did not strictly compel this position, since the Court had confined its ruling to the reach of the Suspension Clause and declined to comment on other constitutional provisions, including the Due Process Clause in the Fifth Amendment. By adopting this interpretation, the Obama administration could use the Court decision to nudge Congress along.

As legislative deliberations unfolded, the administration stressed that commissions would have to be more protective of defendants in order to pass muster in the courts.[9] Once again, policy makers who favored altering the status quo used litigation and judicial intervention to their advantage. By embracing an exaggerated reading of an existing precedent and linking it with the threat of additional lawsuits and judicial reversals, reformers could frame their effort as a legal necessity rather than a policy choice. On this view, revising the MCA was not optional but required. Surely reform proponents in the Obama administration and in Congress understood that approaching the issue this way would help overcome the usual inertia present in the legislative process. It also provided reformers with a counterargument to increasingly common charges from Republicans that President Obama and other Democrats were weak on national security and too concerned with protecting the rights of terrorists.[10]

In October 2009, Congress passed a series of amendments to the MCA. These amendments, enacted as part of the National Defense Authorization Act (NDAA) for 2010, made several key changes to the 2006 military commission statute.[11] First off, the 2009 amendments tightened evidentiary rules in ways that favored the accused. Any statement acquired through the use of "cruel, inhuman, or degrading treatment" was made categorically inadmissible in military commissions. Statements of the accused must be voluntary, with only a limited exception for statements obtained on the battlefield.[12] The rules surrounding hearsay evidence were overhauled so that the government would no longer benefit from a presumption in favor of its reliability, but would instead bear the burden of demonstrating its reliability. The 2009 amendments also went into more detail on the use of classified evidence, largely adopting the framework contained in the Classified Information Procedures Act (CIPA). For decades, federal trial courts followed CIPA in cases involving sensitive issues of national security. Now, military commissions would operate under a similar set of procedures.

The 2009 amendments made a number of other changes to the MCA. It tightened the language regarding defendants' access to counsel to make it available "as soon as practicable," gave commission defendants more freedom to select a military lawyer of their own choosing, and increased the amount of resources allocated to the defense.[13] The revisions also expanded the scope of review exercised by the CMCR and the DC Circuit. The 2006 MCA limited appellate review of commission decisions to questions of law. Under the 2009 amendments, the CMCR was given authority to review questions of law *and* fact—and to examine "the entire record" when doing so. This included allowing the CMCR to "weigh the evidence, judge the credibility of witnesses, and determine controverted questions of fact." In a similar manner, DC Circuit review—though still limited to questions of law—was expanded to include "the sufficiency of the evidence to support the verdict." By giving the CMCR appellate jurisdiction over factual questions and permitting both courts to assess the underlying evidence, the 2009 amendments markedly bolstered the review system for military commission decisions.[14]

The 2009 legislation did not fundamentally overhaul the commission system, but it did represent another significant moment in its ongoing evolution. Several commentators, including some critics of military commissions, noted that the latest suite of reforms brought the commission system extremely close to the model for courts-martial.[15] Many who opposed earlier iterations of commissions—including JAGs—had long advocated for precisely this sort of convergence. After years of litigation and a convoluted back-and-forth involving all three branches of government, many early critics of the Bush administration's military commissions had gotten much of what they wanted. To be sure, objections remained: some observers thought that the taint of illegitimacy could not be removed by incremental adjustments and argued for a complete shift to civilian trials in Article III courts.[16] But whatever one's position on the desirability of using military commissions, the 2009 amendments to the MCA undeniably moved the system in a prodefendant direction once again.

## RESTARTING COMMISSIONS (AGAIN)

Military commission proceedings resumed in 2010 and soon yielded a trio of convictions in cases already in progress when President Obama took office. In July 2010, Ibrahim al Qosi pleaded guilty to conspiracy and material support, spent two more years in confinement, and was repatriated to Sudan in 2012.[17] Canadian Omar Khadr also accepted a plea deal on a number of charges, received an eight-year sentence, and was transferred to Canada in 2012 to complete his sentence.[18] In early 2011, Noor Uthman Muhammed pleaded guilty to conspiracy and material support, served three more years in US custody, and departed Guantánamo in late 2013.[19] But if it seemed like the newly reformed commission system might be hitting its stride, external events soon intervened to shake things up.

One key event that unsettled the policy space was the attempted terrorist attack on Christmas Day 2009. The attempt failed, but the Obama administration's decision to prosecute the would-be bomber in a civilian court rather than a military commission met with criticism from Republicans.[20] And the Christmas Day episode came on the heels of another controversial decision by the Obama administration: in November 2009, the administration had announced its intention to transfer the 9/11 plotters from the military commission system to the criminal justice system and prosecute them in federal district court in New York. That idea was also widely panned by Republicans in Congress.

In response to these moves, some lawmakers began advocating for reforms. Senator Lindsey Graham (R-SC) pushed for a comprehensive statute that would have brought Guantánamo detainees to US soil but preserved military commission trials for at least some higher-value individuals, such as the 9/11 plotters. Graham's plan would have permitted civilian trials for lower-level terrorist suspects. Following a familiar pattern, Graham used the courts for cover: "Judges are begging us to do this. I want Congress and the administration to come up with a detainee policy that will be accepted by courts."[21] Other lawmakers took a harder line, rallying behind a proposal by Senators John McCain (R-AZ) and Joseph Lieberman (I-CT) that would have required that *all* noncitizen enemy belligerents receive military trials.[22] The McCain-Lieberman proposal failed to gain the support of many national security experts, including some former Bush administration officials, who opposed removing civilian prosecution from the set of options for incapacitating terrorists.[23] That proposal and the Graham proposal ultimately foundered in the face of this pushback and widespread Democratic opposition.

Still, the Democratic Congress did not remain completely silent on matters related to Guantánamo Bay. In late 2010, it enacted limits on spending money to transfer or release detainees held there, including flatly prohibiting the use of funds to transfer Guantánamo detainees to American soil for any reason—including prosecution.[24] Prior to the enactment of this provision, transfers to the United States for prosecution were permitted. The Obama administration had already completed one such transfer: Ahmed Khalfan Ghailani was brought to the United States for a civilian trial and sentenced to life in prison. Despite the life sentence, Ghailani was acquitted of all but one of the nearly three hundred charges against him. Critics seized on this, claiming that the acquittals demonstrated the risk involved in using Article III courts to prosecute Guantánamo detainees. Viewed against the backdrop of the Obama administration's plan to try the 9/11 defendants in a civilian court, the Ghailani episode provided many lawmakers with the motivation to enact the restrictions.[25] Although Congress was controlled by members of President Obama's own party at this time, the legislature charted a course at odds with his administration. As a result, military commissions became the only prosecution venue for individuals held at Guantánamo Bay.

Following the enactment of the new statutory limits, Attorney General Eric Holder announced that the administration would use military commissions for the 9/11 defendants after all.[26] Charges against them were refiled in the spring of 2011.[27] Charges were also brought against another high-profile detainee, Abd al-Rahim al-Nashiri, around this time.[28] Nashiri was a member of al-Qaeda and a suspect in the 2000 terrorist attack on the USS *Cole*. Pretrial proceedings in these two major cases moved extremely slowly. As they inched forward, the commission system delivered another conviction: in February 2012, Majid Shoukat Khan pleaded guilty to a handful of charges. By agreeing to cooperate with the US government and testify in future commission prosecutions against other detainees, Khan was able to keep his sentence under twenty years.[29] Khan's was the seventh conviction produced by the commission system, and the fifth to come via guilty plea. More than a decade after their initial creation, then, military commissions had still conducted trials for only two detainees: Salim Hamdan and Ali al Bahlul. Both of those convictions were soon in trouble in the DC Circuit Court of Appeals.

## THE JUDICIARY REENTERS THE FRAY

Back in the summer of 2008, DC District Court judge James Robertson had dismissed a legal challenge from Salim Hamdan, allowing his military commission trial under the 2006 MCA to proceed. Hamdan was convicted shortly thereafter. But as it turned out, the legal saga involving Hamdan was far from over. His attorneys quickly seized on a potential problem: Hamdan was convicted of providing material support for terrorism, but the viability of charging that offense in a military commission was unclear. The subject had been debated before. In fact, during legislative hearings on the 2009 amendments to the MCA, executive branch lawyers were concerned enough about the legal status of material support to recommend that Congress remove it from the MCA's list of offenses triable by military commission. The congressional testimony tracked a May 2009 Office of Legal Counsel (OLC) memo concluding that material support convictions were unlikely to survive appellate review.[30] David Kris, the assistant attorney general for DOJ's National Security Division, warned members of Congress in July 2009 that there was "a significant risk that appellate courts will ultimately conclude that material support for terrorism is not a traditional law of war offense, thereby reversing hard-won convictions and leading to questions about the system's legitimacy."[31] Congress ignored that advice, but Kris's warning turned out to be prescient.

The appeal of Hamdan's conviction proceeded at a remarkably slow pace. After his conviction in 2008 the commission decision was forwarded to the convening authority, who approved the verdict in the summer of 2009. Hamdan then availed himself of review in the CMCR. A panel of CMCR judges heard oral argument in January 2010. After a long delay caused by personnel issues involving the recusal and retirement of CMCR judges, the court elected to rehear the case en banc before issuing a ruling. This required a new round of oral argument, which did not take place until March 2011.[32] On June 24, 2011, the CMCR finally handed down a decision unanimously upholding Hamdan's conviction for material support.[33] The CMCR opinion began by confronting Hamdan's most sweeping legal argument: that the Define and Punish Clause in Article I of the Constitution prohibited Congress from making material support triable by military commission. The text of Article I gives Congress the power "to define and punish Piracies and Felonies committed on the high Seas, and Offences against the Law of Nations." According to Hamdan's lawyers, this clause had a limiting effect on legislative power: Congress could codify only law of war offenses that were well established and widely recognized as such by the international community. Material support, they held, did not meet that criterion.

The CMCR disagreed with Hamdan's restrictive interpretation of the Define and Punish Clause. It found "no constitutional prerequisite of universal, international, or scholarly unanimity before Congress may act" to codify an offense against the law of war.[34] The Define and Punish Clause was not so rigid; what mattered, in the court's view, was whether some precedent existed for charging material support as a law of war offense. And according to the CMCR, it did. The bulk of its nearly ninety-page opinion canvassed a variety of international and domestic precedents and found some degree of historical support for material support charges or charges akin to them. The CMCR's reasoning also undercut Hamdan's argument that his conviction for conduct predating the 2006 MCA violated the Constitution's Ex Post Facto Clause. Because the CMCR located some historical precedent for material support as a war crime, it held that Congress was merely clarifying this preexisting state of affairs when it enacted the MCA, not creating a brand-new offense. The CMCR noted that the MCA contained a passage stating that its list of offenses included only those "that have traditionally been triable by military commissions." The MCA continued: "This chapter does not establish new crimes that did not exist before its enactment, but rather codifies those crimes for trial by military commission. . . . [It] does not preclude trial for crimes that occurred before the date of the enactment." The CMCR took Congress at its word.

A few months after the CMCR upheld Hamdan's conviction, it handed down a very similar ruling in an appeal brought on behalf of the second individual convicted in a military commission—the al-Qaeda propagandist Ali al Bahlul.[35] The Bahlul case differed slightly from Hamdan's, because in addition to material support Bahlul was convicted of conspiracy and solicitation offenses. But both of those offenses were open to the same legal objections as material support. The CMCR reached the same conclusion: like material support, solicitation and conspiracy to commit war crimes were recognizable law of war offenses prior to the MCA's enactment and Bahlul's alleged conduct. Congress was therefore acting appropriately when it included all three offenses in the MCA's list of offenses triable by military commissions.

It took approximately three years for the Court of Military Commission Review to finally uphold the first two verdicts rendered by military commissions. In the meantime, legal uncertainty prevailed. Military commission prosecutors faced with crucial decisions about whom to charge and which charges to use could not be sure which offenses would ultimately survive appellate review. And even after the CMCR weighed in, litigation continued. Under the congressionally created review scheme for commission decisions, defendants were entitled to another round of review in the DC Circuit Court of Appeals. Before the DC Circuit heard Hamdan's appeal, DOJ did something unusual: it dropped an argument that was central to its case before the CMCR and substituted a new one in its place.[36] Before the CMCR, the government successfully argued that material support was an offense against the international law of war—a subset of the "law of nations" mentioned in the Constitution's Define and Punish Clause. Now, in the DC Circuit, the government was no longer willing to make this argument.[37] Instead, it argued that material support was an accepted violation, not of the *international* law of war, but of a *domestic* common law of war. To buttress its position, the government cited examples of past US military commissions trying offenses similar to material support.

More than five months elapsed between oral argument and the DC Circuit's decision in what came to be called *Hamdan II*. The case had far-reaching implications for the future of the military commission system: the government did not possess evidence linking many Guantánamo detainees to specific plots or attacks, and material support offered commission prosecutors a broad, catch-all charge with which to go after lower-level suspects—individuals who, like Salim Hamdan, had been participating members of al-Qaeda but could not be directly tied to specific acts of violence. Furthermore, depending on the court's reasoning, a ruling against the government in *Hamdan II* might spell trouble for the solicitation and conspiracy charges at issue in Bahlul's appeal, which was pending in the DC Circuit before a different three-judge panel. According to Charlie Savage, a court ruling against conspiracy and material support charges would mean roughly two dozen Guantánamo detainees could no longer be prosecuted in military commissions. Instead, they would have to be detained without trial or transferred out of Guantánamo, since statutory restrictions prevented bringing Guantánamo detainees to US soil for civilian prosecutions in Article III courts (where material support and conspiracy charges are quite common).[38]

In October 2012, a DC Circuit panel voted 3–0 to reverse the CMCR decision and vacate Hamdan's conviction for material support.[39] Writing for the unanimous panel, Judge Brett Kavanaugh explained that at the time of Hamdan's alleged conduct, the jurisdiction of military commissions was circumscribed by the Uniform Code of Military Justice (UCMJ). The UCMJ did not list specific offenses triable by military commissions, but it confined their jurisdiction to offenses against the "law of war." The DC Circuit panel held that the phrase "law of war" referred to the international law of war, not a domestic common law of war as the government had contended. And—as the government itself now admitted—material support was not recognized as an offense against the international law of war. Thus, Hamdan's conviction had to fall.

The *Hamdan II* ruling demonstrated the robustness of the congressionally created review process for commission decisions. The CMCR may have been deferential to the government, but the DC Circuit was not. Despite the generally progovernment stance adopted by the DC Circuit in post-*Boumediene* detention litigation (see chapter 3), the court was willing to rule against the government in the first-ever appeal of a military commission verdict.[40] Moreover, given the panel's reasoning in *Hamdan II*, the ruling called into question the viability of solicitation and conspiracy charges. The government quickly conceded this point in the *Bahlul* litigation, where it was also relying on the domestic common law of war argument the *Hamdan II* panel rejected. In January 2013 the three-judge panel in *Bahlul* accordingly issued a one-page per curiam order vacating Bahlul's convictions.[41]

The government was not yet willing to jettison the domestic common law of war argument for good, however. Instead, it asked for en banc review in *Bahlul*, in hopes that the full DC Circuit might reach a different result than the *Hamdan II* panel—at least with respect to the conspiracy offense, for which the government believed its legal arguments to be strongest. The decision to keep fighting on the conspiracy issue was controversial inside the executive branch, which was divided into two camps. On one side were top officials in the State and Defense Departments and the chief prosecutor for military commissions, Mark Martins, who favored abandoning conspiracy charges for pre-MCA conduct. Faced with the uncertain legal status of conspiracy, this group worried about the prospect of another adverse court ruling that would further weaken the legitimacy of the commission system. The other camp included Assistant Attorney General for National Security Lisa Monaco and career attorneys at DOJ, who thought the benefits of trying to keep conspiracy charges in play outweighed the costs of more legal wrangling. These officials were convinced that the full DC Circuit might rule differently or, alternatively, that Justice Anthony Kennedy might provide a fifth vote for the government's domestic common law of war theory in a potential Supreme Court appeal.[42]

The second camp ultimately won the debate. The Obama administration announced that it would move ahead with an appeal in an effort to salvage conspiracy charges in military commissions. In a highly unusual move, Attorney

General Eric Holder reversed Solicitor General Donald Verrilli, who initially sided with the first group.[43] In April 2013, the DC Circuit agreed to an en banc rehearing in *Bahlul.* Few observers envisioned the government prevailing.[44] It took until the summer of 2014 for the DC Circuit to issue a decision. But far from bringing long-overdue clarity to the situation, the court perpetuated the legal uncertainty surrounding military commissions at Guantánamo Bay. Unlike Judge Kavanaugh's tidy opinion for a unanimous panel in *Hamdan II*, the *Bahlul* appeal generated a complex split decision.[45] All seven DC Circuit judges voted to vacate Bahlul's convictions for material support and solicitation to commit war crimes. But six out of seven judges voted to sustain Bahlul's conspiracy conviction. Given the case's significance for the future of military commissions, the decision is worth exploring.

Judge Karen LeCraft Henderson wrote the lead opinion, which was joined by three other judges: Merrick Garland, David Tatel, and Thomas Griffith. The four-judge majority made an important procedural move at the outset, holding that the proper standard of review in the case was "plain error" review—a highly deferential standard. By essentially boycotting his military commission trial, Bahlul had failed to raise the Ex Post Facto Clause argument he was now making. Thus, unless Bahlul's conviction was clearly and obviously unlawful, it would survive review under the majority's approach. The decision to conduct their review under this looser standard was highly consequential, because it limited the applicability of the ruling to the specifics of Bahlul's challenge. It would do little to clear up the legal uncertainty in future cases where defendants mounted active defenses in their military commission trials. Whatever the DC Circuit decided, then, more legal challenges were virtually guaranteed.

Under the plain error standard, the four-judge majority struck down the material support and solicitation convictions but upheld the conviction for conspiracy. The central question was whether the three charges could be applied to pre-MCA conduct without violating the Ex Post Facto Clause of the US Constitution, which prohibits punishing individuals for actions that were not illegal at the time they were carried out. (The logically prior question, of course, was whether the Ex Post Facto Clause even applied at Guantánamo Bay. Because the government took the position that it did, the majority "assume[d] without deciding" that this was so.) Bahlul's challenge to his conspiracy conviction failed under plain error review for two reasons. First, the majority pointed to the existence of a domestic statute criminalizing conspiracy at the time of Bahlul's conduct, holding that it was not "plain" or obvious that trying that offense by military commission instead of an Article III court violated the Ex Post Facto Clause. Second, the majority thought it at least plausible that the UCMJ's "law of war" language might include more than just the international law of war. For support, Judge Henderson's opinion cited the 2006 Supreme Court decision in *Hamdan v. Rumsfeld.* Although four justices found that conspiracy was not a triable offense under the UCMJ, three justices took the opposite view, and neither position garnered a majority. This uncertainty, combined with scattered historical examples that arguably showed American military commissions meting out conspiracy convictions, convinced the majority to uphold Bahlul's conspiracy conviction under plain error review.

The convictions for material support and solicitation were a different story. Even under the plain error standard, the majority concluded that there was "inadequate" precedent for trying these two offenses in military commissions.[46] Unlike the treatment of conspiracy, the effects of this part of the ruling were quite clear and would apply beyond the present case. Barring a contrary decision by the Supreme Court, military commission prosecutors would no longer be able to use material support or solicitation charges for conduct predating the MCA. Because almost every Guantánamo detainee had been captured and brought to the facility prior to the MCA's passage, this was an important holding. It made the government's job more difficult in prospective commission prosecutions and imperiled existing convictions, including Salim Hamdan's.

The other three DC Circuit judges took issue with the majority's approach. Judge Judith Rogers filed a dissenting opinion disagreeing with the majority's use of plain error review and its handling of the conspiracy charge. According to Judge Rogers, the UCMJ's reference to the "law of war" could not be read to include a US common law of war. Hers was the only vote against sustaining Bahlul's conspiracy conviction. The remaining two judges—Janice Rogers Brown and Brett Kavanaugh—voted with the majority to uphold Bahlul's conspiracy conviction, but dissented from other portions of the majority opinion. Both were highly critical of the use of plain error review. Framing the case as an opportunity for the government to receive "clarification of the prosecutorial tools it can employ in the war on terror," Judge Brown condemned the majority for "minimiz[ing] the value its opinion might provide to the government in future prosecutions."[47] Later in her opinion, she continued the thought: "The court disposes of this case without providing the government clear guidance for prosecuting the remaining detainees at Guantanamo. Thus, it may be many years before the government receives a definitive answer on whether it can charge the September 11 perpetrators with conspiracy."[48] Judge Kavanaugh echoed this lament, claiming that the court had a duty to decide wartime cases with "clarity and expedition" and bemoaning the majority's refusal to provide "guidance . . . going forward" on the legal status of conspiracy charges.[49]

Judges Brown and Kavanaugh favored de novo review, and they would both have upheld Bahlul's conspiracy conviction under that more exacting standard. Kavanaugh's opinion was surprising, because it seemed at odds with his opinion for the unanimous panel in *Hamdan II*. At various points in that opinion, Kavanaugh declined to adopt the domestic common law of war argument proffered by the government. Now, in *Bahlul*, Kavanaugh declared that "conspiracy has long been proscribed under U.S. law as a war crime triable by military commission."[50] Brown and Kavanaugh would also have answered other outstanding legal questions that the majority punted back to the original *Bahlul* panel. In addition to the Ex Post Facto claim, Bahlul's attorneys had made arguments under the Define and Punish Clause, the First Amendment, the Fifth Amendment, and Article III of the Constitution. Kavanaugh and Brown wanted to resolve all of these issues once and for all. Instead, those arguments would be confronted by the DC Circuit panel on remand.

Reaction to the *Bahlul* decision was mixed. Critics of military commissions seized on the ruling as another indication of the system's flaws and called for shutting it down. For example, Daphne Eviatar of Human Rights First urged Congress and the president to respond to the judicial decision by repealing the Guantánamo transfer restrictions and bringing detainees to the United States for civilian trials.[51] Stephen Vladeck underscored the differences between the DC Circuit ruling and the rulings from the CMCR and Bahlul's military commission, arguing that the disparity reflected poorly on the commission system. In his view, the fact that the DC Circuit unanimously rejected both the material support and solicitation convictions—even under an extraordinarily deferential standard of review—did not reflect well on the initial commission or the CMCR, both of which had upheld them.[52]

Other observers offered a different take. Jack Goldsmith argued that the government—and the commission system—did better than many believed.[53] For one thing, *Bahlul* marked the first time that a commission conviction was upheld by an Article III court. Moreover, Goldsmith noted that beneath all of the complicated legal wrangling lay an underlying judicial acceptance of the commission system. The DC Circuit judges skirmished over the details, but the court appeared to embrace military commissions as a legitimate mechanism for handling some subset of wartime prosecutions. For Goldsmith, disagreement among the judges about the precise size and character of that subset of cases ought not obscure the more fundamental point of agreement. On this view, military commissions were experiencing growing pains, but they were also on a path to becoming a legitimate, widely accepted tool in the government's national security toolbox.

## THE PERSISTENCE OF ADVERSARIAL LEGALISM

Whichever way one chose to view the *Bahlul* decision, the commission system continued to be buffeted by the forces of adversarial legalism in its wake. Defense attorneys in the Nashiri and 9/11 cases have continued to file a blizzard of pretrial motions, pushing trial dates back by several years. Those efforts were aided by the 2014 release of the Senate Intelligence Committee report on the CIA's rendition, detention, and interrogation (RDI) program, which gave defense lawyers more fodder to challenge their clients' treatment while in American custody.[54] In the meantime, litigation in the CMCR and the DC Circuit has persisted, casting a continued shadow over the commission system. The interbranch tug-of-war over military commissions has largely ceased, but adversarial legalism endures.

The DC Circuit ruling in 2014 sustaining Bahlul's conspiracy conviction against an Ex Post Facto Clause challenge did not end the *Bahlul* litigation. The case was remanded to a DC Circuit panel, which considered Bahlul's other legal arguments against his conviction. These included a claim that Article III of the Constitution—the article that establishes the power of the judicial branch—prevents Congress from giving military commissions the power to try domestic common law of war offenses like conspiracy. In June 2015 a DC Circuit panel agreed, voting 2–1 to throw out Bahlul's conspiracy conviction.[55] In a sweeping opinion written by Judge Judith Rogers and joined by Judge David Tatel, the majority held that conspiracy charges in military commissions were prohibited even if authorized by the legislature. Judge Rogers framed the challenge as a clash between the elected branches and the judiciary, and she argued for regular de novo review instead of the more relaxed plain error standard used in the prior case. According to Rogers, "Such searching, *de novo* review is appropriate because Bahlul's Article III challenge implicates the power of the political branches to sideline the federal courts. . . . The Article III challenge in Bahlul's case goes to the heart of the judiciary's status as a coordinate branch of government."[56]

Judge Rogers then endorsed the core of Bahlul's Article III argument: that the jurisdiction of military commissions solely encompasses violations of the international law of war and that Congress may not constitutionally allow commissions to try domestic law offenses such as conspiracy. Article III vests judicial power in courts staffed by judges with life tenure and salary protections, and it guarantees trial by jury for all crimes (with an explicit exception for impeachment). However, as Judge Rogers noted, over time the judiciary has recognized certain limited, implicit exceptions to Article III's requirements—including one for military courts. The question, then, concerned the precise contours of this exception. Rogers turned to *Ex parte Quirin* for help.[57] In that 1942 case, the Supreme Court held that military commissions could try violations of the "law of war." Rogers cited language in the opinion that referred to the law of war as "a branch of international law." Thus, Rogers concluded that since there was no clear precedent for conspiracy as a violation of the international law of war, that offense was outside the constitutional purview of military commissions. It did not matter that the MCA expressly listed conspiracy as an offense triable by military commission. Rogers adopted a restrictive interpretation of the Article I Define and Punish Clause: "Congress cannot, pursuant to the Define and Punish Clause, declare an offense to be an international war crime when the international law of war concededly does not." Military commissions could try only offenses recognized by the international community as war crimes; other crimes, such as conspiracy, were to be tried only in Article III courts. Bahlul's conviction had to be overturned on these grounds.

The decision was a sweeping one. In separation-of-powers terms, it limited the authority of Congress and the executive over military commissions. In terms of policy impact, the ruling made military commissions a less useful tool for the government moving forward. If upheld, the panel decision meant that common counterterrorism charges like material support and conspiracy could not be employed in military commissions ever again. Even for conduct postdating the MCA's enactment, material support and conspiracy charges would be off the table for military commission prosecutors. This would limit the future utility of commissions and make civilian prosecutions much more attractive by comparison. Broader, catchall offenses like conspiracy are regularly utilized in Article III courts. Indeed, Judge Tatel referred to this fact in a concurring opinion, noting that conspiracy has been used repeatedly in civilian trials for terrorists with great success. He contrasted the strong record of Article III courts in terrorism prosecutions to the struggles of the commission system, highlighting its small number of convictions and vulnerability to appeals. Tatel apparently made this observation without irony. What he neglected to mention, of course, was that federal judges were key contributors to the spotty track record of the commission system—and that now, his own vote in the case at hand threatened to make that track record even more underwhelming.

Yet again, a court issued a ruling devoid of deference on a key matter of national security. As Judge Henderson pointed out in a searing dissent, the ruling was unusual for contradicting not one but *both* elected branches on a wartime policy issue. Henderson was unsparing, taking the majority to task for its refusal to defer to the national security judgments of Congress and the president. And she was incredulous that the majority was using its interpretation of international law to constrain the other branches of government. Calling Congress's decision to include conspiracy in the MCA "consistent with international law—even if not a perfect match," Henderson refused to accept that the legislature was strictly confined to codifying offenses recognized as war crimes by international consensus. In addition to her pointed criticism of the majority's legal analysis, Henderson expressed concern about the consequences of the decision. She wondered whether the government would still be able to punish Bahlul, whom she deemed clearly guilty of serious crimes. And Judge Henderson worried about the prospective consequences of the ruling for military operations against ISIS, which had begun one year earlier.

Bahlul's legal saga was still not over. The government appealed, and the DC Circuit again reheard the case en banc. In October 2016, it handed down a 6–3 decision reversing the panel below and reinstating Ali al Bahlul's conviction for conspiracy.[58] Once again, the court's decision created more uncertainty than it did clarity. Although a six-judge majority voted to sustain Bahlul's conviction, there was disagreement over the rationale for doing so. Because of this disagreement, the ruling was heavily contingent on the specific facts of Bahlul's challenge and offered little clarity for other military commission cases. A plurality of four judges—Kavanaugh, Brown, Griffith, and Henderson—thought Bahlul's conviction for conspiracy to commit war crimes posed no constitutional problem under Article III or the Define and Punish Clause.

Employing de novo review, the plurality first dispensed with the Define and Punish Clause argument. Even if that clause limited Congress to codifying broadly accepted international law of war offenses—a point they were unwilling to concede—the plurality maintained that Congress's other Article I war powers were not so constrained. Citing the Declare War Clause, the Necessary and Proper Clause, and others, Judge Kavanaugh wrote, "The Constitution does not give foreign nations (acting through the international law of war or otherwise) a de facto veto over Congress's determination of which war crimes may be tried by U.S. military commissions."[59] Then, pivoting to historical practice and the *Quirin* decision, the plurality found precedents supporting the use of conspiracy charges and other non–international law of war offenses in past American military commissions. This was enough confirmation that conspiracy charges could be used in military commissions without violating Article III's jury trial requirements.

If the plurality opinion had garnered just one more vote, the *Bahlul* litigation would have ended with a clear legal outcome: conspiracy charges would be available in military commissions, now and in the future, for all prospective defendants. But because the other two judges who voted with the plurality rejected its reasoning, such clarity proved elusive. Judges Patricia Millett and Robert Wilkins issued narrow concurring opinions affirming Bahlul's conviction but declining to endorse the plurality's arguments. Judge Millett was alone in believing that the proper standard of review in the case was plain error review. Under this more deferential standard, she held that Bahlul's conviction should be sustained. Judge Wilkins took a slightly different tack: he argued for de novo review, but claimed that Bahlul had actually been convicted of more than "ordinary, inchoate conspiracy." Scanning the commission's verdict and the text of the MCA, Wilkins maintained that Bahlul had committed specific offenses that exceeded the vague offense of conspiracy—and that the MCA's definition of conspiracy resembled other crimes that were widely accepted as international law of war violations. He declared, "When I look at what Bahlul was really convicted of, I see a war crime."[60] Judge Millett agreed with Judge Wilkins on this point. But while they were both willing to affirm Bahlul's conviction, neither of them provided the decisive fifth vote for upholding conspiracy as an offense triable by military commission in all future cases. And the three remaining judges—Rogers, Tatel, and Cornelia Pillard—filed a lengthy dissent arguing that Bahlul's conspiracy conviction exceeded Congress's authority and violated Article III. They would have upheld the prior panel decision.

Shortly after the full DC Circuit decided Bahlul's case, the Supreme Court denied certiorari. Nearly eight years after Ali al Bahlul's conviction by military commission, his legal challenge was finally settled. Bahlul remains imprisoned at Guantánamo Bay. But the underlying legal uncertainty surrounding the commission system would prevail. Bahlul's lawsuit was just one of several legal challenges during this period. The litigation played out in three arenas: the military commissions themselves, the CMCR, and the DC Circuit Court of Appeals. As a result of the DC Circuit's jurisprudence, Noor Uthman Mohammed's military commission conviction for material support, like Hamdan's, was thrown out.[61] David Hicks saw his commission verdict overturned as well.[62] A pair of lawsuits challenged the composition of the CMCR, on the grounds that the judges serving on it had been improperly appointed or were insufficiently independent. In both of those cases, the DC Circuit refused to intervene until the underlying legal issues were confronted by the commission and the CMCR, prolonging uncertainty on these questions.[63]

The DC Circuit adopted a similar approach in an important 2016 case. Lawyers for Abd al-Rahim al-Nashiri—whose military commission was still mired in pretrial proceedings—argued that the military commission lacked authority to try him. They maintained that the attacks to which he was linked—the 2000 bombing of the U.S.S. *Cole* and the 2002 bombing of a French ship called the *Limburg*—were not part of the US armed conflict with al-Qaeda, and therefore that neither the MCA nor the Constitution permitted his trial by military commission. Nashiri sought a court order to end the proceedings, but a divided DC Circuit panel sided with the government. The majority held that the proper course of action was abstention: it would allow the military commission process to play out and address Nashiri's arguments first, and Nashiri could avail himself of the MCA's review scheme after his trial was complete. To distinguish the case from *Hamdan v. Rumsfeld*, where the Supreme Court intervened before a trial took place, the majority opinion cited the reforms undertaken in the wake of that ruling. "Much has changed since *Hamdan*," Judge Griffith wrote, including the introduction of "significant procedural and evidentiary safeguards" in commissions and the guarantee of judicial review in an Article III court afterward. Once again, then, key questions about the jurisdictional scope of military commissions went unanswered.

The sluggishness of military commission proceedings for the 9/11 conspirators is largely attributable to the wide array of pretrial motions filed by their defense attorneys, which have challenged virtually every imaginable aspect of the commission system. For example, in 2015 Deputy Secretary of Defense Robert Work followed the advice of Convening Authority Vaughn Ary and issued an order instructing commission judges to relocate to Guantánamo Bay. The objective was to speed up proceedings by having judges on site instead of a plane ride away. Lawyers for the 9/11 defendants challenged the order as an exercise of unlawful command influence over the commission system, and the commission judge, Colonel James Pohl, agreed. Judge Pohl halted the proceedings until DOD revoked the order, and the convening authority promptly resigned his post.[64] A variety of other logistical issues and legal challenges have continued to plague the 9/11 case. As a result, nearly two decades after the attack these defendants allegedly helped plan and carry out, their military commission is still in pretrial proceedings.

## MILITARY COMMISSIONS UNDER TRUMP: THE STATUS QUO PREVAILS

During the 2016 presidential campaign, Donald Trump spoke approvingly of using military commissions to prosecute suspected terrorists. He even suggested that he might favor military trials for US citizens, despite the MCA's express limitation to noncitizens.[65] After his election and inauguration, President Trump's attorney general, Jeff Sessions, made remarks that seemed to indicate a preference for using detention and military commissions at Guantánamo for newly captured enemy fighters—a break with the Obama administration's approach, which eschewed both of those policy options for new captures.[66] But just as President Obama found it difficult to make significant policy changes, President Trump was similarly constrained. The reformed military commission system that Trump currently presides over is largely insulated from presidential control.

As of this writing, the Trump administration has not brought a single new individual to Guantánamo Bay for detention or a military commission trial. In a pair of particularly high-profile episodes in the fall of 2017, the Trump administration followed the Obama administration's practice of pursuing prosecutions in Article III courts. When US commandos in Libya captured Mustafa al-Imam, a suspect in the 2012 Benghazi embassy attack, the Trump administration elected to bring him to the United States for a civilian trial.[67] Just days later, a man named Sayfullo Saipov drove a truck onto a bike path in New York

City, killing eight and wounding eleven. Despite an initial remark by President Trump that he was open to sending the culprit to Guantánamo, Saipov—a noncitizen jihadist apparently inspired by ISIS—was quickly charged in federal court in Manhattan.[68]

For detainees already in American custody when Trump took office, the story has been similar. In December 2017, military commission prosecutors attempted to bring new charges against three existing Guantánamo detainees for their connections to terrorist plots in Southeast Asia. But when the charges reached the convening authority, he declined to approve them.[69] The basis for the refusal was not revealed. Adding to the instability, Convening Authority Harvey Rishikof and his legal adviser were removed not long after for undisclosed reasons.[70]

The Trump administration inherited three ongoing military commission cases from its predecessor: one for the 9/11 defendants, one for Nashiri, and one for a man named Abdul Hadi al Iraqi. All three moved at a remarkably slow pace. The Nashiri proceedings have been particularly troubled: in the fall of 2017, Nashiri's civilian defense team resigned en masse, citing an inability to be certain of attorney-client confidentiality.[71] The commission judge in the case, Colonel Vance Spath, expressed extreme frustration with the defense team's maneuver, and in February 2018 he halted the Nashiri proceedings entirely.[72] A variety of problems have hindered progress in the other two cases as well.[73] It is not only litigation that has caused delay in the commission system. Setting up a court system largely from scratch created a host of logistical issues: there have been several internal setbacks and mishaps, including high-profile disputes over closing the proceedings to protect classified information and the discovery of potential government monitoring of defense teams.[74] But internal and external legal challenges have certainly been the leading contributor to the extraordinary amount of delay and uncertainty that continues to afflict the military commission system.

## CONCLUSION

Though we are now far removed from President George W. Bush's November 2001 order creating them, the battle over military commissions continues. Inside the commissions themselves, through a dizzying array of defense motions, and outside the commissions, in litigation in the CMCR and the DC

Circuit, legal challenges are unceasing. Since Majid Khan's February 2012 plea agreement, commissions have produced just one more conviction: Ahmed Muhammed Haza al-Darbi entered a guilty plea in February 2014 for offenses related to the bombings of the USS *Cole* in 2000 and a French ship in 2002. He received a lighter sentence in return for his cooperation in the case against Nashiri.[75]

Al-Darbi's guilty plea brought the number of military commission convictions to eight, where it still stands as of this writing. And those eight convictions have been highly vulnerable to appellate attack. Any future convictions are virtually certain to give rise to lengthy appeals as well. While policy makers and national security experts continue to disagree about the utility of military commissions, all agree that their operation to date has been extraordinarily rocky—and that, consequently, they have failed to fulfill their original purpose.[76] Some have blamed their troubles on the novelty of the system, as compared to the tried-and-true method of prosecution in Article III courts. For example, Charlie Savage has written that "traditional institutions and practices that evolved over time should not be lightly tossed aside for untested replacements because it's hard to make a complex new system work."[77] There is certainly some truth to Savage's observation, but it does ignore an important fact: military commissions are not actually new. The United States has used them before: during the Civil War their use was widespread, and they were employed again in World War II. Aside from an 1866 Supreme Court ruling narrowing their jurisdiction over American citizens, lawsuits challenging military commissions in these periods largely failed. It is only now, in the twenty-first-century United States, that commissions have spawned such wide-ranging—and often successful—legal attacks.

Something has changed, in other words, and it isn't military commissions. After all, President Bush's initial executive order creating commissions was modeled on President Roosevelt's 1942 order establishing a military commission to try Nazi saboteurs. FDR's move was unanimously upheld by the Supreme Court. One might therefore have expected, as Bush administration lawyers did, that Bush's action would survive judicial scrutiny. But even after a series of regulatory modifications that made the post-9/11 commissions more protective of defendants and more insulated from White House control than the FDR commission, Bush was repudiated in court. Moreover, more than a decade after the Supreme Court invalidated the commissions and Congress responded—not once, but twice—with reforms, the system remains subject to an array of legal challenges.

When one examines the creation and evolution of military commissions since 2001, it is clear that the American system of "separated institutions sharing powers" has carried the day. The institutional tug-of-war over military commissions has repeatedly derived energy from lawsuits and court decisions. This is surprising, since national security policy has often been thought of as an area characterized by a high degree of presidential unilateralism and few checks and balances. Congress and, to an even greater extent, the courts have traditionally been viewed as deferential to White House positions on matters of war and peace. But the development of laws and policies surrounding military commissions is a different story. Commissions were created unilaterally by presidential order in the wake of 9/11 with the goal of meting out swift convictions and lengthy sentences. But they have been anything but swift, and the handful of sentences they have produced have generally not been very lengthy. The structure and functioning of commissions has diverged considerably from the original vision held by the Bush White House *and* its critics, who took the White House at its word and predicted that quick trials and harsh punishments would turn commissions into "kangaroo courts" devoid of legitimacy.

Legal and policy developments have been the product of a convoluted back and forth between the three branches of government. And that back-and-forth has been spurred on by the ever-present threat, and reality, of litigation and judicial intervention. Even in the national security space, policy making is increasingly decentralized and legalized, and it is subject to the same sorts of interbranch interactions that have long characterized domestic policy making. Central to these interactions is the role of litigation and courts. While the Supreme Court's *Hamdan* decision in 2006 receives the most attention, there is much more to be said about the judiciary's broader involvement in reshaping the commission system. As this chapter in particular shows, the DC Circuit Court of Appeals has been an especially influential actor. And court decisions have been consequential not simply for what they have expressly held, but also for the ways in which they have been leveraged by other actors, in Congress and in the bureaucracy, to push policy in their preferred direction. Furthermore, the influence of litigation turns out to be even greater than that, because the threat of a future lawsuit always looms over policy makers. Adversarial legalism and the interbranch tug-of-war have made military commissions more independent from the president and more protective of the rights of the accused.

Changes to the commission system have not come without costs. Court decisions described in this chapter have shrunk the jurisdiction of military commissions, and other changes to the system have made prosecution by military commission more difficult, and therefore less appealing, for the government. One of the policy tools in the executive branch's post-9/11 toolbox has been significantly degraded to the point of near uselessness. Moreover, to the extent that there are current or future detainees who might therefore be subject to treatment offering fewer protections than military commissions—such as prolonged detention without charges or prosecution in other nations with dubious commitments to due process—it is not clear that they have benefited, either.

As military commissions have continued to struggle, another method for removing suspected terrorists from the battlefield has increasingly taken center stage: ordinary criminal prosecutions in Article III courts. All three presidential administrations since 9/11 have used this tool in certain circumstances, and it has been highly effective.[78] But for the detainees who remain at Guantánamo, civilian prosecutions inside the United States are not an option: they are prohibited by legislative restrictions barring the transfer of Guantánamo detainees to US soil. Furthermore, although military commissions in their current form bear a close resemblance to Article III courts, there are still at least a few differences that may make military commissions more desirable in certain situations. As Robert Chesney notes, the most important of these is the more relaxed standard for introducing hearsay evidence in military commissions.[79] Even here the rules for military commissions have converged somewhat with Article III court procedures, but the commission rules are at least slightly more favorable to the government. In some small subset of cases, including Nashiri's, that difference might be decisive.[80]

The convergence between military commissions and Article III courts is noteworthy, for it is more or less what President Bush's critics clamored for from the outset. And for those who complained that Bush's 2001 executive order violated the separation of powers, Congress—with a shove from the judiciary—has now provided a clear and detailed statutory foundation for commissions. The review process for commission decisions has been significantly enhanced to include multiple appellate review bodies, one of which is an Article III court—making the appeals process for commission decisions more rigorous than the review process for courts-martial.[81] Transparency has increased, with commission proceedings at Guantánamo now broadcast via closed-circuit television at Fort Meade in Maryland. Procedures for handling classified information in commissions mirror the ones that have been used in federal courts for decades. Statements obtained involuntarily are as a rule no longer admissible. And the sentences handed down by commissions are on average shorter than the sentences produced by civilian courts in terrorism cases.

Viewed against these developments, much of the debate over military commissions now seems divorced from reality. For national security hawks, it is no longer accurate to praise commissions as vastly preferable or a necessary alternative to ordinary civilian trials in most cases. For the system's critics, military commissions in their current form cannot credibly be labeled "kangaroo courts." Both these lines of argument have been substantially undercut by events since 2001. It is no longer clear that commissions offer the government advantages over regular criminal proceedings. And instead of fretting that commission prosecutions would be engineered to produce swift progovernment verdicts, critics now make precisely the opposite argument: that commissions are too slow, and that justice delayed is justice denied.[82]

The result of all this is a rather odd situation. The United States has a new and improved military commission system, repeatedly vetted and embraced by all three branches of government and presidents from both political parties. But that system has become a seldom-used, deeply troubled tool for national security policy makers. Despite retaining them, President Obama eschewed their use for newly captured suspects, and his successor—an unorthodox president whose campaign rhetoric suggested a renewed commitment to commissions—has nevertheless followed in Obama's footsteps. Though a few cases remain in the works, it is not clear whether military commissions will have staying power beyond these proceedings or whether they are destined to wither away. But one thing does seem certain: litigation over military commissions will not end anytime soon.

# Conclusion

In considering the evolution of enemy combatant policies first formulated in the wake of the September 11, 2001, terrorist attack, the central takeaway is that lawsuits and court rulings have repeatedly generated significant policy changes. These changes have had major consequences for policy makers tasked with managing the war effort and for suspected enemy fighters. The initial decision in November 2001 to authorize detention and military commissions was made unilaterally by President George W. Bush. Since then, however, policies have emerged not from White House edicts, but from an extended back-and-forth among a variety of actors. And courts have played a key role in that process. On numerous occasions, actors in Congress and the bureaucracy used judicial decisions and the specter of litigation to carve out a role for themselves and move policies in their preferred direction. The consequences included increased checks on presidential authority and greater levels of due process for suspected belligerents held in US custody. But the slow pace of litigation and persistent legal uncertainty meant that many individuals in US custody were kept in limbo for long periods of time. And as it became increasingly difficult for the government to sustain detentions and military commission prosecutions, policy makers turned to other mechanisms for handling suspected adversaries—policies with costs of their own for both the government and the individuals it seeks to combat.

## THE FUTURE OF DETENTION AND MILITARY COMMISSIONS

Nearly two decades removed from the events of 9/11, the United States is still at war with al-Qaeda and various other terrorist organizations. Forty individuals remain at Guantánamo Bay. Of these forty individuals, seven have military commission proceedings in progress, two have been convicted by a military commission, and five are recommended for transfer subject to security agreements. The remaining twenty-six continue to be detained indefinitely, unable to be prosecuted but considered too dangerous to release.[1] At the very least, the policies discussed in this book retain their relevance in light of these numbers. But given the disinclination on the part of the Obama and

Trump administrations to use detention and military commissions for newly captured individuals, one might wonder: Aren't these merely legacy issues left over from the Bush administration's policy decisions in the early stages of the war? Why bother studying them now, if they've essentially run their course?

First, it is important to note that detention and military commissions remain readily available to policy makers who may wish to use them in the future. Precisely because enemy combatant policies have been repeatedly vetted and reformed, policy makers who see fit to deploy them will presumably be on firm legal ground in doing so. Detention and military trials have been sanctioned by presidents from both parties, multiple Congresses, and several courts—including the US Supreme Court. To be sure, there remains some legal uncertainty regarding the proper scope of these two policy tools, and future uses of them would surely give rise to litigation. But the widespread endorsement of detention and military commissions—the underlying acceptance that they are legitimate exercises of government power in certain contexts—means that they are likely to remain politically and legally viable options for future policy makers.

The current conflict has already evolved considerably over time. We should expect that as this war continues to change shape, policy makers will adapt to realities on the ground. What if a future president determines that it will take more than targeted air strikes to dislodge a terrorist cell from a safe haven halfway across the globe? If significant numbers of ground forces were deployed, it is not hard to imagine the United States again capturing hundreds of rank-and-file terrorist suspects. What then? If the country in which the intervention takes place does not have a functioning justice system, handing captured fighters over is a nonstarter. Flying a small number of individuals to the United States and prosecuting them for broad offenses such as material support has worked reasonably well for high-level terrorist suspects, but is it really feasible to start prosecutions for hundreds at once? Furthermore, if individuals are taken into custody in the heat of battle, careful collection of evidence may be difficult or impossible. Under these conditions, detention without trial or prosecution in military commissions, where evidentiary rules are more flexible, might become the most palatable options.

It is possible, then, to imagine future scenarios in which the benefits of using detention or military trials might outweigh the benefits of alternative policy options. Presidents Obama and Trump have favored a hybrid approach of brief military custody followed by prosecution in Article III courts for high-level terrorist suspects, but there may be situations in which prolonged military custody is preferable. Moreover, it is by no means clear that the practice of turning detention and prosecution responsibilities for lower-level fighters over to other nations—nations that may have little commitment to due process, interests that diverge from American interests, or both—is an optimal course, either. Resorting to lethal force has serious downsides, too: it certainly does no favors to the individual being targeted, and it may result in the United States forfeiting an opportunity to gather valuable intelligence.

## DIFFERENT POLICY AREAS, SIMILAR PATTERNS

Whether or not detention or military commissions continue to play a role in the armed conflict against terrorist groups, the patterns of policy development discussed in this book are generalizable to other wartime policy areas.

### *Surveillance*

One of the most infamous episodes of George W. Bush's presidency concerned a legal rift within the executive branch over a wartime surveillance program established after 9/11. When the Office of Legal Counsel and Deputy Attorney General James Comey (then acting as attorney general because Attorney General John Ashcroft was hospitalized with a serious health problem) declined to reauthorize the program, White House officials protested. What happened next sounds like a scene from a movie: White House counsel Alberto Gonzales and President Bush's chief of staff, Andrew Card, drove to the hospital where Ashcroft was in intensive care and attempted to get him to overrule the Department of Justice's (DOJ) position. The bedridden Ashcroft declined, pointing to Comey—who had rushed to the hospital when he learned of Card and Gonzales's plan—and declaring that Comey was the attorney general.[2] When the Bush White House suggested it might proceed with the surveillance program over DOJ's legal objections, DOJ officials threatened to resign and the White House backed down. The controversial program was reformed.[3] In this instance, internal executive branch disagreement on matters of law had generated policy changes.

In a second example from several years later, litigation helped spur reforms to the National Security Agency surveillance program that relied on the government's bulk collection of metadata. After its exposure by Edward Snowden in 2013, the program became the subject of multiple lawsuits and met with judicial pushback in the lower courts. In May 2015, a unanimous Second Circuit panel ruled that the bulk collection program lacked statutory authorization.[4] In the wake of the ruling, Congress—already faced with a legislative deadline to reauthorize the program or let it lapse—enacted the USA Freedom Act, making a series of changes to the program. The judiciary had provided proponents of reform with a powerful tool in support of their cause.[5]

*Interrogation*

Court decisions in the areas of detention and military commissions had ripple effects on interrogation policies. The Supreme Court's 2004 ruling in *Rasul v. Bush*, finding statutory habeas corpus rights applicable at Guantánamo Bay, generated a congressional response. The Detainee Treatment Act (DTA) of 2005 overrode the Court's interpretation, stripping statutory habeas jurisdiction over Guantánamo. But the DTA also contained limits on the harsh interrogation tactics employed by the Bush administration in the early years of the conflict. Without the 2004 Supreme Court ruling, it is questionable whether Congress would have summoned the requisite political will to enact the DTA.

Then, in 2006, the Supreme Court ruling in *Hamdan v. Rumsfeld* that the Bush administration's version of military commissions was unlawful had further implications for interrogation policies. In the course of finding the military commission system illegal, the Court concluded that Common Article 3 of the Geneva Conventions applies to the armed conflict against al-Qaeda and other terrorist organizations. Common Article 3 contains language barring "outrages upon personal dignity, in particular humiliating and degrading treatment."[6] The Bush administration, worried that this language could be used to prosecute individuals involved in interrogations, moved to suspend the CIA's controversial interrogation program. By applying a portion of the Geneva Conventions to the ongoing war, the *Hamdan* ruling cast a pall over the CIA's enhanced interrogation program and helped lead to its demise. The story did not end there: on entering office, President Obama immediately issued an executive order restricting the use of coercive interrogation methods.[7] Congress later codified stringent interrogation limits in legislation.[8] And despite recurring remarks from President Trump that he wished to resume the use of coercive interrogation techniques, including waterboarding, there is no evidence that his administration has done so—more confirmation of the effectiveness of constraints on presidential unilateralism.[9]

*Targeted Killing*

One also sees the effects of litigation and court decisions in the realm of targeted killing. Here, the effects are largely indirect: courts have been reluctant to reach the merits in cases challenging specific uses of lethal force against terrorist suspects.[10] However, as Jack Goldsmith has noted, court rulings dealing with detention have influenced decisions regarding the use of lethal force.[11] This is because many lethal force operations—including the Obama administration's drone strike against US citizen Anwar al-Awlaki, a senior member of al-Qaeda offshoot Al-Qaeda in the Arabian Peninsula (AQAP)—are carried out pursuant to the 2001 AUMF. And courts have repeatedly interpreted the 2001 AUMF in the context of habeas corpus litigation brought by detainees. Goldsmith points out that in the detention litigation, courts have held that the AUMF's grant of "all necessary and appropriate force" could apply to American citizens, was not subject to geographic restrictions, and encompassed "associated forces" aligned with al-Qaeda. These interpretations of the AUMF arguably pointed toward the legality of targeting Awlaki (among other noncitizen terrorist suspects).[12]

Evidence shows that judicial constructions of the AUMF's scope have shaped internal debates within the executive branch about who can and cannot be targeted with lethal force. During Barack Obama's presidency, recurring disagreements arose among administration officials over the proper scope of the drone program. Both Daniel Klaidman and Charlie Savage have documented internal debates between State Department legal adviser Harold Koh and Defense Department general counsel Jeh Johnson over which individuals and groups could be targeted under the 2001 AUMF. Legal considerations had a constraining impact on the drone program: in one episode, Koh's interpretation of the AUMF prevented a targeted killing operation from taking place. Koh successfully argued that an individual tied to the Somali terrorist group Al Shabab could not be targeted under the AUMF.[13] Ultimately, Goldsmith describes the process for targeted killing decisions as "executive deliberation guided by judicial precedent and subject to congressional oversight."[14] In other words, all three branches are involved, and despite the lack of direct intervention from the judiciary, lawsuits and court decisions in an adjacent policy area have played an important role in shaping policy outcomes.

*Travel Ban*

One of Donald Trump's first acts as president was to issue an executive order banning travel to the United States from several Muslim-majority nations. The policy, justified as a national security measure, provoked immediate litigation in multiple courts.[15] On January 28, just one day after President Trump promulgated his executive order, a federal judge in New York temporarily blocked parts of the policy. One day after that, a federal judge in Massachusetts made a similar move. As these initial rulings were handed down, the Trump administration moved on February 2 to loosen the travel ban's application to green card holders. A day after that policy adjustment, a federal judge in Washington State blocked the travel ban on a nationwide basis, and that nationwide injunction was quickly upheld by the US Court of Appeals for the Ninth Circuit. Rather than appeal to the Supreme Court, the Trump administration announced that it would revise the travel ban policy. The new executive order, President Trump declared, would be "very much tailored" to reflect the court decisions.

The revised travel ban was enacted on March 6, 2017.[16] Again, adversarial legalism kicked in right away: the state of Hawaii filed a lawsuit on March 7, and the following week—one day before the revised version was set to go into effect—a federal district court in Hawaii issued a nationwide injunction stopping the policy in its tracks. A district court in Maryland reached a similar conclusion the next day. Appellate courts largely agreed, but legal uncertainty increased when the Supreme Court narrowed the injunctions, allowing the policy to be enforced against "foreign nationals who lack any bona fide relationship with a person or entity in the United States" while legal challenges on the merits moved forward. In the meantime, more litigation ensued over the meaning and application of the "bona fide relationship" language used by the Supreme Court.

Before the Supreme Court could weigh in on the merits of the second version of the travel ban, however, the Trump administration issued a third version of the policy. This version, announced on September 24, 2017, weakened some of the prior versions' provisions. But it also made the ban more enduring, and it added non–Muslim-majority nations to the list—likely in part an effort to blunt First Amendment Establishment Clause challenges, which claimed the policy was an unconstitutional "Muslim ban."[17] Not only had adversarial legalism produced delay and legal uncertainty, it had led to the unintended consequence of extending the travel ban's application in key respects. Version three was blocked again by lower courts, but the volley between the executive branch and the judiciary finally ended when the Supreme Court upheld the third version of the policy by a 5–4 vote in June 2018.[18]

## THE BIG PICTURE

For much of this book we have been deep in the weeds, tracing the evolution of enemy combatant policies through subtle regulatory changes, complex lower court rulings, and obscure statutory provisions. I conclude by zooming out and briefly examining the bigger picture. At a time when it is common to hear complaints that our governing institutions are not working well, the story told in the preceding pages offers some cause for optimism. There is, however, plenty to regret in the US government's response to the 9/11 terrorist attack. The Bush administration's sweeping legal theories of presidential power, if endorsed by the other two branches, could have seriously undermined the separation of powers and checks and balances so central to our constitutional structure. The early images of detainees being transported to Guantánamo Bay exacted a toll on America's reputation as a protector of human rights. The report of the Senate Select Committee on Intelligence on the CIA's rendition, detention, and interrogation program is a sobering and at times stomach-turning read. Though estimates vary as to their number, it is clear that the proliferation of drone strikes has resulted in civilian casualties. Any complete accounting of the United States' conduct post-9/11 must reckon with these realities. Moreover, as we have seen, even the reforms to enemy combatant policies have come with costs of their own.

But if the US response to 9/11 has been far from perfect, I have also argued here that our system of checks and balances has largely prevailed—and that lawsuits and court rulings have been a major reason why. The wartime presidency of today is a remarkably powerful institution, but litigation—both the threat and the reality of it—has helped to discipline it. As judicial intervention in national security matters becomes more commonplace, presidents must anticipate the potential for judicial review at a later date when they are making decisions. And the ability of other actors and institutions to check the presidency has been augmented by the rise of litigation and judicial involvement. Bureaucrats and legislators have repeatedly used the specter of litigation and court decisions as openings to intervene in the policy-making process.

Ultimately, this study demonstrates the value of adopting an interbranch perspective and applying it to the national security sphere—an area often thought to be dominated by the executive. A narrow focus on the presidency may create a misleading impression that we have witnessed the return of the imperial president, liberated from checks and balances and capable of unilaterally dictating national security policy. Indeed, many scholars have argued exactly that.[19] But by widening our lens, we develop a more comprehensive and more accurate understanding of the policy-making process and the presidency's position in that process. In particular, we gain a rich appreciation for the extraordinary role that litigation and court decisions have played in reshaping the post-9/11 national security policy landscape. As Jeb Barnes has written of the influence of courts on policy making, "snapshots of judicial decision making—however sophisticated the lens—can provide an incomplete picture."[20] Snapshots of presidential decision-making are liable to the same objection: focusing exclusively on executive branch legal memos or executive orders without examining their implementation over time yields a distorted understanding of policy making.

As a result of the many institutional interactions detailed in this book, enemy combatant policies are now more insulated from presidential control and more protective of suspected combatants. Will this state of affairs endure? It is hard to say. That it has endured thus far under the Trump presidency despite campaign promises to the contrary may be a testament to its staying power.[21] But what if the United States experiences another terrorist attack on the scale of 9/11? Or an even more deadly attack or series of attacks? Perhaps the patterns and policies discussed in this book would give way to unilateral presidential action and draconian measures. As this book has shown, however, such moves would almost certainly generate widespread litigation. Lawyers seeking to challenge them would be armed with a variety of legal arguments and precedents with which to push back. Future administrations would bump up against statutory limitations and might well face resistance from within the executive branch itself. Lawsuits and court rulings would in all likelihood energize our system of "separated institutions sharing powers," making it very difficult for presidential unilateralism and extreme policies to be implemented and sustained. Litigation and judicial intervention would come with drawbacks, too. Above all, it is to be hoped that the lessons learned after 9/11 and discussed in this book will be applied—by lawyers, judges, legislators, bureaucrats, presidents, and ordinary citizens—to make our government work as well as possible when it confronts a similar crisis in the future.

# *Timeline of Significant Events*

September 11, 2001: The United States is attacked by the al-Qaeda terrorist organization. Nearly three thousand Americans are killed. A week later, President George W. Bush signs into law the Authorization for Use of Military Force (2001 AUMF). Under the 2001 AUMF, the president is authorized to use "all necessary and appropriate force" against those linked to the 9/11 attack.

November 2001: President Bush issues an executive order authorizing the detention of enemy combatants and creating military commissions to try certain unlawful enemy combatants for war crimes.

February 2002: A federal district court finds that it does not have jurisdiction to entertain the habeas corpus petitions of detainees held at Guantánamo Bay. Other lower courts soon reach the same conclusion.

July 2003: For the first time, a group of Guantánamo detainees is designated as eligible to be tried in military commissions. It takes another year for charges to be filed and pretrial proceedings to begin.

June 2004: The Supreme Court hands down decisions in cases challenging the Bush administration's detention policies. The Court rules that noncitizens detained at Guantánamo Bay have a statutory right to habeas corpus hearings in federal court (*Rasul v. Bush*), and that a US citizen captured in Afghanistan can be detained by the US military on American soil but must receive more due process than the Bush administration has provided to date (*Hamdi v. Rumsfeld*).

July 2004: The Bush administration creates combatant status review tribunals (CSRTs), administrative bodies tasked with reviewing enemy combatant classifications at Guantánamo Bay.

November 2004: The DC District Court finds the Bush administration's version of military commissions to be unlawful.

December 2005: Congress passes the Detainee Treatment Act (DTA). Among other things, the DTA overrides the Supreme Court's statutory interpretation in *Rasul v. Bush* and creates a limited form of judicial review in the DC Circuit Court of Appeals for CSRT determinations and military commission decisions.

June 2006: The Supreme Court decides *Hamdan v. Rumsfeld,* finding the Bush administration's system of military commissions unlawful.

October 2006: Congress passes the Military Commissions Act (2006 MCA). A response to the Supreme Court's decision in *Hamdan v. Rumsfeld,* the MCA offers explicit congressional authorization for a reformed system of military commissions.

March 2007: The military commission system produces its first-ever conviction: David Hicks pleads guilty to material support. His conviction is later overturned.

June 2008: In *Boumediene v. Bush,* the Supreme Court rules that the Constitution guarantees noncitizen detainees held at Guantánamo Bay a right to challenge their detentions in habeas corpus hearings in federal court. It also finds that the existing review scheme crafted by the Bush administration and Congress is an inadequate substitute for habeas corpus.

August 2008: In the first military commission to go to trial, Salim Hamdan is acquitted of conspiracy but found guilty of material support. The conviction is later overturned.

November 2008: Ali al-Bahlul becomes the second individual to undergo a full military commission trial. He is found guilty on charges of conspiracy, material support, and solicitation. The material support and solicitation charges are later thrown out, but his conviction for conspiracy is upheld on narrow grounds by the DC Circuit Court of Appeals.

January 2009: Barack Obama is inaugurated as president of the United States. Despite having campaigned in favor of overhauling enemy combatant policies, he is unable to close Guantánamo and continues military commissions with some modifications.

April 2009: The DC District Court rules that non-Afghan detainees held by the US military in Afghanistan are entitled to habeas corpus hearings in federal court. The DC Circuit Court of Appeals ultimately reverses, but before it does so the Obama administration makes changes to detention policy that are more protective of the interests of detainees held in Afghanistan.

October 2009: Congress follows the wishes of President Obama, enacting amendments to the 2006 MCA that make military commissions more favorable to defendants. The commissions yield a handful of guilty pleas during Obama's presidency.

March 2011: President Obama issues an executive order creating periodic review boards (PRBs) for Guantánamo detainees. A reformed version of earlier review panels created by the Bush administration, the PRBs function like parole boards, assessing whether individuals subject to detention can be safely transferred out of Guantánamo Bay.

December 2011: Congress enacts the National Defense Authorization Act for 2012 (NDAA 2012). The legislation contains a provision explicitly authorizing detention for the first time. It also strengthens previously enacted restrictions on transferring detainees out of Guantánamo Bay.

October 2012: A DC Circuit Court of Appeals panel vacates Salim Hamdan's military commission conviction for material support.

May 2013: President Obama delivers a speech in which he promises to speed up efforts to empty the Guantánamo detention facility. By the time he leaves office, his administration has reduced the population at Guantánamo from 242 to 41.

July 2014: The full DC Circuit Court of Appeals vacates Ali al-Bahlul's conviction for material support and solicitation but upholds his conviction for conspiracy on narrow grounds.

June 2015: A DC Circuit Court of Appeals panel uses a new legal argument to vacate Ali al-Bahlul's conspiracy conviction. An en banc ruling the following year narrowly reinstates the conviction, but the future of conspiracy charges in military commissions remains unclear.

November 2016: Donald J. Trump is elected president of the United States. His vows to increase the population at Guantánamo and make greater use of detention and military commissions have thus far gone unfulfilled.

# *Notes*

## INTRODUCTION

1. Oyez, "2003–2004 Term," accessed May 18, 2020, https://www.oyez.org/cases/2003. The cases are Missouri v. Seibert, 542 U.S. 600 (2004); United States v. Patane, 542 U.S. 630 (2004); and Holland v. Jackson, 542 U.S. 649 (2004).

2. Some scholars have challenged the conventional wisdom that the judiciary has almost invariably exhibited deference or restraint in wartime cases. While courts have certainly been reluctant to issue sweeping constitutional decisions in wartime cases, these scholars note that judges have on occasion been willing to rule against the government on narrower grounds. See Samuel Issacharoff and Richard H. Pildes, "Between Civil Libertarianism and Executive Unilateralism: An Institutional Process Approach to Rights during Wartime," *Theoretical Inquiries in Law* 5, no. 1 (February 2004). See also a pair of articles by David J. Barron and Martin S. Lederman, "The Commander in Chief at the Lowest Ebb—Framing the Problem, Doctrine, and Original Understanding," *Harvard Law Review* 121, no. 3 (January 2008), and "The Commander in Chief at the Lowest Ebb—A Constitutional History," *Harvard Law Review* 121, no. 4 (February 2008). Whatever the merits of this argument, it is hard to deny that something fundamental has changed. First, as Jack Goldsmith has noted, the Supreme Court's rulings against the government in 2004, 2006, and 2008 were in tension with World War II–era precedents that suggested the government would likely win the cases. See Jack Goldsmith, *Power and Constraint: The Accountable Presidency after 9/11* (New York: W. W. Norton, 2012), 163–166 and 178–179. Second, the lack of deferential language in the opinions of the Supreme Court and certain lower court judges in post-9/11 cases is impossible to ignore. See Ganesh Sitaraman and Ingrid Wuerth, "The Normalization of Foreign Relations Law," *Harvard Law Review* 128, no. 7 (May 2015): 1921–1924. Judicial intervention in the war on terror cannot simply be treated as a story of continuity.

3. Throughout this book, I use the term "war on terror" to refer to the ongoing armed conflict between the United States and al-Qaeda and its associates. I do so primarily for the sake of convenience and consistency, but also because the Obama administration's decision to stop using the term was almost entirely symbolic. On the two most fundamental questions—first, whether the United States is at war, and second, with whom we are at war—the Obama administration's positions were substantially similar, if not identical, to those of the Bush administration. The Trump administration has adopted a similar stance on those two questions, though it too has varied the terminology, sometimes opting to refer to the conflict as a war on radical Islam. Note also that I exclude the Iraq War from this account, choosing to treat it as a separate military conflict largely discrete from what I am calling the war on terror.

4. See, for example, C. Neal Tate and Torbjörn Vallinder, eds., *The Global Expansion*

*of Judicial Power* (New York: New York University Press, 1995); Robert A. Kagan, *Adversarial Legalism: The American Way of Law* (Cambridge, MA: Harvard University Press, 2001); W. A. Bogart, *Consequences: The Impact of Law and Its Complexity* (Toronto: University of Toronto Press, 2002); Ran Hirschl, *Towards Juristocracy: The Origins and Consequences of the New Constitutionalism* (Cambridge, MA: Harvard University Press, 2004); Gordon Silverstein, *Law's Allure: How Law Shapes, Constrains, Saves, and Kills Politics* (New York: Cambridge University Press, 2009); and Thomas F. Burke and Jeb Barnes, eds., *Varieties of Legal Order: The Politics of Adversarial and Bureaucratic Legalism* (New York: Routledge, 2018).

5. Jeb Barnes and Thomas F. Burke, *How Policy Shapes Politics: Rights, Courts, Litigation, and the Struggle over Injury Compensation* (New York: Oxford University Press, 2015), 4–5.

6. Barnes and Burke, *How Policy Shapes Politics*, 6–7. See generally Martin Shapiro, "Political Jurisprudence," reprinted in *On Law, Politics, and Judicialization*, ed. Martin Shapiro and Alec Stone Sweet (New York: Oxford University Press, 2002), 19–54.

7. Authorization for Use of Military Force, Pub. L. No. 107–40, 115 Stat. 224 (2001).

8. Though Congress authorized the war in the 2001 AUMF, the conflict never received a formal declaration of war from Congress. The last time Congress issued a declaration of war was World War II.

9. The inclusion of "associated forces" was controversial, since the 2001 AUMF did not include that phrase. In 2012, Congress codified the "associated forces" language in the National Defense Authorization Act. See chapter 3 of this volume.

10. See the State Department memo to Senate Foreign Relations Committee Chairman Bob Corker, August 2, 2017, at the following link: https://assets.documentcloud.org/documents/3911844/8-2-17-Corker-Response.pdf.

11. Gerald N. Rosenberg, *The Hollow Hope: Can Courts Bring About Social Change?* (Chicago: University of Chicago Press, 1991). Rosenberg's account does not address national security policy, where the judiciary is commonly assumed to be at its weakest. For an article casting doubt on the idea that courts have played an influential role in checking the presidency and shaping national security policy after 9/11, see Kim Lane Scheppele, "The New Judicial Deference," *Boston University Law Review* 92, no. 1 (January 2012).

12. For an example of pre-9/11 scholarship arguing that court rulings influence the policy-making process in the foreign affairs realm, see Gordon Silverstein, *Imbalance of Powers: Constitutional Interpretation and the Making of American Foreign Policy* (New York: Oxford University Press, 1997), 6–7, 15–17, and 215–217. Silverstein found that "judicial decisions . . . have shaped the way those in the other branches of the government understand the Constitution, and have shaped the national debate over constitutional interpretation in every area, including foreign policy." His conclusions, however, are mostly at odds with my own: Silverstein argued that the judiciary had become increasingly deferential to the executive when Congress had legislated in vague terms or been silent. As we will see, the judiciary—and the Supreme Court, in particular—often did exactly the opposite after 9/11, declining to give the executive the benefit of the doubt

in the face of statutory ambiguity or congressional silence. The 2006 Supreme Court ruling in *Hamdan v. Rumsfeld* is the best example. See chapter 5 of this volume.

13. The term comes from Arthur M. Schlesinger Jr., *The Imperial Presidency* (Boston: Houghton Mifflin, 1973). For more recent works updating and reapplying Schlesinger's thesis to the twenty-first-century presidency, see Andrew Rudalevige, *The New Imperial Presidency: Renewing Presidential Power after Watergate* (Ann Arbor: University of Michigan Press, 2005); Charlie Savage, *Takeover: The Return of the Imperial Presidency and the Subversion of American Democracy* (New York: Back Bay Books, 2007); Frederick A. O. Schwarz Jr. and Aziz Z. Huq, *Unchecked and Unbalanced: Presidential Power in a Time of Terror* (New York: New Press, 2007); Peter M. Shane, *Madison's Nightmare: How Executive Power Threatens American Democracy* (Chicago: University of Chicago Press, 2009); and Bruce Ackerman, *The Decline and Fall of the American Republic* (Cambridge, MA: Belknap Press, 2010).

14. James Madison, "Helvidius Number IV," in *The Pacificus-Helvidius Debates of 1793–1794,* ed. Morton J. Frisch (Indianapolis: Liberty Fund, 2007), 87.

15. For examples of the sweeping legal arguments made by the Office of Legal Counsel (OLC), see Chris Edelson, *Emergency Presidential Power: From the Drafting of the Constitution to the War on Terror* (Madison: University of Wisconsin Press, 2013). Edelson helpfully reproduces excerpts from OLC memos. See, for example, pages 131–138 and 211–221.

16. Jeb Barnes and Mark C. Miller, "Putting the Pieces Together: American Lawmaking from an Interbranch Perspective," in *Making Policy, Making Law: An Interbranch Perspective,* ed. Mark C. Miller and Jeb Barnes (Washington, DC: Georgetown University Press, 2004), 11.

17. Richard E. Neustadt, *Presidential Power and the Modern Presidents: The Politics of Leadership from Roosevelt to Reagan* (New York: Free Press, 1990), 29.

18. Silverstein, *Law's Allure,* 2.

19. Another good example of a work that envisions American government in similar terms is Louis Fisher, *Constitutional Dialogues: Interpretation as Political Process* (Princeton, NJ: Princeton University Press, 1988). Fisher's account focuses mainly on the Constitution and constitutional interpretation. On pages 3–4, he writes, "Constitutional law is not a monopoly of the judiciary. It is a process in which all three branches converge and interact with their separate interpretations. . . . A purely technical approach to the law misses the constant, creative interplay between the judiciary and the political system." Later, on pages 275–276, he makes a claim that fits the post-9/11 Supreme Court rulings particularly well: "Usually the Court makes a series of exploratory movements followed by backing and filling—a necessary and sensible policy for resolving constitutional issues that have profound political, social, and economic ramifications."

20. James Q. Wilson, *Bureaucracy: What Government Agencies Do and Why They Do It* (New York: Basic Books, 1989). See especially chapters 3–6.

21. See generally Goldsmith, *Power and Constraint,* and Charlie Savage, *Power Wars: Inside Obama's Post-9/11 Presidency* (New York: Little, Brown, 2015). See also Jack

Goldsmith, *The Terror Presidency: Law and Judgment inside the Bush Administration* (New York: W. W. Norton, 2007).

22. There is plenty of scholarly debate on this point. Some scholars have maintained that the limits imposed by other actors on the presidency have not been particularly meaningful in practice. See, for example, Chris Edelson, *Power without Constraint: The Post-9/11 Presidency and National Security* (Madison: University of Wisconsin Press, 2016), 3–7. On page 3, Edelson writes, "The Obama administration, like the Bush administration, has failed to recognize meaningful limits on presidential national security power." See also Shane, *Madison's Nightmare,* 58 and 141.

23. A search turned up only two articles that make brief references to "adversarial legalism" in the context of foreign affairs and national security policy. The author of both these articles is none other than John Yoo, the Office of Legal Counsel (OLC) lawyer who wrote some of the most controversial legal memos in the early stages of the war on terror. See John Yoo, "Federal Courts as Weapons of Foreign Policy: The Case of the Helms-Burton Act," *Hastings International and Comparative Law Review* 20, no. 4 (Summer 1997): 763, and "Foreign Affairs Federalism and the Separation of Powers," *Villanova Law Review* 46, no. 5 (December 2001): 1348.

24. Kagan, *Adversarial Legalism,* 7. See also 55–56.

25. Kagan, 12, 49, and 57.

26. Kagan, 22.

27. Kagan, 22–23.

28. Kagan, 3 and 22–25. Not every post-9/11 judicial decision has made it easier for terrorist suspects to access courts and win their cases. See, for example, Ashcroft v. Iqbal, 556 U.S. 662 (2009).

29. Kagan, *Adversarial Legalism,* 25–33.

30. Silverstein, *Law's Allure,* 9–10.

31. See, for example, Benjamin Wittes, *Detention and Denial: The Case for Candor after Guantánamo* (Washington, DC: Brookings Institution Press, 2011), 4–6 and 23–27.

32. For the latest statistics, see Office of the Director of National Intelligence (DNI), "Summary of the Reengagement of Detainees Formerly Held at Guantanamo Bay, Cuba," November 26, 2019, https://www.dni.gov/index.php/newsroom/reports-publications/item/2079-summary-of-the-reengagement-of-detainees-formerly-held-at-guantanamo-bay-cuba.

33. See, for example, Mary B. McCord, "Federal Prosecution Is a Viable Option for Enemy Combatants," Lawfare, July 24, 2017, https://www.lawfareblog.com/federal-prosecution-viable-option-enemy-combatants.

34. Goldsmith, *Power and Constraint,* 177–179. Goldsmith highlights these and other factors as possible explanations for why the Supreme Court appeared to discard long-standing precedents in its post-9/11 wartime jurisprudence.

35. Tate and Vallinder, *Global Expansion.*

36. See, for example, Kagan, *Adversarial Legalism,* and Bogart, *Consequences.*

37. Bogart, *Consequences,* 5.

38. Thomas F. Burke, *Lawyers, Lawsuits, and Legal Rights: The Battle over Litigation in American Society* (Berkeley: University of California Press, 2002), 4.

39. Thomas M. Keck, *Judicial Politics in Polarized Times* (Chicago: University of Chicago Press, 2014), 4. But see the book generally.

40. Keck, *Judicial Politics in Polarized Times*, 9.

41. On the centrality of rights, see Mary Ann Glendon, *Rights Talk: The Impoverishment of Political Discourse* (New York: Free Press, 1991).

42. Charles R. Epp, *The Rights Revolution: Lawyers, Activists, and Supreme Courts in Comparative Perspective* (Chicago: University of Chicago Press), 2.

43. Robert A. Kagan, "American Courts and the Policy Dialogue: The Role of Adversarial Legalism," in *Making Policy, Making Law,* ed. Miller and Barnes, 32.

44. See, for example, Robert A. Kagan, "A Consequential Court: The U.S. Supreme Court in the Twentieth Century," in *Consequential Courts: Judicial Roles in Global Perspective,* ed. Diana Kapiszewski, Gordon Silverstein, and Robert A. Kagan (New York: Cambridge University Press, 2013), 219.

45. Malcolm M. Feeley and Edward L. Rubin, *Judicial Policy Making and the Modern State: How the Courts Reformed America's Prisons* (New York: Cambridge University Press, 1998), 176.

46. Epp, *The Rights Revolution,* 2–3.

47. Interestingly, the judiciary's openness to the claims of noncitizen terrorist suspects is in tension with recent scholarship on "judicial retrenchment," which has detailed ways in which Congress, the courts, and other actors have scaled back access to the courts in many areas in recent decades. See Sarah Staszak, *No Day in Court: Access to Justice and the Politics of Judicial Retrenchment* (New York: Oxford University Press, 2015), especially 5–8 and 29–30, and Stephen B. Burbank and Sean Farhang, *Rights and Retrenchment: The Counterrevolution against Federal Litigation* (New York: Cambridge University Press, 2017), especially 2–3, 130–131, and 220–223.

48. Goldsmith, *Power and Constraint,* 34–35. For a detailed examination of the congressional response to Vietnam and Watergate, see James L. Sundquist, *The Decline and Resurgence of Congress* (Washington, DC: Brookings Institution Press, 1981).

49. See generally Savage, *Power Wars.* Scholars disagree about how effective these internal legal checks are. See Trevor W. Morrison, "Constitutional Alarmism," *Harvard Law Review* 124, no. 7 (May 2011). Morrison's article is a lengthy review—and critique—of Ackerman, *Decline and Fall.*

50. Mark A. Graber, "The Nonmajoritarian Difficulty: Legislative Deference to the Judiciary," *Studies in American Political Development* 7, no. 1 (Spring 1993).

51. Jeb Barnes, "Bringing the Courts Back In: Interbranch Perspectives on the Role of Courts in American Politics and Policy Making," *Annual Review of Political Science* 10 (2007): 26. Also, see generally Barnes and Miller, "Putting the Pieces Together."

52. Barnes, "Bringing the Courts Back In," 27–28.

53. Barnes, 26.

54. Barnes, 26.

55. Kagan, *Adversarial Legalism*, 14. Nathan Alexander Sales has made this point in the specific context of national security policy. According to Sales, the ever-present prospect of lawsuits causes national security policy makers to act with more self-restraint and caution than we might expect. See Nathan Alexander Sales, "Self-Restraint and National Security," *Journal of National Security Law & Policy* 6, no. 1 (2012): 230.

56. For an extended treatment of the value and importance of descriptive analysis in political science, see John Gerring, "Mere Description," *British Journal of Political Science* 42, no. 4 (October 2012).

## CHAPTER 1. "THE LEAST WORST PLACE"

1. Adam R. Pearlman, "Meaningful Review and Process Due: How Guantanamo Detention Is Changing the Battlefield," *Harvard National Security Journal* 6, no. 1 (February 2015): 258.

2. Donald Rumsfeld, *Known and Unknown: A Memoir* (New York: Sentinel, 2011), 556, 565, and 606. See also Richard B. Myers, *Eyes on the Horizon: Serving on the Front Lines of National Security* (New York: Simon & Schuster, 2009), 200.

3. Condoleezza Rice, *No Higher Honor: A Memoir of My Years in Washington* (New York: Crown Publishers, 2011), 105.

4. Rice, *No Higher Honor*, 105. See also Rumsfeld, *Known and Unknown*, 568–569.

5. Jeff A. Bovarnick, "Detainee Review Boards in Afghanistan," Department of the Army Pamphlet 27-50-445, *Army Lawyer* (June 2010): 12–15. See also Myers, *Eyes on the Horizon*, 198, and Steven Lee Myers and James Dao, "Marines Set Up Pens for Wave of Prisoners," *New York Times*, December 15, 2001.

6. Rumsfeld, *Known and Unknown*, 559–560 and 565. See also Myers, *Eyes on the Horizon*, 198–199, and George W. Bush, *Decision Points* (New York: Crown Publishers, 2010), 166.

7. Quoted in Katharine Q. Seelye, "U.S. to Hold Taliban Detainees in 'the Least Worst Place,'" *New York Times*, December 28, 2001. See also Rumsfeld, *Known and Unknown*, 566, and Rice, *No Higher Honor*, 106–107.

8. Rumsfeld, *Known and Unknown*, 566–567, and Bush, *Decision Points*, 166. See also Dick Cheney, with Liz Cheney, *In My Time: A Personal and Political Memoir* (New York: Threshold Editions, 2011), 354.

9. Patrick F. Philbin and John C. Yoo, "Memorandum for William J. Haynes, II, General Counsel, Department of Defense," December 28, 2001, http://nsarchive.gwu.edu/torturingdemocracy/documents/20011228.pdf.

10. Pearlman, "Meaningful Review and Process Due," 268.

11. Katharine Q. Seelye, "For America's Captives, Home Is a Camp in Cuba, with Goggles and a Koran," *New York Times*, January 20, 2002, and Katharine Q. Seelye, "Criticized, U.S. Brings Visitors to Prison Camp," *New York Times*, January 26, 2002.

12. Pearlman, "Meaningful Review and Process Due," 258–259.

13. Quoted in Tim Golden, "Administration Officials Split over Stalled Military Tribunals," *New York Times*, October 25, 2004.

14. Jess Bravin, *The Terror Courts: Rough Justice at Guantanamo Bay* (New Haven, CT: Yale University Press, 2013), 80–81. See also Philip Shenon, "Britain Defends U.S. Treatment of Detainees at Guantánamo," *New York Times*, January 22, 2002, and Katharine Q. Seelye, "Rumsfeld Defends U.S. Treatment of Detainees in Cuba," *New York Times*, January 23, 2002.

15. Bravin, *The Terror Courts*, 80–81, and Philip Shenon, "Suit to Be Filed on Behalf of Three Detainees in Cuba," *New York Times*, February 19, 2002.

16. Coalition of Clergy v. Bush, 189 F. Supp. 2d 1036 (C.D. Ca. 2002).

17. Johnson v. Eisentrager, 339 U.S. 763 (1950).

18. Coalition of Clergy v. Bush, 189 F. Supp. 2d 1036 (C.D. Ca. 2002), at 1048.

19. Rasul v. Bush, 215 F. Supp. 2d 55 (D.D.C. 2002).

20. Katharine Q. Seelye, "Move Likely for Inmate Who May Be American," *New York Times*, April 5, 2002, and Katharine Q. Seelye, "Believed to Be a U.S. Citizen, Detainee Is Jailed in Virginia," *New York Times*, April 6, 2002.

21. Mike Dorning, "U.S. Releases Details in Case against Padilla," *Chicago Tribune*, June 2, 2004.

22. Hamdi v. Rumsfeld, 243 F. Supp. 2d 527 (E.D. Va. 2002).

23. Hamdi v. Rumsfeld, 294 F.3d 598 (4th Cir. 2002).

24. Hamdi v. Rumsfeld, 296 F.3d 278 (4th Cir. 2002).

25. Hamdi v. Rumsfeld, 296 F.3d 278 (4th Cir. 2002), at 282.

26. "Declaration of Michael H. Mobbs, Special Advisor to the Under Secretary of Defense for Policy," *Frontline*, October 16, 2003, https://www.pbs.org/wgbh/pages/frontline/shows/sleeper/tools/mobbshamdi.html.

27. Hamdi v. Rumsfeld, 243 F. Supp. 2d 527 (E.D. Va. 2002), at 532–533.

28. Hamdi v. Rumsfeld, 243 F. Supp. 2d 527 (E.D. Va. 2002), at 535.

29. Padilla v. Bush, 233 F. Supp. 2d 564 (S.D.N.Y. 2002).

30. Authorization for Use of Military Force, Pub. L. No. 107–40, 115 Stat. 224 (2001).

31. Padilla v. Bush (S.D.N.Y. 2002), at 602.

32. Padilla v. Rumsfeld, 243 F. Supp. 2d 42 (S.D.N.Y. 2003).

33. Padilla v. Rumsfeld, 243 F. Supp. 2d 42 (S.D.N.Y. 2003), at 52–53.

34. Padilla v. Rumsfeld, 243 F. Supp. 2d 42 (S.D.N.Y. 2003), at 57.

35. Rice, *No Higher Honor*, 274.

36. Golden, "Administration Officials Split." See also Rumsfeld, *Known and Unknown*, 568–569, and Rice, *No Higher Honor*, 275.

37. Rice, *No Higher Honor*, 275–276.

38. Katharine Q. Seelye, "Some Guantánamo Prisoners Will Be Freed, Rumsfeld Says," *New York Times*, October 23, 2002, and Golden, "Administration Officials Split."

39. Golden, "Administration Officials Split."

40. Carlotta Gall, "U.S. Returns 18 Guantánamo Detainees to Afghanistan," *New York Times*, March 24, 2003.

41. Rumsfeld, *Known and Unknown*, 569.

42. Gall, "U.S. Returns 18 Guantánamo Detainees," and Neil A. Lewis, "Detainees from the Afghan War Remain in a Legal Limbo in Cuba," *New York Times*, April 24, 2003.

43. Coalition of Clergy v. Bush, 310 F.3d 1153 (9th Cir. 2002).

44. Al Odah v. United States, 321 F.3d 1134 (D.C. Cir. 2003).

45. Hamdi v. Rumsfeld, 316 F.3d 450 (4th Cir. 2003). By finding legal authorization in a statute passed by Congress, the Fourth Circuit avoided the need to answer a separate legal question: whether the president's constitutional authority under Article II entitled him to detain enemy combatants, including citizens like Hamdi.

46. Padilla v. Rumsfeld, 352 F.3d 695 (2nd Cir. 2003).

47. Padilla v. Rumsfeld, 352 F.3d 695 (2nd Cir. 2003), at 723.

48. 18 U.S.C. §4001 (1971). The law represented an effort to prevent another episode like the Japanese internment during World War II.

49. Neil A. Lewis, "Try Detainees or Free Them, 3 Senators Urge," *New York Times*, December 13, 2003.

50. Gherebi v. Bush, 374 F.3d 727 (9th Cir. 2004).

51. Neal Kumar Katyal, "*Hamdan v. Rumsfeld:* The Legal Academy Goes to Practice," *Harvard Law Review* 120, no. 1 (November 2006): 90.

52. Oral argument in *Rasul v. Bush* can be listened to at "Rasul v. Bush," Oyez, accessed May 20, 2020, https://www.oyez.org/cases/2003/03–334.

53. Laura K. Donohue, *The Cost of Counterterrorism: Power, Politics, and Liberty* (New York: Cambridge University Press, 2008), 84–85.

54. Maria Newman, "Reviews of Guantánamo Detainees to Begin Soon, Navy Says," *New York Times*, June 23, 2004. For more on ARBs, see Benjamin Wittes, *Law and the Long War: The Future of Justice in the Age of Terror* (New York: Penguin Books, 2008), 66–67.

55. Jeb Barnes and Mark C. Miller, "Putting the Pieces Together: American Lawmaking from an Interbranch Perspective," in *Making Policy, Making Law: An Interbranch Perspective*, ed. Mark C. Miller and Jeb Barnes (Washington, DC: Georgetown University Press, 2004), 11.

56. Rasul v. Bush, 542 U.S. 466 (2004).

57. Rasul v. Bush, 542 U.S. 466 (2004), at 475.

58. Rasul v. Bush, 542 U.S. 466 (2004) (Kennedy, J., concurring), at 487.

59. Rasul v. Bush, 542 U.S. 466 (2004) (Scalia, J., dissenting).

60. Rasul v. Bush, 542 U.S. 466 (2004), at 497–498.

61. Rasul v. Bush, 542 U.S. 466 (2004), at 506.

62. Hamdi v. Rumsfeld, 542 U.S. 507 (2004).

63. Hamdi v. Rumsfeld, 542 U.S. 507 (2004) (Thomas, J., dissenting). Justice Thomas also believed that the president had constitutional authority as commander in chief to detain enemy fighters. Because the plurality found statutory authorization, it did not reach the constitutional question.

64. Hamdi v. Rumsfeld, 542 U.S. 507 (2004) (plurality opinion of Justice O'Connor), at 518.

65. The plurality did add to this analysis a potentially significant warning, however. Acknowledging that the current war differs from more traditional armed conflicts

between nation-states, O'Connor wrote: "Our understanding is based on longstanding law-of-war principles. If the practical circumstances of a given conflict are entirely unlike those of the conflicts that informed the development of the law of war, that understanding may unravel. But that is not the situation we face as of this date. Active combat operations against Taliban fighters apparently are ongoing in Afghanistan." It appears that the understanding has yet to "unravel." For example, in July 2015 the DC District Court rejected a challenge from a Guantánamo detainee with links to the Taliban, holding that hostilities against the Taliban in Afghanistan were ongoing despite the Obama administration's repeated public statements that the US combat role had ended. See the opinion of Judge Royce Lamberth in Al Warafi v. Obama, Civil Action No. 09–2368 (D.D.C. 2015).

66. Mathews v. Eldridge, 424 U.S. 319 (1976).

67. Hamdi v. Rumsfeld, 542 U.S. 507 (2004) (plurality opinion of Justice O'Connor), at 536 and 533.

68. Hamdi v. Rumsfeld, 542 U.S. 507 (2004), at 536.

69. Hamdi v. Rumsfeld, 542 U.S. 507 (2004) (Thomas, J., dissenting).

70. Hamdi v. Rumsfeld, 542 U.S. 507 (2004) (Souter, J., dissenting in part).

71. Rumsfeld v. Padilla, 542 U.S. 426 (2004).

72. Rumsfeld v. Padilla, 542 U.S. 426 (2004) (Stevens, J., dissenting).

73. Paul Wolfowitz, "Memorandum for the Secretary of the Navy, Subject: Order Establishing Combatant Status Review Tribunal," July 7, 2004, https://www.law.utoronto.ca/documents/Mackin/MuneerAhmad_ExhibitV.pdf.

74. Wolfowitz, "Memorandum." The "associated forces" and "support" prongs proved to be controversial on account of their breadth. For a critical account of the sorts of individuals who could be deemed enemy combatants under this definition, see Joseph Margulies, *Guantánamo and the Abuse of Presidential Power* (New York: Simon & Schuster, 2006), 63–84.

75. Wittes, *Law and the Long War*, 66–67.

76. Pearlman, "Meaningful Review and Process Due," 271.

77. Wittes, *Law and the Long War*, 66. For more on CSRTs, see Wittes, 74–81, and Darren A. Wheeler, *Presidential Power in Action: Implementing Supreme Court Detainee Decisions* (New York: Palgrave Macmillan, 2008), 36–40.

78. Quoted in Neil A. Lewis, "U.S. Is Readying Review for Detainees in Cuba," *New York Times*, July 17, 2004.

79. Lewis, "U.S. Is Readying Review."

80. Some scholars have questioned the rigor of CSRT proceedings and claimed that in practice they fell short of truly "meaningful" review procedures. See, for example, Mark Denbeaux et al., "No-Hearing Hearings: An Analysis of the Proceedings of the Combatant Status Review Tribunals at Guantánamo," *Seton Hall Law Review* 41, no. 4 (2011).

81. Wheeler, *Presidential Power in Action*, 39.

82. Wheeler, 39.

83. Joel Brinkley and Eric Lichtblau, "U.S. Releases Saudi-American It Had

Captured in Afghanistan," *New York Times*, October 12, 2004. Shafiq Rasul, the plaintiff named in *Rasul v. Bush*, had experienced a similar fate: Rasul and a handful of fellow British nationals were released to the UK earlier in 2004, before the Court's decision in *Rasul* was handed down. See "At-a-glance: Guantanamo Bay Britons," *BBC News*, March 9, 2004, http://news.bbc.co.uk/2/hi/uk_news/3089395.stm.

84. James Risen, "35 Guantánamo Detainees Are Given to Pakistan," *New York Times*, September 19, 2004. See also Rice, *No Higher Honor*, 276–277.

85. See Rumsfeld, *Known and Unknown*, 565–569 and 607, and Douglas Jehl, "Pentagon Seeks to Transfer More Detainees from Base in Cuba," *New York Times*, March 11, 2005.

86. Quoted in Jehl, "Pentagon Seeks to Transfer More Detainees."

87. Michael Greenberger, "You Ain't Seen Nothin' Yet: The Inevitable Post-*Hamdan* Conflict between the Supreme Court and the Political Branches," *Maryland Law Review* 66, no. 3 (2007): 818.

88. Neil A. Lewis, "Guantánamo Detainees Make Their Case," *New York Times*, March 24, 2005. For an overview of the CSRT proceedings, see Denbeaux et al., "No-Hearing Hearings."

89. Jehl, "Pentagon Seeks to Transfer More Detainees."

90. Aziz Z. Huq, "What Good Is Habeas?," *Constitutional Commentary* 26, no. 3 (Summer 2010): 406–407.

91. Pearlman, "Meaningful Review and Process Due," 279–280. See especially footnote 135.

92. Again, it is important to note that some observers questioned whether the administrative review mechanisms actually imposed meaningful accountability on presidential decision making. See Denbeaux et al., "No-Hearing Hearings."

## CHAPTER 2. DETAINING ENEMY COMBATANTS AMID LEGAL UNCERTAINTY (2005–2008)

1. For an overview of this detention litigation, see Larkin Reynolds, The Harvard Law School National Security Research Committee, Benjamin Wittes, and Robert M. Chesney, "The Emerging Law of Detention 2.0: The Guantánamo Habeas Cases as Lawmaking" (April 2012), https://www.brookings.edu/research/the-emerging-law-of-detention-2-0-the-guantanamo-habeas-cases-as-lawmaking/. The paper is part of the Project on Law and Security by Harvard Law School and the Brookings Institution.

2. Khalid v. Bush, 355 F. Supp. 2d 311 (D.D.C. 2005).

3. Khalid v. Bush, 355 F. Supp. 2d 311 (D.D.C. 2005), at 314.

4. In re Guantánamo Detainee Cases, 355 F. Supp. 2d 443 (D.D.C. 2005).

5. In re Guantánamo Detainee Cases, 355 F. Supp. 2d 443 (D.D.C. 2005), at 454.

6. Paul Wolfowitz, "Memorandum for the Secretary of the Navy, Subject: Order Establishing Combatant Status Review Tribunal," July 7, 2004, https://www.law.utoronto.ca/documents/Mackin/MuneerAhmad_ExhibitV.pdf.

7. Hamdi v. Rumsfeld, 542 U.S. 507 (2004), at 516.

8. Scott Shane, "Judge Blocks the Transfer of 13 Detainees From Guantánamo," *New York Times*, March 13, 2005.

9. Neil A. Lewis, "Hunger Strike by Detainees Goes to Court," *New York Times*, September 22, 2005, and Neil A. Lewis, "Guantánamo Detainees Gain in Ruling," *New York Times*, October 27, 2005.

10. Detainee Treatment Act, Pub. L. No. 109–148, 119 Stat. 2739 (2005).

11. Detainee Treatment Act, Pub. L. No. 109–148, 119 Stat. 2739 (2005), at 2742.

12. See, for example, Mark A. Graber, "The Nonmajoritarian Difficulty: Legislative Deference to the Judiciary," *Studies in American Political Development* 7, no. 1 (Spring 1993): 35–73.

13. Detainee Treatment Act, Pub. L. No. 109–148, 119 Stat. 2739 (2005), at 2742.

14. Detainee Treatment Act, Pub. L. No. 109–148, 119 Stat. 2739 (2005), at 2742.

15. Quoted in Eric Schmitt and Tim Golden, "Lawmakers Back Use of Evidence Coerced from Detainees," *New York Times*, December 17, 2005.

16. Boumediene v. Bush, 476 F.3d 981 (D.C. Cir. 2007).

17. Hamdan v. Rumsfeld, 548 U.S. 557 (2006).

18. Military Commissions Act, Pub. L. No. 109–366, 120 Stat. 2600 (2006).

19. See, for example, Neil A. Lewis and Kate Zernike, "Measures Seek to Restrict Detainees' Access to Courts," *New York Times*, September 21, 2006.

20. U.S. Constitution art. 1, sec. 9, cl. 2.

21. Reuters, "Bush Speaks of Closing Guantánamo Prison," *New York Times*, May 8, 2006.

22. Tim Golden and Eric Schmitt, "A Growing Afghan Prison Rivals Bleak Guantánamo," *New York Times*, February 26, 2006.

23. Golden and Schmitt, "A Growing Afghan Prison."

24. Julia Preston, "Judge Orders U.S. to Supply Prisoner Names," *New York Times*, January 24, 2006.

25. Thom Shanker, "Pentagon Plans to Tell Names of Detainees," *New York Times*, February 26, 2006.

26. Scott Shane and Margot Williams, "Yemenis Freed after Transfer from Secret Prisons, Report Says," *New York Times*, April 5, 2006.

27. Condoleezza Rice, *No Higher Honor: A Memoir of My Years in Washington* (New York: Crown Publishers, 2011), 497–498.

28. Rice, *No Higher Honor*, 501–502.

29. George W. Bush, "President Discusses Creation of Military Commissions to Try Suspected Terrorists," September 6, 2006, http://georgewbush-whitehouse.archives.gov/news/releases/2006/09/20060906-3.html. Litigation concerns were not the only reason for the transfer. Bush's speech included a call for Congress to pass a law reforming and authorizing military commissions. Some observers speculated that the detainee transfer was partly intended to pressure Congress to act. President Bush seemed to confirm this in his memoir, writing that bringing the CIA detainees to Guantánamo was "a way to highlight the stakes of passing the [Military Commissions Act]." See

George W. Bush, *Decision Points* (New York: Crown Publishers, 2010), 178. The speech also contained an assertion that the CIA's intelligence collection efforts for these detainees had run their course.

30. Hamdan v. Rumsfeld, 548 U.S. 557 (2006).

31. For the full text of Common Article 3, see Associated Press, "Common Article 3 of the Geneva Conventions," https://archive.nytimes.com/www.nytimes.com/ref/us/AP-Guantanamo-Geneva-Conventions.html.

32. The program technically remained open for business, but only a few detainees passed through it over the next couple of years. See, for example, Mark Mazzetti, "C.I.A. Secretly Held Qaeda Suspect, Officials Say," *New York Times*, March 15, 2008. Upon taking office, President Barack Obama quickly issued an executive order discontinuing the program.

33. Boumediene v. Bush, 476 F.3d 981 (D.C. Cir. 2007).

34. Boumediene v. Bush, 476 F.3d 981 (D.C. Cir. 2007), at 989–990.

35. Boumediene v. Bush, 476 F.3d 981 (D.C. Cir. 2007) (Rogers, J., dissenting).

36. Boumediene v. Bush, 476 F.3d 981 (D.C. Cir. 2007) (Rogers, J., dissenting), at 1005.

37. Linda Greenhouse, "Supreme Court Denies Guantánamo Appeal," *New York Times*, April 3, 2007.

38. The dissent from the denial of certiorari can be found at http://www.scotusblog.com/archives/BoumedieneDenial.pdf.

39. See, for example, Aziz Z. Huq, "What Good Is Habeas?," *Constitutional Commentary* 26, no. 3 (Summer 2010): 425, and William Glaberson, "In Shift, Justices Agree to Review Detainees' Case," *New York Times*, June 30, 2007.

40. William Glaberson, "Unlikely Adversary Arises to Criticize Detainee Hearings," *New York Times*, July 23, 2007.

41. Robert M. Gates, *Duty: Memoirs of a Secretary at War* (New York: Alfred A. Knopf, 2014), 250–251.

42. Gates, *Duty.* See also Thom Shanker and David Johnston, "Legislation Could Be Path to Closing Guantánamo," *New York Times*, July 3, 2007.

43. David Stout, "Senate Blocks Detainees' Rights Bill," *New York Times*, September 19, 2007.

44. Tim Golden, "Foiling U.S. Plan, Prison Expands in Afghanistan," *New York Times*, January 7, 2008.

45. Bismullah v. Gates, 501 F.3d 178 (D.C. Cir. 2007).

46. Bismullah v. Gates, 503 F.3d 137 (D.C. Cir. 2007).

47. Bismullah v. Gates, 503 F.3d 137 (D.C. Cir. 2007), at 142.

48. William Glaberson, "U.S. Mulls New Status Hearings for Guantánamo Inmates," *New York Times*, October 15, 2007.

49. Bismullah v. Gates, 514 F.3d 1291 (D.C. Cir. 2008).

50. Bismullah v. Gates, 514 F.3d 1291 (D.C. Cir. 2008), at 1296. This was a response to Judge Henderson, who at one point in her dissent contrasted the extensive access to information demanded in the *Bismullah I* and *II* decisions to the more limited record

for courts in reviewing administrative agency decisions and in probable cause hearings for criminal suspects.

51. Bismullah v. Gates, 514 F.3d 1291 (D.C. Cir. 2008), at 1296–1297.

52. Bismullah v. Gates, 514 F.3d 1291 (D.C. Cir. 2008), at 1298–1299.

53. Linda Greenhouse, "A 2nd Case on Detainees Complicates Deliberations," *New York Times*, February 6, 2008.

54. Boumediene v. Bush, 128 S. Ct. 2229 (2008).

55. Boumediene v. Bush, 128 S. Ct. 2229 (2008), at 2252.

56. Boumediene v. Bush, 128 S. Ct. 2229 (2008), at 2259.

57. Boumediene v. Bush, 128 S. Ct. 2229 (2008), at 2259–2260.

58. Boumediene v. Bush, 128 S. Ct. 2229 (2008), at 2261.

59. Boumediene v. Bush, 128 S. Ct. 2229 (2008), at 2266.

60. Boumediene v. Bush, 128 S. Ct. 2229 (2008), at 2272.

61. Boumediene v. Bush, 128 S. Ct. 2229 (2008), at 2275. See also the concurring opinion of Justice Souter, stressing that the dissenters were not sufficiently responsive to this length-of-detention issue.

62. Boumediene v. Bush, 128 S. Ct. 2229 (2008) (Scalia, J., dissenting), at 2294.

63. Boumediene v. Bush, 128 S. Ct. 2229 (2008), at 2307.

64. Boumediene v. Bush, 128 S. Ct. 2229 (2008) (Roberts, C. J., dissenting), at 2279.

65. Boumediene v. Bush, 128 S. Ct. 2229 (2008), at 2279.

66. Boumediene v. Bush, 128 S. Ct. 2229 (2008), at 2282.

67. See generally Reynolds et al., "The Emerging Law of Detention 2.0."

68. Boumediene v. Bush, 128 S. Ct. 2229 (2008) (Roberts, C. J., dissenting), at 2293.

69. The recent elevation of Brett Kavanaugh to the Supreme Court makes the possibility of judicial reversal at least marginally more likely. While serving on the D.C. Circuit Court of Appeals, Kavanaugh's jurisprudence in national security cases was largely deferential to the government. See Stephen I. Vladeck, "One Huge Difference between Kavanaugh and Kennedy: Their Guantanamo Records," *Washington Post*, July 11, 2018. However, it should be noted that the Supreme Court has not taken a Guantánamo detention case in several years despite many opportunities to do so.

70. William Glaberson, "Despite Ruling, Detainee Cases Facing Delays," *New York Times*, October 4, 2008.

71. Steven Lee Myers, "Bush Decides to Keep Guantánamo Open," *New York Times*, October 21, 2008.

72. William Glaberson, "Detention Camp Remains, but Not Its Rationale," *New York Times*, June 13, 2008.

73. William Glaberson and Margot Williams, "Next President Will Face Test on Detainees," *New York Times*, November 3, 2008.

74. Gates, *Duty*, 252.

75. Myers, "Bush Decides to Keep Guantánamo Open."

76. William Glaberson, "Judge Orders 17 Detainees at Guantánamo Freed," *New York Times*, October 8, 2008.

77. Glaberson, "Judge Orders 17 Detainees."

78. William Glaberson, "Judge Declares Five Detainees Held Illegally," *New York Times*, November 20, 2008.

79. William Glaberson, "U.S. Is Set to Release 3 Detainees from Base," *New York Times*, December 16, 2008.

80. Gates, *Duty*, 279.

81. Quoted in Myers, "Bush Decides to Keep Guantánamo Open."

## CHAPTER 3. DETENTION POLICY IN A POST-*BOUMEDIENE* WORLD (2009–2017)

1. Mark Mazzetti and William Glaberson, "Obama Issues Directive to Shut Down Guantánamo," *New York Times*, January 22, 2009.

2. Daniel Klaidman, *Kill or Capture: The War on Terror and the Soul of the Obama Presidency* (New York: Houghton Mifflin Harcourt, 2012), 33. See also Robert M. Gates, *Duty: Memoirs of a Secretary at War* (New York: Alfred A. Knopf, 2014), 281–282.

3. Charlie Savage, *Power Wars: Inside Obama's Post-9/11 Presidency* (New York: Little, Brown, 2015), 103–105.

4. "Final Report: Guantanamo Review Task Force," January 22, 2010, 12, https://www.justice.gov/sites/default/files/ag/legacy/2010/06/02/guantanamo-review-final-report.pdf. See also Savage, *Power Wars*, 21 and 106.

5. For a complete accounting of Guantánamo detainees—those currently held, as well as those transferred out of the facility—see "The Guantánamo Docket," *New York Times*, data last changed May 2, 2018, https://www.nytimes.com/interactive/projects/guantanamo.

6. John Ashcroft, *Never Again: Securing America and Restoring Justice* (New York: Center Street, Hachette Book Group USA, 2006), 168–169.

7. Al-Marri v. Wright, No. 06–7427 (4th Cir. 2007).

8. Al-Marri v. Pucciarelli, 534 F.3d 213 (4th Cir. 2008).

9. Adam Liptak, "Early Test of Obama View on Power over Detainees," *New York Times*, January 3, 2009.

10. The only other case involving a citizen-detainee, *Hamdi v. Rumsfeld*, did produce a Supreme Court ruling (see chapter 1), but unlike Padilla and al-Marri, Hamdi was captured on the battlefield in Afghanistan. These three men are the only individuals who have been detained inside the U.S. as enemy combatants since 9/11.

11. Padilla v. Hanft, 423 F.3d 386 (4th Cir. 2005).

12. Padilla v. Rumsfeld, 352 F.3d 695 (2nd Cir. 2003).

13. Padilla v. Hanft, No. 05-6396 (4th Cir. 2005).

14. Linda Greenhouse, "Justices Let U.S. Transfer Padilla to Civilian Custody," *New York Times*, January 5, 2006. See also David Stout, "Justices, 6–3, Sidestep Ruling on Padilla Case," *New York Times*, April 3, 2006.

15. David Johnston and Neil A. Lewis, "U.S. Will Give Qaeda Suspect a Civilian Trial," *New York Times*, February 27, 2009.

16. Missy Ryan, "Qatari Man, Once Held as Enemy Combatant, Is Quietly Released from Supermax Prison," *Washington Post*, January 20, 2015.

17. Jose Padilla's sentence was increased in 2014, after an appeals court found that his initial sentence of seventeen and a half years was too lenient. See Department of Justice, "Jose Padilla Re-Sentenced to 21 Years in Prison for Conspiracy to Murder Individuals Overseas, Providing Material Support to Terrorists," press release, updated October 7, 2014, https://www.justice.gov/opa/pr/jose-padilla-re-sentenced-21-years-prison-conspiracy-murder-individuals-overseas-providing.

18. Klaidman, *Kill or Capture*, 46–47.

19. Quoted in Savage, *Power Wars*, 117.

20. Savage, *Power Wars*, 117. For a broader overview of the continuity between Obama and Bush, see Jack Goldsmith, *Power and Constraint: The Accountable Presidency after 9/11* (New York: W. W. Norton, 2012), chapters 1–2.

21. Savage, *Power Wars*, 107–108.

22. Larkin Reynolds, The Harvard Law School National Security Research Committee, Benjamin Wittes, and Robert M. Chesney, "The Emerging Law of Detention 2.0: The Guantánamo Habeas Cases as Lawmaking," April 2012, 26, https://www.brookings.edu/research/the-emerging-law-of-detention-2–0-the-guantanamo-habeas-cases-as-lawmaking/. The paper is part of the Project on Law and Security by Harvard Law School and the Brookings Institution. See also Adam R. Pearlman, "Meaningful Review and Process Due: How Guantanamo Detention Is Changing the Battlefield," *Harvard National Security Journal* 6, no. 1 (February 2015): 274, and Klaidman, *Kill or Capture*, 58–60.

23. Quoted in Del Quentin Wilbur and Peter Finn, "U.S. Retires 'Enemy Combatant,' Keeps Broad Right to Detain," *Washington Post*, March 14, 2009.

24. William Glaberson, "U.S. Won't Label Terror Suspects as 'Combatants,'" *New York Times*, March 14, 2009.

25. Savage, *Power Wars*, 118–120.

26. Savage, *Power Wars*, 64–65.

27. Savage, *Power Wars*, 65–66.

28. Savage, *Power Wars*, 67.

29. Savage, *Power Wars*, 63 and 693–694.

30. Al Maqaleh v. Gates, 604 F. Supp. 2d 205 (D.D.C. 2009).

31. Al Maqaleh v. Gates, 604 F. Supp. 2d 205 (D.D.C. 2009), at 220.

32. Al Maqaleh v. Gates, 604 F. Supp. 2d 205 (D.D.C. 2009), at 222.

33. Savage, *Power Wars*, 109–110.

34. Quoted in Eric Schmitt, "U.S. to Expand Detainee Review in Afghan Prison," *New York Times*, September 13, 2009.

35. For a terrific overview of the review boards and how they evolved over time, see generally Jeff A. Bovarnick, "Detainee Review Boards in Afghanistan," *Army Lawyer*, Department of the Army Pamphlet 27-50-445 (June 2010): 9–49. The summary of policy changes that follows draws on Bovarnick, 16–24 and 28–33, unless otherwise noted.

36. Over 400 witnesses appeared at DRB hearings between March and June of 2010. See Bovarnick, "Detainee Review Boards," 44.

37. Bovarnick, 39.

38. Bovarnick, 46. See also Savage, *Power Wars*, 120–121.

39. Al Maqaleh v. Gates, 605 F.3d 84 (D.C. Cir. 2010).

40. Alissa J. Rubin, "U.S. Readies New Facility for Afghan Detainees," *New York Times*, November 16, 2009. For more on this, see Bovarnick, "Detainee Review Boards," 9 and 25.

41. Alissa J. Rubin and Sangar Rahimi, "Bagram Detainees Named by U.S.," *New York Times*, January 16, 2010.

42. Barack Obama, "Remarks by the President on National Security," May 21, 2009, https://obamawhitehouse.archives.gov/the-press-office/remarks-president-national-security-5-21-09.

43. William Glaberson, "U.S. Judge Challenges Evidence on a Detainee," *New York Times*, July 23, 2009, and Chisun Lee, "Their Own Private Guantánamo," *New York Times*, July 22, 2009.

44. Klaidman, *Kill or Capture*, 89–90.

45. David Johnston, "Compromise Is Reached on Detainees," *New York Times*, October 8, 2009, and David Stout, "House Backs Detainee Transfers," *New York Times*, October 16, 2009.

46. Klaidman, *Kill or Capture*, 97–99.

47. William Glaberson and Robert F. Worth, "Yemen Dispute Slows Closing of Guantánamo," *New York Times*, April 24, 2009. See also Klaidman, *Kill or Capture*, 93–95.

48. Peter Baker and Charlie Savage, "Terror Attempt May Hinder Plans to Close Guantánamo," *New York Times*, December 31, 2009.

49. "Final Report: Guantánamo Review Task Force," 18. For a discussion of the internal debates leading up to this move, see Savage, *Power Wars*, 138–139 and 147–148.

50. Savage, *Power Wars*, 80.

51. Klaidman, *Kill or Capture*, 153, and Charlie Savage, "Senator Proposes Deal on Handling of Detainees," *New York Times*, March 3, 2010.

52. For example, see the ACLU, "Close Guantánamo," accessed May 27, 2020, https://www.aclu.org/feature/close-guantanamo. According to the ACLU, the proposed transfer of Guantánamo detainees to the United States for continued detention "was never the way to close Guantánamo" and "would just create 'Guantánamo North' on American soil."

53. Charlie Savage, "Closing Guantánamo Fades as a Priority," *New York Times*, June 25, 2010.

54. Quoted in Savage, "Closing Guantánamo Fades."

55. Charlie Savage, "Vote Hurts Obama's Push to Empty Cuba Prison," *New York Times*, December 22, 2010.

56. For recent statistics, see the report from the Office of the Director of National Intelligence, "Summary of the Reengagement of Detainees Formerly Held at Guantanamo Bay, Cuba," November 26, 2019, https://www.dni.gov/index.php/newsroom/reports-publications/item/2079-summary-of-the-reengagement-of-detainees-formerly-held-at-guantanamo-bay-cuba.

57. Charlie Savage, "Obama May Bypass Guantánamo Rules, Aides Say," *New York Times*, January 3, 2011, and Charlie Savage, "New Measure to Hinder Closing of Guantánamo," *New York Times*, January 7, 2011.

58. Evidence of the strategy's effectiveness could be seen in Massachusetts, where Republican Scott Brown improbably won a special election to fill the late Democratic senator Ted Kennedy's seat. Though many commentators focused on Brown's opposition to President Obama's increasingly unpopular health care legislation moving through Congress, Brown campaign officials later insisted that it was Brown's oft-stated resistance to "giving rights to terrorists" that polled the best and may have ultimately tipped the scales in their favor. See Savage, *Power Wars*, 76–77 and 83.

59. Charlie Savage, "Ghailani Verdict Reignites Debate over the Proper Court for Terrorism Trials," *New York Times*, November 18, 2010.

60. Scott Shane and Benjamin Weiser, "U.S. Drops Plan for a 9/11 Trial in New York City," *New York Times*, January 29, 2010.

61. For an overview of the habeas cases in the DC District and Circuit Courts, see Reynolds et al., "Emerging Law of Detention."

62. Savage, *Power Wars*, 299–300.

63. Savage, *Power Wars*, 300, 311–313, and 320–324.

64. Charlie Savage, "Reversal Upholds Detention of Yemeni at Guantánamo," *New York Times*, July 13, 2010. The DC Circuit Court had already upheld lower court decisions denying the writ. See, for example, Al-Bihani v. Obama, 590 F.3d 866 (D.C. Cir. 2010).

65. Al-Adahi v. Obama, 613 F.3d 1102 (D.C. Cir. 2010).

66. This so-called mosaic approach to considering evidence was repeatedly endorsed by the DC Circuit in other cases. See Reynolds et al., "Emerging Law of Detention," 116–121.

67. Latif v. Obama, 666 F.3d 746 (D.C. Cir. 2011).

68. In August 2018, Judge David Tatel wrote an opinion in a denial of en banc rehearing in *Qassim v. Trump* making the same argument. According to Tatel, "Six years [of detention] have become sixteen, and the prospect of relief remains largely illusory. . . . Petitioner believes something has gone awry in this court's jurisprudence, and I agree that the en banc court has reason to consider whether we have faithfully implemented *Boumediene*'s holding." It remains to be seen whether the DC Circuit will do so in future litigation. See Qassim v. Trump, No. 18-5148 (D.C. Cir. 2018) (Tatel, Circuit Judge, concurring).

69. See, for example, Linda Greenhouse, "Gitmo Fatigue at the Supreme Court," *New York Times*, April 6, 2011; Adam Liptak, "Justices Decline to Hear Appeal from Chinese Detainees," *New York Times*, April 18, 2011; and Adam Liptak, "The 'Fill in the Blanks' Court Game of Indefinite Detention," *New York Times*, December 12, 2011.

70. See, for example, the New York Times editorial, "Reneging on Justice at Guantánamo," November 19, 2011, and Linda Greenhouse, "Lessons Maybe Learned," *New York Times*, September 7, 2011.

71. Linda Greenhouse, "Goodbye to Gitmo," *New York Times*, May 16, 2012.

72. See generally Benjamin Wittes, *Detention and Denial: The Case for Candor after Guantánamo* (Washington, DC: Brookings Institution Press, 2011). But see especially 20–24. For a similar argument, see Jack Goldsmith, "The Shell Game on Detainees and Interrogation," *Washington Post*, May 31, 2009.

73. Pearlman, "Meaningful Review and Process Due," 282–283. For a specific example of a situation in 2009 where the apparent lack of a clear capture-and-detain option may have contributed to a decision to kill instead of capture a suspected terrorist, see Klaidman, *Kill or Capture*, 122–128.

74. Klaidman, *Kill or Capture*, 117–118.

75. Quoted in Michael Hirsh, "Slow Dance: Obama's Romance with the CIA," *Atlantic*, May 13, 2011.

76. Quoted in Jo Becker and Scott Shane, "Secret 'Kill List' Proves a Test of Obama's Principles and Will," *New York Times*, May 29, 2012.

77. Pearlman, "Meaningful Review and Process Due," 295–297.

78. Quoted in Ken Dilanian, "U.S. Has Slashed Its Terrorism Interrogation Role," *Los Angeles Times*, April 10, 2011.

79. Eli Lake, "Somalia's Prisons: The War on Terror's Latest Front," *Daily Beast*, June 27, 2012.

80. Kenneth Anderson and Benjamin Wittes, *Speaking the Law: The Obama Administration's Addresses on National Security Law* (Stanford, CA: Hoover Institution Press, 2015), 117–118.

81. Quoted in Anderson and Wittes, *Speaking the Law*, 117–118.

82. Scott Shane and Mark Landler, "Obama Clears Way for Guantánamo Trials," *New York Times*, March 7, 2011. For a good overview of PRBs and the internal debate leading up to the executive order, see Klaidman, *Kill or Capture*, 138–143 and 233–234.

83. The official website for Periodic Review Boards, https://www.prs.mil/, lays out these and other details.

84. See "The Guantánamo Docket."

85. Charlie Savage and Eric Schmitt, "U.S. to Prosecute a Somali Suspect in Civilian Court," *New York Times*, July 5, 2011, and Charlie Savage, "U.S. Tests New Approach to Terrorism Cases on Somali Suspect," *New York Times*, July 6, 2011.

86. Klaidman, *Kill or Capture*, 249, and Savage, *Power Wars*, 340–345. For an overview of the early hypothetical discussions about these sorts of situations, see Savage, 294–296. No definitive decision was reached until Warsame's capture finally forced the administration's hand.

87. Klaidman, *Kill or Capture*, 249–251.

88. Savage, *Power Wars*, 342–343.

89. Savage, *Power Wars*, 346–348.

90. Adam Goldman and Benjamin Weiser, "How Civilian Prosecution Gave the U.S. a Key Informant," *New York Times*, January 27, 2017.

91. Charlie Savage, "G.O.P. Pushes Military Custody for Terror Suspects," *New York Times*, October 27, 2011, and Charlie Savage, "Levin and McCain Strike Deal over Detainee Handling," *New York Times*, November 15, 2011.

92. Graham Cronogue, "A New AUMF: Defining Combatants in the War on Terror," *Duke Journal of Comparative and International Law* 22, no. 3 (April 2012): 402.

93. Quoted in Reynolds et al., "Emerging Law of Detention," 27.

94. Charlie Savage, "Senate Declines to Clarify Rights of American Qaeda Suspects Arrested in U.S.," *New York Times*, December 1, 2011.

95. Mark A. Graber, "The Nonmajoritarian Difficulty: Legislative Deference to the Judiciary," *Studies in American Political Development* 7, no. 1 (Spring 1993).

96. Savage, "Senate Declines to Clarify Rights."

97. Barack Obama, "Statement by the President on H.R. 1540," The White House: Office of the Press Secretary (December 31, 2011). For the full signing statement, see https://obamawhitehouse.archives.gov/the-press-office/2011/12/31/statement-president-hr-1540.

98. Barack Obama, "Presidential Policy Directive—Requirements of the National Defense Authorization Act," The White House: Office of the Press Secretary (February 28, 2012). For the full document, see https://obamawhitehouse.archives.gov/the-press-office/2012/02/28/presidential-policy-directive-requirements-national-defense-authorizatio.

99. Savage, *Power Wars*, 481.

100. Charlie Savage, "Two Guantánamo Detainees Freed, the First in 15 Months," *New York Times*, April 19, 2012.

101. Savage, *Power Wars*, 494–495.

102. Charlie Savage, "Despair Drives Guantánamo Detainees to Revolt," *New York Times*, April 24, 2013.

103. Savage, "Despair Drives Guantánamo Detainees."

104. Charlie Savage and Matthew Rosenberg, "Republican Report Criticizes Transfers from Guantánamo," *New York Times*, February 9, 2012.

105. Savage, *Power Wars*, 331.

106. Savage, *Power Wars*, 508–509.

107. Savage, *Power Wars*, 510.

108. Leon Panetta, *Worthy Fights: A Memoir of Leadership in War and Peace* (New York: Penguin Books, 2014), 414.

109. See, for example, Graham Bowley, "U.S. Puts Transfer of Detainees to Afghans on Hold," *New York Times*, September 9, 2012; Rod Nordland, "Karzai Orders Afghan Forces to Take Control of American-Built Prison," *New York Times*, November 19, 2012; Rod Nordland and Charlie Savage, "U.S. Again Delays Transfer of Bagram Prison to Afghan Forces," *New York Times*, March 9, 2013; and Rod Nordland, Michael R. Gordon, and Alissa J. Rubin, "Karzai Has Nothing but Praise for U.S. upon Bagram Prison Transfer," *New York Times*, March 25, 2013.

110. Matthew Rosenberg, "With Release of Prisoners, Afghan Leader Again Defies U.S. Wishes," *New York Times*, January 9, 2014.

111. Savage, *Power Wars*, 533–534.

112. Barack Obama, "Remarks by the President at the National Defense University," May 23, 2013, https://www.whitehouse.gov/the-press-office/2013/05/23/remarks

-president-national-defense-university. The remainder of this paragraph summarizes the speech.

113. Charlie Savage, "U.S. to Send 2 at Guantánamo Back to Algeria, Saying Security Conditions Are Met," *New York Times*, July 26, 2013; Charlie Savage, "Two Guantánamo Detainees Are Involuntarily Repatriated to Algeria," *New York Times*, December 5, 2013; Charlie Savage, "Two Saudi Prisoners Sent Home from Guantánamo," *New York Times*, December 16, 2013; and Charlie Savage, "U.S. Frees Last of the Chinese Uighur Detainees from Guantánamo Bay," *New York Times*, December 31, 2013.

114. Charlie Savage, "Pentagon Denies Money for Guantánamo Overhaul," *New York Times*, September 24, 2013.

115. Charlie Savage, "Panel Recommends Transferring Yemeni from Guantánamo," *New York Times*, January 9, 2014.

116. Aamer v. Obama, 742 F.3d 1023 (D.C. Cir. 2014). For an excellent discussion of the case and its broader implications, see Steve Vladeck, "The True Significance of Judge Tatel's Opinion in the Force-Feeding Appeal," *Just Security*, February 11, 2014, https://www.justsecurity.org/7016/true-significance-judge-tatels-opinion-force-feeding-appeal/.

117. Charlie Savage, "Appeals Court Allows Challenges by Detainees at Guantánamo Prison," *New York Times*, February 11, 2014.

118. Savage, *Power Wars*, 526–529.

119. Charlie Savage and Helene Cooper, "Under Pressure, Hagel Promises to Act on Guantánamo Transfers," *New York Times*, May 29, 2014.

120. Charlie Savage, "5 Guantánamo Inmates Are Sent to Eastern Europe," *New York Times*, November 20, 2014, and Helene Cooper, "Five Guantánamo Prisoners Are Released to Kazakhstan," *New York Times*, December 30, 2014. See also Savage, *Power Wars*, 529–530.

121. See, for example, Alex Ely, "PRB Recommends Repatriation for One Saudi Detainee, Continued Detention for Another," Lawfare, October 21, 2014, https://www.lawfareblog.com/prb-recommends-repatriation-one-saudi-detainee-continued-detention-another, and Carol Rosenberg, "Guantánamo Parole Board Clears Another 'Forever Prisoner,'" *Miami Herald*, March 18, 2015. See also Charlie Savage, "Frustrated in Efforts to Close Guantánamo Prison, Officials Look to Reduce Population," *New York Times*, December 2, 2015.

122. Savage, *Power Wars*, 528.

123. See, for example, Al Warafi v. Obama, No. 09–2368 (D.D.C. 2015).

124. Al-Alwi v. Trump, No. 17–5067 (D.C. Cir. 2018).

125. Charlie Savage, "Lawyers for a Guantánamo Detainee Cite Failing Health in Seeking His Release," *New York Times*, April 7, 2014.

126. Charlie Savage and Steven Erlanger, "Shaker Aamer Is Released from Guantánamo Prison after 13 Years," *New York Times*, October 30, 2015.

127. Benjamin Wittes, "Interesting New Habeas Argument in the D.C. Circuit," Lawfare, July 11, 2014, https://www.lawfareblog.com/interesting-new-habeas-argument-dc-circuit.

128. Jane Chong, "D.C. Circuit Upholds Security Policies in Hatim v. Obama,"

Lawfare, August 1, 2014, https://www.lawfareblog.com/dc-circuit-upholds-security-policies-hatim-v-obama.

129. Charlie Savage, "Guantánamo Population Drops to 93 after 10 Prisoners Go to Oman," *New York Times*, January 14, 2016; Charlie Savage, "9 Guantánamo Prisoners from Yemen Are Sent to Saudi Arabia," *New York Times*, April 16, 2016; Charlie Savage, "15 Guantánamo Detainees Are Sent to Emirates in Largest Obama-Era Transfer," *New York Times*, August 15, 2016; Charlie Savage, "10 More Detainees Are Transferred From Guantánamo Prison," *New York Times*, January 16, 2017; and Charlie Savage, "Obama Transfers 4 from Guantánamo, Leaving 41 There as Term Ends," *New York Times*, January 19, 2017.

130. Quoted in Charlie Savage, "Harsher Security Tactics? Obama Left Door Ajar, and Donald Trump Is Knocking," *New York Times*, November 13, 2016.

131. Charlie Savage, "U.S. Transfers First Guantánamo Detainee Under Trump, Who Vowed to Fill It," *New York Times*, May 2, 2018.

132. For a good overview of this approach to ISIS detainees, see Robert Chesney, "The Expeditionary Targeting Force in Iraq: Putting the Short-Term Military Detention Model to the Test," Lawfare, March 2, 2016, https://www.lawfareblog.com/expeditionary-targeting-force-iraq-putting-short-term-military-detention-model-test.

133. Charlie Savage, "ISIS Detainees May Be Held at Guantánamo, Document Shows," *New York Times*, February 8, 2017.

134. Rebecca R. Ruiz, Adam Goldman, and Matt Apuzzo, "Terror Suspect Brought to U.S. for Trial, Breaking from Trump Rhetoric," *New York Times*, July 21, 2017.

135. Adam Goldman and Eric Schmitt, "Benghazi Attacks Suspect Is Captured in Libya by U.S. Commandos," *New York Times*, October 30, 2017.

136. See Robert Chesney, "Perhaps Guantánamo Won't Get New Detainees After All? An Update on Efforts to Capture Islamic State Leaders," Lawfare, June 26, 2017, https://www.lawfareblog.com/perhaps-guantanamo-wont-get-new-detainees-after-all-update-efforts-capture-islamic-state-leaders.

137. Eric Schmitt and Charlie Savage, "American Held as ISIS Suspect, Creating a Quandary for the Trump Administration," *New York Times*, October 6, 2017, and Dana Priest, Devlin Barrett, and Matt Zapotosky, "Case of Suspected American ISIS Fighter Captured in Syria Vexes U.S.," *Washington Post*, October 29, 2017.

138. Charlie Savage, "Military Ordered to Notify A.C.L.U. before Transferring American ISIS Suspect," *New York Times*, January 24, 2018.

139. Charlie Savage, "Appeals Court Bars U.S. from Transferring American ISIS Suspect," *New York Times*, May 9, 2018.

140. Charlie Savage, Rukmini Callimachi, and Eric Schmitt, "American ISIS Suspect Is Freed after Being Held More Than a Year," *New York Times*, October 29, 2018.

141. Quoted in Savage, Callimachi, and Schmitt, "American ISIS Suspect Is Freed."

142. Ramzi Kassem, "A View from Gitmo," *New York Times*, June 7, 2014.

143. Aisha I. Saad and Zoe A.Y. Weinberg, "Remember Guantánamo?," *New York Times*, March 15, 2018.

144. Richard E. Neustadt, *Presidential Power and the Modern Presidents: The Politics of Leadership from Roosevelt to Reagan* (New York: Free Press, 1991), 29.

## CHAPTER 4. "KANGAROO COURTS?"

1. George W. Bush, "Detention, Treatment, and Trial of Certain Non-Citizens in the War Against Terrorism," *Federal Register* 66, no. 222 (November 16, 2001), http://georgewbush-whitehouse.archives.gov/news/releases/2001/11/20011113-27.html.

2. Jess Bravin, *The Terror Courts: Rough Justice at Guantanamo Bay* (New Haven, CT: Yale University Press, 2013), 21.

3. Tim Golden, "After Terror, a Secret Rewriting of Military Law," *New York Times*, October 24, 2004. For good treatments of the Nazi saboteur episode, see Louis Fisher, *Military Tribunals and Presidential Power: American Revolution to the War on Terrorism* (Lawrence: University Press of Kansas, 2005), 91–129, and David Glazier, "The Development of an Exceptional Court: The History of the American Military Commission," in *Guantánamo and Beyond: Exceptional Courts and Military Commissions in Comparative Perspective*, ed. Fionnuala Ní Aoláin and Oren Gross (New York: Cambridge University Press, 2013), 47–52, but see the chapter generally. In his dissent in *Hamdi v. Rumsfeld*, Justice Antonin Scalia referred to *Quirin* as "not this Court's finest hour." Military commissions have a checkered history in the United States, as the accounts cited above make clear.

4. Patrick F. Philbin, "Legality of the Use of Military Commissions to Try Terrorists," November 6, 2001, https://nsarchive2.gwu.edu/torturingdemocracy/documents/20011106.pdf.

5. Bravin, *The Terror Courts*, 22 and 47.

6. Bravin, 112–114.

7. Condoleezza Rice, *No Higher Honor: A Memoir of My Years in Washington* (New York: Crown Publishers, 2011), 105.

8. Darren A. Wheeler, *Presidential Power in Action: Implementing Supreme Court Detainee Decisions* (New York: Palgrave Macmillan, 2008), 116–118.

9. Bravin, *The Terror Courts*, 39, and Golden, "After Terror, a Secret Rewriting."

10. Golden, "After Terror, a Secret Rewriting." And see Fisher, *Military Tribunals and Presidential Power*, 91–129, for a critical review of the *Quirin* ruling.

11. This summary is drawn from the account provided by Barton Gellman and Jo Becker in "'A Different Understanding with the President,'" *Washington Post*, June 24, 2007. On the last point, see also Rice, *No Higher Honor*, 106.

12. Rice, *No Higher Honor*, 106.

13. Dick Cheney, with Liz Cheney, *In My Time: A Personal and Political Memoir* (New York: Threshold Editions, 2011), 357.

14. Fisher, *Military Tribunals and Presidential Power*, 168–169. See also Glenn Sulmasy, "*Ex parte Quirin* and Military Commissions under the Obama Administration," *University of Toledo Law Review* 41, no. 4 (Summer 2010).

15. This "not practicable" finding was important because it referred to provisions in the UCMJ, 10 U.S.C. Ch. 47. In particular, §836 read:

> (a) Pretrial, trial, and post-trial procedures, including modes of proof, for cases arising under this chapter triable in courts-martial, military commissions and other military tribunals, and procedures for courts of inquiry, may be prescribed by the President by regulations which shall, so far as he considers practicable, apply the principles of law and the rules of evidence generally recognized in the trial of criminal cases in the United States district courts, but which may not be contrary to or inconsistent with this chapter. (b) All rules and regulations made under this article shall be uniform insofar as practicable.

It has since been amended slightly by the Military Commissions Act (MCA), Pub. L. No. 109–366, 120 Stat. 2600 (2006).

16. For an overview of the legal issues associated with military commissions, especially their relationship to the 2001 AUMF, see Curtis A. Bradley and Jack L. Goldsmith, "Congressional Authorization and the War on Terrorism," *Harvard Law Review* 118, no. 7 (May 2005).

17. For more on the vagueness of the order and the considerable amount of discretion delegated to the secretary of defense, see Bernard Horowitz and Harvey Rishikof, "Enemy Combatant Detainees," in *Congress and the Politics of National Security*, ed. David P. Auerswald and Colton C. Campbell (Cambridge: Cambridge University Press, 2012), 174; Wheeler, *Presidential Power in Action*, 116; and Matthew Purdy, "Bush's New Rules to Fight Terror Transform the Legal Landscape," *New York Times*, November 25, 2001.

18. Wheeler, *Presidential Power in Action*, 118.

19. Golden, "After Terror, a Secret Rewriting."

20. For more on these developments, see Fisher, *Military Tribunals and Presidential Power*, 174–179. See also Wheeler, *Presidential Power in Action*, 118–119, and Bravin, *The Terror Courts*, 53–54.

21. Golden, "After Terror, a Secret Rewriting."

22. Bravin, *The Terror Courts*, 59.

23. Department of Defense, "Military Commission Order No. 1," March 21, 2002. The remainder of this section summarizing the contents of MCO No. 1 draws on the text of this document unless otherwise noted. The full text of Military Commission Order No. 1 can be found at http://www.mc.mil/Portals/0/milcomord1.pdf.

24. Bravin, *The Terror Courts*, 63.

25. Bravin, 41–42.

26. Bravin, 59–60.

27. Dawn E. Johnsen, "The Story of *Hamdan v. Rumsfeld:* Trying Enemy Combatants By Military Commission," in *Presidential Power Stories*, ed. Christopher H. Schroeder and Curtis A. Bradley (New York: Thomson West Foundation Press, 2009), 466.

28. Neil A. Lewis, "Rules on Tribunal Require Unanimity on Death Penalty," *New York Times*, December 28, 2001.

29. Lewis, "Rules on Tribunal."

30. Bravin, *The Terror Courts*, 40.

31. Golden, "After Terror, a Secret Rewriting."

32. Donald Rumsfeld, *Known and Unknown: A Memoir* (New York: Sentinel, 2011), 589.

33. Rumsfeld, *Known and Unknown*, 590.

34. James Q. Wilson, *Bureaucracy: What Government Agencies Do and Why They Do It* (New York: Basic Books, 1989). See especially chs. 3–6.

35. Rebecca Ingber, "Interpretation Catalysts and Executive Branch Legal Decision-making," *Yale Journal of International Law* 38, no. 2 (Summer 2013): 362, 369–370, and 421.

36. Jack Goldsmith, *Power and Constraint: The Accountable Presidency after 9/11* (New York: W. W. Norton, 2012), 187 and 228. But see the book generally. See also Neal Kumar Katyal, "Internal Separation of Powers: Checking Today's Most Dangerous Branch from Within," *Yale Law Journal* 115, no. 9 (July 2006), for a similar argument.

37. Purdy, "Bush's New Rules."

38. Rumsfeld, *Known and Unknown*, 590.

39. Department of Defense, "Military Commission Order No. 2," June 21, 2003, http://www.mc.mil/Portals/0/milcomord2.pdf.

40. Department of Defense, "Military Commission Order No. 5," March 15, 2004, http://www.mc.mil/Portals/0/milcomord5.pdf.

41. See Department of Defense, "Military Commission Instructions" Nos. 2, 5, and 8, April 30, 2003, http://www.mc.mil/LEGALRESOURCES/MilitaryCommissionsDocuments/HistoricalDocuments.aspx.

42. Rumsfeld, *Known and Unknown*, 590, and Rice, *No Higher Honor*, 275.

43. See Department of Defense, "Military Commission Instructions" Nos. 3, 4, and 9, respectively.

44. Bravin, *The Terror Courts*, 69–70. See also 83–84, 93–94, and 140–141.

45. John Mintz, "6 Could Be Facing Military Tribunals; U.S. Says Detainees Tied to Al Qaeda," *Washington Post*, July 4, 2003.

46. Bravin, *The Terror Courts*, 126–127. See also "Briton Condemns Proposed U.S. Trials," *New York Times*, June 26, 2004, and Tim Golden, "Administration Officials Split over Stalled Military Tribunals," *New York Times*, October 25, 2004. The British were especially critical of the lack of civilian review of commission decisions.

47. Neil A. Lewis, "First War-Crimes Case Opens at Guantánamo Base," *New York Times*, August 25, 2004.

48. U.S. Library of Congress, Congressional Research Service, *The Department of Defense Rules for Military Commissions: Analysis of Procedural Rules and Comparison with Proposed Legislation and the Uniform Code of Military Justice*, by Jennifer Elsea, RL31600 (August 4, 2005): 2.

49. Bravin, *The Terror Courts*, 211.

50. Joshua L. Dratel, "How I Learned to Stop Worrying and Love the Military Commissions," *Seton Hall Law Review* 41, no. 4 (Fall 2011): 1356.

51. Quoted in Raymond Bonner, "Marine Defends Guantánamo Detainee, and Surprises Australians," *New York Times*, March 28, 2004.

52. Quoted in Neil A. Lewis, "Lawyer Says Detainees Face Unfair System," *New York Times*, January 22, 2004.

53. Quoted in Neil A. Lewis, "U.S. Charges Two at Guantánamo With Conspiracy," *New York Times*, February 25, 2004. See also Golden, "Administration Officials Split."

54. Golden, "Administration Officials Split."

55. Bravin, *The Terror Courts*, 184.

56. Bravin, 191 and 194.

57. Neil A. Lewis, "Terror Tribunal Defendant Demands to Be Own Lawyer," *New York Times*, August 27, 2004.

58. Lewis, "Terror Tribunal Defendant." For a longer summary of the episode, see Bravin, *The Terror Courts*, 195–201.

59. Bravin, *The Terror Courts*, 217.

60. Neil A. Lewis, "Suit Contests Military Trials of Detainees at Cuba Base," *New York Times*, April 8, 2004.

61. Neal K. Katyal and Laurence H. Tribe, "Waging War, Deciding Guilt: Trying the Military Tribunals," *Yale Law Journal* 111, no. 6 (April 2002).

62. Bravin, *The Terror Courts*, 213–214.

63. Maureen O'Hagan, "Yemeni's Lawsuit Contends Special Tribunal Violates Constitution," *Seattle Times*, May 19, 2004. See also Bravin, *The Terror Courts*, 214.

64. Hamdan v. Rumsfeld, 344 F. Supp. 2d 152 (D.D.C. 2004).

65. UCMJ, §821.

66. George W. Bush, "Humane Treatment of Taliban and al Qaeda Detainees," February 7, 2002, http://www.pegc.us/archive/White_House/bush_memo_20020207_ed.pdf.

67. Hamdan v. Rumsfeld, 344 F. Supp. 2d 152 (D.D.C. 2004), at 161.

68. Hamdan v. Rumsfeld, 344 F. Supp. 2d 152 (D.D.C. 2004), at 161–162.

69. For the full text of Common Article 3, see Associated Press, "Common Article 3 of the Geneva Conventions," accessed June 22, 2020, https://archive.nytimes.com/www.nytimes.com/ref/us/AP-Guantanamo-Geneva-Conventions.html.

70. See Bush, "Humane Treatment of Taliban and al Qaeda Detainees." As a matter of policy, however, the administration's position was not so clear-cut. It vowed that it would "continue to treat detainees humanely and, to the extent appropriate and consistent with military necessity, in a manner consistent with the principles of Geneva." This represented one of several instances in which the administration's legal position and policy decision seemingly diverged. However, it is not clear how great this divergence was, since the qualifier "to the extent appropriate and consistent with military necessity" provided the administration with room to depart from Geneva's principles.

71. Hamdan v. Rumsfeld, 344 F. Supp. 2d 152 (D.D.C. 2004), at 27.

72. Bravin, *The Terror Courts*, 219–220.

73. Bravin, 222–223. The remainder of this paragraph draws on Bravin's account.

74. Bravin, 240.

75. Bravin, 244.

76. Bravin, 240–241.

77. Hamdan v. Rumsfeld, 415 F.3d 33 (D.C. Cir. 2005).

78. Hamdan v. Rumsfeld, 415 F.3d 33 (D.C. Cir. 2005) (Williams, J., concurring).

79. Neil A. Lewis, "Detainee Trials to Resume Soon, Rumsfeld Says," *New York Times*, July 18, 2005.

80. Neil A. Lewis, "Two Prosecutors Faulted Trials for Detainees," *New York Times*, August 1, 2005.

81. Department of Defense, "Military Commission Order No. 1" (revised), August 31, 2005, https://www.mc.mil/Portals/0/milcomord1%20(as%20amended).pdf.

82. Bravin, *The Terror Courts*, 273.

83. Neil A. Lewis, "U.S. Alters Rules for War Crime Trials," *New York Times*, September 1, 2005.

84. Bravin, *The Terror Courts*, 273–275. Solicitor General Paul Clement cited the revisions in a brief to the Court urging it to deny certiorari in *Hamdan v. Rumsfeld*.

85. Department of Defense, "Military Commission Instruction No. 10," March 24, 2006, https://www.mc.mil/Portals/0/milcominstn010.pdf.

86. Thom Shanker, "Barring Evidence from Torture Is Considered," *New York Times*, March 23, 2006.

87. Tim Golden, "Boycott Threat Roils Guantánamo Hearing," *New York Times*, April 6, 2006. See also Bravin, *The Terror Courts*, 277–278.

88. Bravin, *The Terror Courts*, 65.

89. Golden, "Boycott Threat Roils." See also Bravin, *The Terror Courts*, 275–276.

90. David S. Cloud, "Terror Suspect Upsets Plan to Resume Trials in Cuba," *New York Times*, January 12, 2006.

## CHAPTER 5. THE SUPREME COURT INTERVENES

1. See Linda Greenhouse, "Detainee Case Hits on Limits of Presidency," *New York Times*, January 10, 2006, and Linda Greenhouse, "Detainee Case Will Pose Delicate Question for Court," *New York Times*, March 27, 2006.

2. Quoted in Associated Press, "Supreme Court Is Asked to Block Terror Tribunals," *New York Times*, August 9, 2005.

3. Detainee Treatment Act, Pub. L. No. 109–148, 119 Stat. 2739 (2005).

4. Stephen I. Vladeck, "Exceptional Courts and the Structure of American Military Justice," in *Guantánamo and Beyond: Exceptional Courts and Military Commissions in Comparative Perspective*, ed. Fionnuala Ní Aoláin and Oren Gross (New York: Cambridge University Press, 2013), 172.

5. Detainee Treatment Act, §1005 (e).

6. An audio recording and transcript of the *Hamdan* oral argument can be found at "Hamdan v. Rumsfeld," Oyez, accessed June 1, 2020, http://www.oyez.org/cases/2000–2009/2005/2005_05_184.

7. Hamdi v. Rumsfeld, 542 U.S. 507 (2004), at 536.

8. This is a common theme in major presidential power cases: the government often presses particularly aggressive claims in the lower courts, only to moderate them before the Supreme Court. See, for example, Patricia L. Bellia, "The Story of the *Steel Seizure* Case," in *Presidential Power Stories*, ed. Christopher H. Schroeder and Curtis A. Bradley (New York: Thomson West Foundation Press, 2009), 234 and 249–251; Curtis A. Bradley, "The Story of *Ex parte Milligan*: Military Trials, Enemy Combatants, and Congressional Authorization," in *Presidential Power Stories*, ed. Schroeder and Bradley, 110; Trevor W. Morrison, "The Story of *United States v. United States District Court (Keith)*: The Surveillance Power," in *Presidential Power Stories*, ed. Schroeder and Bradley, 308–309; and David J. Barron and Martin S. Lederman, "The Commander in Chief at the Lowest Ebb—Framing the Problem, Doctrine, and Original Understanding," *Harvard Law Review* 121, no. 3 (January 2008): 764.

9. Hamdan v. Rumsfeld, 548 U.S. 557 (2006).

10. Hamdan v. Rumsfeld, 548 U.S. 557 (2006) (Scalia, J., dissenting), at 655.

11. It is surprising that the question of whether the DTA constituted legislative authorization for the Bush administration's version of military commissions did not receive more attention in the *Hamdan* opinions. After all, one could certainly view Congress's decision in the DTA to set up a review mechanism for commission decisions as indicating at least some degree of legislative assent for the existing commission system.

12. For more on this point, see Michael Greenberger, "You Ain't Seen Nothin' Yet: The Inevitable Post-*Hamdan* Conflict between the Supreme Court and the Political Branches," *Maryland Law Review* 66, no. 3 (2007): 806–807.

13. For the full text of Common Article 3, see Associated Press, "Common Article 3 of the Geneva Conventions," *New York Times*, accessed June 1, 2020, https://archive.nytimes.com/www.nytimes.com/ref/us/AP-Guantanamo-Geneva-Conventions.html.

14. David Hicks was also charged with aiding the enemy and attempted murder. See Neil A. Lewis, "First War-Crimes Case Opens at Guantánamo Base," *New York Times*, August 25, 2004.

15. Jess Bravin, *The Terror Courts: Rough Justice at Guantanamo Bay* (New Haven, CT: Yale University Press, 2013), 128–130.

16. Uniform Code of Military Justice (UCMJ), 10 U.S.C. ch. 47, §821 (italics not in original).

17. Hamdan v. Rumsfeld, 548 U.S. 557 (2006) (Thomas, J., dissenting), at 678.

18. Quoted in Dawn E. Johnsen, "The Story of *Hamdan v. Rumsfeld*: Trying Enemy Combatants by Military Commission," in *Presidential Power Stories*, ed. Schroeder and Bradley, 472.

19. Linda Greenhouse, "Justices, 5–3, Broadly Reject Bush Plan to Try Detainees," *New York Times*, June 30, 2006.

20. Greenberger, "You Ain't Seen Nothin' Yet," 805.

21. Neal Kumar Katyal, "*Hamdan v. Rumsfeld*: The Legal Academy Goes to Practice," *Harvard Law Review* 120, no. 1 (November 2006): 66.

22. Quoted in David E. Sanger and Scott Shane, "Court's Ruling Is Likely to Force Negotiations over Presidential Power," *New York Times*, June 30, 2006.

23. Hamdan v. Rumsfeld, 548 U.S. 557 (2006) (Breyer, J., concurring), at 636. The "blank check" language was a reference to *Hamdi v. Rumsfeld*, but I have omitted Justice Breyer's citation for the sake of readability.

24. Darren A. Wheeler, *Presidential Power in Action: Implementing Supreme Court Detainee Decisions* (New York: Palgrave Macmillan, 2008), 133.

25. Quoted in Sanger and Shane, "Court's Ruling Is Likely to Force Negotiations."

26. Quoted in Robin Toner, "Lawmakers Seek Action after Ruling on Detainees," *New York Times*, July 3, 2006.

27. Quoted in Toner, "Lawmakers Seek Action."

28. For more on this point, see Mark Tushnet, "The Political Constitution of Emergency Powers: Some Lessons from *Hamdan*," *Minnesota Law Review* 91, no. 5 (May 2007): 1456; Wheeler, *Presidential Power in Action*, 133–135; and Mark Mazzetti and Kate Zernike, "White House Says Terror Detainees Hold Basic Rights," *New York Times*, July 12, 2006.

29. David S. Cloud and Sheryl Gay Stolberg, "White House Bill Proposes System to Try Detainees," *New York Times*, July 26, 2006.

30. Paul A. Diller, "When Congress Passes an Intentionally Unconstitutional Law: The Military Commissions Act of 2006," *Southern Methodist University Law Review* 61, no. 2 (Spring 2008): 316–317. See also Wheeler, *Presidential Power in Action*, 133–134.

31. Quoted in Kate Zernike, "White House Prods Congress to Curb Detainee Rights," *New York Times*, July 13, 2006.

32. Quoted in Kate Zernike and Neil A. Lewis, "Plan for Tribunals Would Hew to the First Series," *New York Times*, September 7, 2006.

33. Carl Hulse, Kate Zernike, and Sheryl Gay Stolberg, "How 3 G.O.P. Veterans Stalled Bush Detainee Bill," *New York Times*, September 17, 2006.

34. For a helpful summary of the legislative timeline surrounding the MCA, see Carlos Manuel Vázquez, "The Military Commissions Act, the Geneva Conventions, and the Courts: A Critical Guide," *American Journal of International Law* 101, no. 1 (January 2007): 74–75.

35. Military Commissions Act, Pub. L. No. 109–366, 120 Stat. 2600 (2006). For these particular provisions, see 2611–2613.

36. U.S. Library of Congress, Congressional Research Service, *The Military Commissions Act of 2006: Analysis of Procedural Rules and Comparison with Previous DOD Rules and the Uniform Code of Military Justice*, by Jennifer Elsea, RL33688 (October 12, 2006).

37. See, for example, David Glazier, "A Self-Inflicted Wound: A Half-Dozen Years of Turmoil over the Guantánamo Military Commissions," *Lewis & Clark Law Review* 12, no. 1 (Spring 2008): 185–187.

38. Benjamin Wittes, *Law and the Long War: The Future of Justice in the Age of Terror* (New York: Penguin Books, 2008), 140.

39. Glazier, "A Self-Inflicted Wound," 135.

40. Bravin, *The Terror Courts*, 317.

41. Neil A. Lewis, "Officials Plan to Move Quickly for Terrorism Trials in Spring," *New York Times*, September 30, 2006.

42. Neil A. Lewis, "Officials See Qaeda Trials Using New Law in 2007," *New York Times*, November 3, 2006.

43. Department of Defense, "The Manual for Military Commissions" (2007 edition), January 18, 2007, https://www.mc.mil/Portals/0/MANUAL_FOR_MILITARY_COMMISSIONS_2007_signed.pdf.

44. Wheeler, *Presidential Power in Action*, 138.

45. William Glaberson, "Detainee's Lawyers Seek Removal of Prosecutor," *New York Times*, March 26, 2007.

46. Associated Press, "Australian Is Charged in Terror Case," *New York Times*, March 2, 2007.

47. William Glaberson, "Australian to Serve 9 Months in Terror Case," *New York Times*, March 31, 2007.

48. Bravin, *The Terror Courts*, 312.

49. Wheeler, *Presidential Power in Action*, 26. The decisions are *United States of America v. Omar Ahmed Khadr*, "Order on Jurisdiction" (June 4, 2007), and *United States of America v. Salim Ahmed Hamdan*, "Decision and Order—Motion to Dismiss for Lack of Jurisdiction Corrected Order" (June 4, 2007). The text of the decisions can be found on the Office of Military Commissions website, http://www.mc.mil/CASES.aspx; click on the names of the two detainees. Decisions and orders are sorted by date.

50. William Glaberson, "Military Judges Dismiss Charges for 2 Detainees," *New York Times*, June 5, 2007, and Adam Liptak, "Tribunal System, Newly Righted, Stumbles Again," *New York Times*, June 5, 2007.

51. Glaberson, "Military Judges Dismiss Charges."

52. Jeff Zeleny, "Democrats Hope to Expand Rights at Guantánamo," *New York Times*, June 6, 2007, and Helene Cooper and William Glaberson, "At White House, Renewed Debate on Guantánamo," *New York Times*, June 23, 2007.

53. Glazier, "A Self-Inflicted Wound," 182–183.

54. United States of America v. Omar Ahmed Khadr, CMCR 07–001 (U.S.C.M.C.R. 2007). For the full decision, see the PDF at https://www.mc.mil/Portals/0/53-Khadr%20Court%20Order%20Denying%20Defense%20Motion%20to%20Dismiss,%2019%20September%202007.pdf.

55. See William Glaberson, "New Roadblocks Delay Tribunals at Guantánamo," *New York Times*, April 10, 2008, and William Glaberson, "Hurdles Seen as Capital Charges Are Filed in 9/11 Case," *New York Times*, February 12, 2008.

56. Glaberson, "Hurdles Seen as Capital Charges Are Filed."

57. Efforts to collect the sort of information that would be more likely to hold up at trial began as early as 2006. See Scott Shane and David Johnston, "U.S. Acts to Avert Tactic Expected in Qaeda Trial," *New York Times*, February 13, 2008.

58. See Bravin, *The Terror Courts*, 322–323, for a summary of this episode.

59. Bob Woodward, "Guantanamo Detainee Was Tortured, Says Official Overseeing Military Trials," *Washington Post*, January 14, 2009.

60. See Bravin, *The Terror Courts*, 345–350, for a discussion of these events.

61. Glaberson, "New Roadblocks Delay Tribunals."

62. The following summary is drawn from four sources: Bravin, *The Terror Courts*, 323–324, and a trio of articles in *New York Times* by William Glaberson: "Claim of Pressure for Closed Guantánamo Trials," October 20, 2007; "Former Prosecutor to Testify for Detainee," February 28, 2008; and "Ex-Prosecutor Tells of Push by Pentagon on Detainees," April 29, 2008.

63. William Glaberson, "Judge's Guantánamo Ruling Bodes Ill for System," *New York Times*, May 11, 2008.

64. Quoted in William Glaberson, "Detainee Lawyers to Use Ruling for New Attacks," *New York Times*, June 14, 2008.

65. Boumediene v. Bush, 128 S. Ct. 2229 (2008).

66. Hamdan v. Gates, 565 F. Supp. 2d 130 (D.D.C. 2008).

67. Hamdan v. Gates, 565 F. Supp. 2d 130 (D.D.C. 2008), at 132.

68. Hamdan v. Gates, 565 F. Supp. 2d 130 (D.D.C. 2008), at 135.

69. Hamdan v. Gates, 565 F. Supp. 2d 130 (D.D.C. 2008), at 137.

70. The decisions are *United States of America v. Salim Ahmed Hamdan*, "Ruling on Motion to Dismiss (Ex Post Facto)" (July 14, 2008), and *United States of America v. Salim Ahmed Hamdan*, "Ruling on Motion to Suppress Statements Based on Fifth Amendment" (July 20, 2008). The text of the decisions can be found on the Office of Military Commissions website, http://www.mc.mil/CASES.aspx; click on the names of the two detainees. Decisions and orders are sorted by date. For a brief summary of this episode, see Scott Shane and William Glaberson, "Courts Clear the Way for First Trial at Guantánamo," *New York Times*, July 18, 2008.

71. William Glaberson, "Panel Convicts bin Laden Driver in Split Verdict," *New York Times*, August 7, 2008. For a very useful collection of news articles covering Hamdan's commission trial, see Ben Winograd, "Hamdan Military Commission Coverage," *SCOTUSblog.com*, posted July 22, 2008, and updated thereafter, http://www.scotusblog.com/2008/07/hamdan-military-commission-coverage/. See also Bravin, *The Terror Courts*, 330–345.

72. William Glaberson, "Bin Laden Driver Sentenced to a Short Term," *New York Times*, August 8, 2008.

73. Quoted in Bravin, *The Terror Courts*, 344.

74. Josh White and William Branigin, "Former Bin Laden Driver Hamdan to Leave Guantanamo Bay for Yemen," *Washington Post*, November 25, 2008.

75. William Glaberson, "Detainee Convicted on Terrorism Charges," *New York Times*, November 3, 2008.

76. Bravin, *The Terror Courts*, 345.

77. See, for example, *New York Times* editorial, "First Steps at Guantánamo," January 22, 2009.

## CHAPTER 6. LITIGATION WITHOUT END

1. Charlie Savage, *Power Wars: Inside Obama's Post-9/11 Presidency* (New York: Little, Brown, 2015), 113–114 and 124–125.

2. Barack Obama, "Remarks by the President on National Security," May 21, 2009, https://obamawhitehouse.archives.gov/the-press-office/remarks-president-national-security-5-21-09.

3. Peter Baker and David M. Herszenhorn, "Obama Planning to Keep Tribunals for Detainees," *New York Times*, May 15, 2009.

4. The following summary of Jawad's military commission is drawn from David J. R. Frakt, "Mohammed Jawad and the Military Commissions of Guantánamo," *Duke Law Journal* 60, no. 6 (March 2011): 1367–1412.

5. Quoted in William Glaberson, "U.S. Judge Challenges Evidence on a Detainee," *New York Times*, July 22, 2009. The preceding summary of Jawad's habeas case is drawn from that article and David Frakt, "Mohammed Jawad," 1373–1375.

6. William Glaberson, "Government Might Allow U.S. Trial for Detainee," *New York Times*, July 24, 2009.

7. David J. R. Frakt, "The Practice of Criminal Law in the Guantánamo Military Commissions," *Air Force Law Review* 67 (2011): 38.

8. David Johnston, "In Senate, Debate on Detainee Legal Rights," *New York Times*, July 7, 2009.

9. Johnston, "In Senate, Debate." For more on this point, see Bernard Horowitz and Harvey Rishikof, "Enemy Combatant Detainees," in *Congress and the Politics of National Security*, ed. David P. Auerswald and Colton C. Campbell (Cambridge: Cambridge University Press, 2012), 183; John M. Bickers, "Too Little, Too Late? Why President Obama's Well-Intentioned Reforms of the Military Commissions May Not Be Enough to Save Them," *Whittier Law Review* 31, no. 3 (Spring 2010): 382 and 388; and Josh Gerstein, "Obama Signs Military Commissions Reforms," *Politico*, October 28, 2009.

10. See, for example, Josh Gerstein, "GOP Revives 'Soft on Terror' Charge," *Politico*, January 30, 2010.

11. The statute is Title XVIII of the National Defense Authorization Act for Fiscal Year 2010, H.R. 2647. For a useful discussion of the changes made by the 2009 amendments to the MCA, see U.S. Library of Congress, Congressional Research Service, *The Military Commissions Act of 2006: Analysis of Procedural Rules and Comparison with Previous DOD Rules and the Uniform Code of Military Justice*, by Jennifer Elsea, R41163 (August 4, 2014). The remainder of this section on the 2009 MCA draws on the statute itself and Elsea's piece, unless otherwise noted.

12. The battlefield exception had been controversial during internal executive branch debates on military commission reforms. Military lawyers and DOD argued for it, but some civilian lawyers, led by David Barron, worried that it could provoke legal challenges—particularly if military commissions were, as the administration was planning, moved to US soil, where the Fifth Amendment's prohibition on

self-incrimination would apply. Ultimately the issue was punted to Congress, which sided with the position taken by the military and DOD. Military commission prosecutors and judges would have the discretion to decide whether to admit battlefield statements as evidence. See Savage, *Power Wars*, 131–133.

13. Janet Cooper Alexander, "Military Commissions: A Place Outside the Law's Reach," *Saint Louis University Law Journal* 56, no. 4 (Summer 2012): 1132.

14. For more on this point, see Stephen I. Vladeck, "Exceptional Courts and the Structure of American Military Justice," in *Guantánamo and Beyond: Exceptional Courts and Military Commissions in Comparative Perspective*, ed. Fionnuala Ní Aoláin and Oren Gross (New York: Cambridge University Press, 2013), 174, and Scott L. Silliman, "Prosecuting Alleged Terrorists by Military Commission: A Prudent Option," *Case Western Reserve Journal of International Law* 42, nos. 1–2 (Winter 2009): 295–296.

15. See, for example, Jess Bravin, *The Terror Courts: Rough Justice at Guantanamo Bay* (New Haven, CT: Yale University Press, 2013), 363; Vladeck, "Exceptional Courts," 175; Alexander, "A Place Outside," 1132; Silliman, "Prosecuting Alleged Terrorists," 289; and Reema Shah and Sam Kleiner, "Running Out of Options: Expiring Detention Authority and the Viability of Prosecutions in the Military Commissions under *Hamdan II*," *Yale Law & Policy Review* 32, no. 2 (Spring 2014): 498.

16. See, for example, Eugene R. Fidell, "Charm Offensive in Lilliput: Military Commissions 3.1," *Saint Louis University Law Journal* 56, no. 4 (Summer 2012): 1196–1198. See also Alexander, "A Place Outside,"1117, and Ali Soufan, "Tribunal and Error," *New York Times*, February 11, 2010.

17. Charlie Savage, "Guantánamo Prisoner Is Repatriated to Sudan," *New York Times*, July 11, 2012.

18. Ian Austen, "Sole Canadian Held at Guantánamo Bay Is Repatriated," *New York Times*, September 29, 2012.

19. Charlie Savage, "Sudanese Detainee to Be Sent Home from Guantánamo," *New York Times*, December 4, 2013.

20. See, for example, Benjamin Weiser, "Top Terror Prosecutor Is a Critic of Civilian Trials," *New York Times*, February 19, 2010.

21. Quoted in Charlie Savage, "Senator Proposes Deal on Handling of Detainees," *New York Times*, March 3, 2010.

22. Charlie Savage, "White House Postpones Picking Site of 9/11 Trial," *New York Times*, March 5, 2010.

23. Charlie Savage and Peter Shane, "Experts Urge Keeping Two Options for Terror Trials," *New York Times*, March 8, 2010.

24. U.S. Library of Congress, Congressional Research Service, *Guantanamo Detention Center: Legislative Activity in the 111th Congress*, by Michael John Garcia, R40754 (January 13, 2011): 4.

25. Bravin, *The Terror Courts*, 363–364. See also Charlie Savage, "Ghailani Verdict Reignites Debate over the Proper Court for Terrorism Trials," *New York Times*, November 18, 2010, and "Room for Debate: Prosecuting Terrorists in Federal Court," *New York Times*, November 18, 2010. However, as some observers—and the judge in

the Ghailani case—pointed out, it was doubtful that the evidence obtained via coercion that was excluded in the Ghailani trial would have been admissible in a military commission, under the rules established by the MCA. See Savage, *Power Wars*, 325, for more on this point. Then again, Savage suggests that the military commission outcome may have been different for another reason. The Ghailani jury apparently contained one juror who strongly favored acquittal, and the ensuing split verdict represented a compromise with the holdout. In Savage's view, the likelihood of a holdout on a commission jury exerting this kind of influence was far less likely. See Savage, *Power Wars*, 326.

26. Charlie Savage, "In a Reversal, Military Trials for 9/11 Cases," *New York Times*, April 4, 2011.

27. Associated Press, "9/11 Defendants Charged at Guantánamo with Terrorism and Murder," *New York Times*, May 31, 2011.

28. Associated Press, "New Charges Filed against Suspect in U.S.S. Cole Bombing," *New York Times*, April 20, 2011. Unlike the 9/11 defendants, Nashiri was never slated for a civilian trial. The Obama administration's central public justification for keeping Nashiri in the military commission system was that his attack was carried out against a military target. But Charlie Savage reports that the chief reason for keeping Nashiri in the commission system, as many speculated, was concern about the evidence against him. The government's case against Nashiri rests heavily on hearsay evidence, which remains more readily usable in the military commission system than in Article III courts. See Savage, *Power Wars*, 158–159.

29. Peter Finn, "Guantanamo Detainee Majid Khan Pleads Guilty, Promises Cooperation," *Washington Post*, February 29, 2012.

30. Savage, *Power Wars*, 196–197.

31. Quoted in Stephen Dycus, William C. Banks, and Peter Raven-Hansen, *Counterterrorism Law*, 2nd ed. (New York: Wolters Kluwer Law & Business, 2012), 717.

32. This summary of events leading up to the CMCR's decision is drawn from David Glazier, "The Misuse of History: Conspiracy and the Guantánamo Military Commissions," *Baylor Law Review* 66, no. 2 (Spring 2014): 307–308.

33. United States of America v. Salim Ahmed Hamdan, CMCR 09-002 (U.S.C.M.C.R. 2011). The summary that follows is drawn from the opinion, which can be found at http://jnslp.com/wp-content/uploads/2011/06/09-002-hamdan-uscmcr-decision-june-24-2011-86-pages.pdf.

34. USA v. Salim Hamdan (U.S.C.M.C.R. 2011), at 22.

35. United States of America v. Ali Hamza Ahmad Suliman al Bahlul, CMCR 09-001 (U.S.C.M.C.R. 2011). For the full opinion, see https://www.mc.mil/Portals/0/pdfs/AliHamza09-001/al%20Bahlul%20USCMCR%20Decision%20(Sept.%209,%202011).pdf.

36. This paragraph draws on Steve Vladeck, "Four Big Questions Heading into the Hamdan Argument," Lawfare, May 1, 2012, https://www.lawfareblog.com/four-big-questions-heading-hamdan-argument, and Lawfare Staff, Larkin Reynolds, and Wells Bennett, "Hamdan Oral Argument Preview," Lawfare, May 2, 2012, https://www.law

fareblog.com/hamdan-oral-argument-preview. The latter post contains particularly helpful summaries of the briefs of the two sides.

37. See Steve Vladeck, "My Three Takeaways from the Hamdan Argument," Lawfare, May 3, 2012, https://www.lawfareblog.com/my-three-takeaways-hamdan-argument. For excellent coverage of all of oral argument in *Hamdan II*, see Wells Bennett, "Oral Argument Recap in Hamdan," Lawfare, May 4, 2012, https://www.lawfareblog.com/oral-argument-recap-hamdan.

38. Savage, *Power Wars*, 497.

39. Hamdan v. U.S., 696 F.3d 1238 (D.C. Cir. 2012). The case is often referred to as *Hamdan II*, in order to distinguish it from the earlier case challenging the Bush administration's version of military commissions.

40. Steve Vladeck, "Three (Early) Observations on Judge Kavanaugh's Analysis in Hamdan," Lawfare, October 16, 2012, https://www.lawfareblog.com/three-early-observations-judge-kavanaughs-analysis-hamdan.

41. The preceding paragraph draws heavily on Alan Rozenshtein, "An Explainer on *Hamdan II*, *Al-Bahlul*, and the Jurisdiction of the Guantánamo Military Commissions," Lawfare, April 26, 2013, https://www.lawfareblog.com/explainer-hamdan-ii-al-bahlul-and-jurisdiction-guant%C3%A1namo-military-commissions.

42. The preceding paragraph is drawn from the account provided in Charlie Savage, "U.S. Legal Officials Split over How to Prosecute Terrorism Detainees," *New York Times*, January 7, 2013, and Savage, *Power Wars*, 498.

43. Charlie Savage, "U.S. to Press Fight of Detainee's Appeal," *New York Times*, January 9, 2013, and Savage, *Power Wars*, 499.

44. See, for example, Wells Bennett and Benjamin Wittes, "Breaking News: D.C. Circuit Grants En Banc Rehearing in Al-Bahlul," Lawfare, April 23, 2013, https://www.lawfareblog.com/breaking-news-dc-circuit-grants-en-banc-rehearing-al-bahlul.

45. Al Bahlul v. U.S., 767 F.3d 1 (D.C. Cir. 2014).

46. Al Bahlul v. U.S., 767 F.3d 1 (D.C. Cir. 2014), at 27.

47. Al Bahlul v. U.S., 767 F.3d 1 (D.C. Cir. 2014) (Brown, J., dissenting), at 51.

48. Al Bahlul v. U.S., 767 F.3d 1 (D.C. Cir. 2014) (Brown), at 62.

49. Al Bahlul v. U.S., 767 F.3d 1 (D.C. Cir. 2014) (Kavanaugh, J., dissenting), at 80.

50. Al Bahlul v. U.S., 767 F.3d 1 (D.C. Cir. 2014) (Kavanaugh), at 65.

51. Lyle Denniston, "Are the Guantanamo War Crimes Courts Now Doomed?," *Constitution Daily*, July 22, 2014.

52. Vladeck's remarks on this point are part of an extremely useful Lawfare podcast devoted entirely to unpacking and analyzing the 2014 *Bahlul* decision. Benjamin Wittes, "The Lawfare Podcast, Episode #84: Bahlul, Bahlul, Bahlul," Lawfare, July 19, 2014, https://www.lawfareblog.com/lawfare-podcast-episode-84-bahlul-bahlul-bahlul.

53. Jack Goldsmith, "Bahlul: A Longer View," Lawfare, July 15, 2014, https://www.lawfareblog.com/bahlul-longer-view.

54. David Welna, "'Torture Report' Reshapes Conversation in Guantánamo Courtroom," *Morning Edition*, NPR, February 25, 2015.

55. Al Bahlul v. U.S., 792 F.3d 1 (D.C. Cir. 2015).

56. Al Bahlul v. U.S., 792 F.3d 1 (D.C. Cir. 2015), at 5–6.

57. Ex parte Quirin, 317 U.S. 1 (1942).

58. Al Bahlul v. U.S., 840 F.3d 757 (D.C. Cir. 2016).

59. Al Bahlul v. U.S., 840 F.3d 757 (D.C. Cir. 2016), at 763.

60. Al Bahlul v. U.S., 840 F.3d 757 (D.C. Cir. 2016) (Wilkins, J., concurring), at 804.

61. Carol Rosenberg, "Pentagon Throws Out Foot Soldier's Guantánamo War Court Conviction," *Miami Herald*, January 9, 2015.

62. Matt Apuzzo, "Guantánamo Conviction of Australian is Overturned," *New York Times*, February 18, 2015.

63. See In re al-Nashiri, 791 F3d. 71 (D.C. Cir. 2015) and In re Omar Khadr, No. 14–1227 (D.C. Cir. 2016).

64. Carol Rosenberg, "Pentagon Scraps Judges' Guantánamo Move Order; 9/11 Case Unfrozen," *Miami Herald*, February 27, 2015, and Missy Ryan, "Senior Official Resigns after Flap over Relocating Judges to Guantanamo," *Washington Post*, March 18, 2015.

65. Charlie Savage, "Donald Trump 'Fine' with Prosecuting U.S. Citizens at Guantánamo," *New York Times*, August 12, 2016.

66. Charlie Savage, "Sessions Says Guantánamo Is a 'Very Fine Place' for New Suspects," *New York Times*, March 9, 2017.

67. Adam Goldman and Eric Schmitt, "Benghazi Attacks Suspect Is Captured in Libya by U.S. Commandos," *New York Times*, October 30, 2017.

68. Peter Baker, "Trump Declares Suspect 'Should Get Death Penalty,'" *New York Times*, November 1, 2017. See also Charlie Savage and Adam Goldman, "Following Trump's Lead, Republicans Grow Quiet on Guantánamo," *New York Times*, November 4, 2017.

69. Carol Rosenberg, "Something's Wrong with War Court Prosecutor's Charges in Southeast Asia Terror Plots," *Miami Herald*, December 20, 2017.

70. Charlie Savage, "Fired Pentagon Official Was Exploring Plea Deals for 9/11 Suspects at Guantánamo," *New York Times*, February 10, 2018.

71. Dave Philipps, "Many Say He's the Least Qualified Lawyer Ever to Lead a Guantánamo Case. He Agrees." *New York Times*, February 5, 2018.

72. Charlie Savage, "Frustrated Military Tribunal Judge Indefinitely Halts Cole Bombing Case," *New York Times*, February 16, 2018.

73. See, for example, Scott R. Anderson, "Something Is Rotten with the State of the Military Commissions," Lawfare, March 2, 2018, https://www.lawfareblog.com/something-rotten-state-military-commissions, and Charlie Savage, "Judge Bars Statements Made by Guantánamo Detainees during F.B.I. Interrogations," *New York Times*, August 17, 2018.

74. See Charlie Savage, "Judge Overrules Censors in Guantánamo 9/11 Hearing," *New York Times*, January 30, 2013; Matt Apuzzo, "Covert Inquiry by F.B.I. Rattles 9/11 Tribunals," *New York Times*, April 18, 2014; Carol Rosenberg, "Judge Cancels 9/11 Pretrial Hearing, Considers It Productive," *Miami Herald*, October 15, 2014; and Savage, *Power Wars*, 545.

75. Charlie Savage, "Guantánamo Detainee Pleads Guilty in 2002 Attack on Tanker

Off Yemen," *New York Times*, February 20, 2014. Al-Darbi was sentenced in 2017 and has since been repatriated to Saudi Arabia. See Charlie Savage, "Guantánamo Defendant Is Sentenced, in Rare Success for Military Commission," *New York Times*, October 13, 2017.

76. See the May 2018 report entitled "The U.S. Military Commissions: Looking Forward." The report was the product of a law and policy workshop cosponsored by the American Bar Association Standing Committee on Law and National Security and the George Washington University Law School. The report may be accessed at https://www.americanbar.org/content/dam/aba/administrative/law_national_security/ABAMilitaryCommissionsWorkshopFINAL.authcheckdam.pdf.

77. Savage, *Power Wars*, 547.

78. See, for example, Adam Goldman and Benjamin Weiser, "How Civilian Prosecution Gave the U.S. a Key Informant," *New York Times*, January 27, 2017; Mary B. McCord, "Federal Prosecution Is a Viable Option for Enemy Combatants," Lawfare, July 24, 2017, https://www.lawfareblog.com/federal-prosecution-viable-option-enemy-combatants; and Robert Chesney, "Military Commissions Compared to Civilian Prosecution in Federal Court: A Revealing Snapshot," Lawfare, February 26, 2018, https://www.lawfareblog.com/military-commissions-compared-civilian-prosecution-federal-court-revealing-snapshot.

79. Robert Chesney, "The Least Worst Venue," *Foreign Policy*, January 21, 2011.

80. Chesney, "Least Worst Venue."

81. Vladeck, "Exceptional Courts," 175–176.

82. See, for example, Morris D. Davis, "Guantánamo's Charade of Justice," *New York Times*, March 27, 2015.

## CONCLUSION

1. For a complete accounting of the detainees remaining at Guantánamo Bay, see "The Guantánamo Docket," *New York Times*, data last changed May 2, 2018, https://www.nytimes.com/interactive/projects/guantanamo.

2. Dan Eggen and Paul Kane, "Gonzales Hospital Episode Detailed," *Washington Post*, May 16, 2007.

3. The reformed program remained controversial, and critics would note that changes could not cure past illegality. See, for example, Chris Edelson, *Power without Constraint: The Post-9/11 Presidency and National Security* (Madison: University of Wisconsin Press, 2016), 52–59 and 108–126, reviewing surveillance policy under Presidents Bush and Obama, respectively.

4. Charlie Savage and Jonathan Weisman, "NSA Collection of Bulk Data Is Ruled Illegal," *New York Times*, May 7, 2015.

5. Savage and Weisman, "NSA Collection of Bulk Data." See also Jonathan Weisman and Jennifer Steinhauer, "Court Ruling on N.S.A.'s Data Collection Jolts Both Defenders and Reformers," *New York Times*, May 8, 2015.

6. For the full text of Common Article 3, see Associated Press, "Common Article 3 of the Geneva Conventions," accessed June 5, 2020, https://archive.nytimes.com/www.nytimes.com/ref/us/AP-Guantanamo-Geneva-Conventions.html.

7. Barack Obama, "Ensuring Lawful Interrogations," *Federal Register* 74, no. 16 (January 27, 2009): 4891–4896. In the wake of the executive order, however, the Obama administration Department of Justice elected not to pursue prosecutions of CIA interrogators who may have violated the law before the program was eliminated.

8. Matt Apuzzo and James Risen, "Donald Trump Faces Obstacles to Resuming Waterboarding," *New York Times*, November 28, 2016. The statutory text can be found in Pub. L. No. 114–92, 129 Stat. 977–979 (2015).

9. John J. Farmer and Edward F. Neafsey, "Trump and the Law on Torture," Lawfare, March 1, 2018, https://www.lawfareblog.com/trump-and-law-torture.

10. For an excellent, concise overview of the judiciary's response to targeted killing lawsuits, see Robert Chesney, "Judicial Review of Decisions to Kill American Citizens under the AUMF: The Most Important Case You Missed Last Week," Lawfare, June 18, 2018, https://www.lawfareblog.com/judicial-review-decisions-kill-american-citizens-under-aumf-most-important-case-you-missed-last-week.

11. Jack Goldsmith, "Fire When Ready," *Foreign Policy*, March 20, 2012.

12. Goldsmith, "Fire When Ready." Goldsmith further notes that Congress explicitly signed off on the "associated forces" application of the AUMF when it passed the 2012 NDAA. I cover this development in chapter 3. As Goldsmith points out, Congress knew about the executive branch's targeted killing program and its use of the AUMF to justify the Awlaki strike *before* it passed this legislation. This indicates at least some degree of legislative involvement in, and approval of, targeted killing policies.

13. Daniel Klaidman, *Kill or Capture: The War on Terror and the Soul of the Obama Presidency* (New York: Houghton Mifflin Harcourt, 2012), 221–223, and Charlie Savage, *Power Wars: Inside Obama's Post-9/11 Presidency* (New York: Little, Brown, 2015), 275–278. For another example of a similar episode, see Savage, *Power Wars*, 149–152.

14. Goldsmith, "Fire When Ready."

15. The timeline and summary that follows relies on the following three sources, unless otherwise noted: Steve Almasy and Darran Simon, "A Timeline of President Trump's Travel Bans," March 30, 2017, www.cnn.com/2017/02/10/us/trump-travel-ban-timeline/index.html; the "Timeline of the Muslim Ban," ACLU Washington, accessed June 5, 2020, www.aclu-wa.org/pages/timeline-muslim-ban; and "First Amendment—Establishment Clause—Judicial Review of Pretext—*Trump v. Hawaii*," *Harvard Law Review* 132, no. 1 (November 2018): 327–336.

16. Glenn Thrush, "Trump's New Travel Ban Blocks Migrants from Six Nations, Sparing Iraq," *New York Times*, March 6, 2017.

17. Michael D. Shear, "New Order Indefinitely Bars Almost All Travel from Seven Countries," *New York Times*, September 24, 2017.

18. Adam Liptak and Michael D. Shear, "Trump's Travel Ban Is Upheld by Supreme Court," *New York Times*, June 26, 2018. The case is *Trump v. Hawaii*, 585 U.S. __ (2018).

19. See, for example, Andrew Rudalevige, *The New Imperial Presidency: Renewing*

*Presidential Power after Watergate* (Ann Arbor: University of Michigan Press, 2005); Charlie Savage, *Takeover: The Return of the Imperial Presidency and the Subversion of American Democracy* (New York: Back Bay Books, 2007); Frederick A. O. Schwarz Jr. and Aziz Z. Huq, *Unchecked and Unbalanced: Presidential Power in a Time of Terror* (New York: New Press, 2007); Peter M. Shane, *Madison's Nightmare: How Executive Power Threatens American Democracy* (Chicago: University of Chicago Press, 2009); Bruce Ackerman, *The Decline and Fall of the American Republic* (Cambridge, MA: Belknap Press, 2010); and Edelson, *Power without Constraint.*

20. Jeb Barnes, "Bringing the Courts Back In: Interbranch Perspectives on the Role of Courts in American Politics and Policy Making," *Annual Review of Political Science* 10 (2007): 38.

21. The political rise and subsequent election of Donald J. Trump generated an outpouring of work questioning his commitment to the constitutional separation of powers and checks and balances and highlighting his potential authoritarian tendencies. See, for example, Steven Levitsky and Daniel Ziblatt, *How Democracies Die* (New York: Crown, 2018). My claim about the Trump presidency is limited to the policy areas discussed in this book.

# *Cases Cited*

## ARTICLE III COURT CASES


*Aamer v. Obama*, 742 F.3d 1023 (D.C. Cir. 2014)
*Al-Adahi v. Obama*, 613 F.3d 1102 (D.C. Cir. 2010)
*Al-Alwi v. Trump*, No. 17-5067 (D.C. Cir. 2018)
*Al Bahlul v. U.S.*, 767 F.3d 1 (D.C. Cir. 2014)
*Al Bahlul v. U.S.*, 792 F.3d 1 (D.C. Cir. 2015)
*Al Bahlul v. U.S.*, 840 F.3d 757 (D.C. Cir. 2016)
*Al-Bihani v. Obama*, 590 F.3d 866 (D.C. Cir. 2010)
*Al Maqaleh v. Gates*, 604 F. Supp. 2d 205 (D.D.C. 2009)
*Al Maqaleh v. Gates*, 605 F.3d 84 (D.C. Cir. 2010)
*Al-Marri v. Pucciarelli*, 534 F.3d 213 (4th Cir. 2008)
*Al-Marri v. Wright*, No. 06-7427 (4th Cir. 2007)
*Al Odah v. United States*, 321 F.3d 1134 (D.C. Cir. 2003)
*Al Warafi v. Obama*, No. 09-2368 (D.D.C. 2015)
*Bismullah v. Gates*, 501 F.3d 178 (D.C. Cir. 2007)
*Bismullah v. Gates*, 503 F.3d 137 (D.C. Cir. 2007)
*Bismullah v. Gates*, 514 F.3d 1291 (D.C. Cir. 2008)
*Boumediene v. Bush*, 476 F.3d 981 (D.C. Cir. 2007)
*Boumediene v. Bush*, 128 S. Ct. 2229 (2008)
*Coalition of Clergy v. Bush*, 189 F. Supp. 2d 1036 (C.D. Ca. 2002)
*Coalition of Clergy v. Bush*, 310 F.3d 1153 (9th Cir. 2002)
*Doe v. Mattis*, 288 F. Supp. 3d 195 (D.D.C. 2018)
*Doe v. Mattis*, 889 F. 3d 745 (D.C. Cir. 2018)
*Ex parte Quirin*, 317 U.S. 1 (1942)
*Gherebi v. Bush*, 374 F.3d 727 (9th Cir. 2004)
*Hamdan v. Gates*, 565 F. Supp. 2d 130 (D.D.C. 2008)
*Hamdan v. Rumsfeld*, 344 F. Supp. 2d 152 (D.D.C. 2004)
*Hamdan v. Rumsfeld*, 415 F.3d 33 (D.C. Cir. 2005)
*Hamdan v. Rumsfeld*, 548 U.S. 557 (2006)
*Hamdan v. U.S.*, 696 F.3d 1238 (D.C. Cir. 2012)
*Hamdi v. Rumsfeld*, 243 F. Supp. 2d 527 (E.D. Va. 2002)
*Hamdi v. Rumsfeld*, 294 F.3d 598 (4th Cir. 2002)
*Hamdi v. Rumsfeld*, 296 F.3d 278 (4th Cir. 2002)
*Hamdi v. Rumsfeld*, 316 F.3d 450 (4th Cir. 2003)
*Hamdi v. Rumsfeld*, 542 U.S. 507 (2004)
*Hamlily v. Obama*, 616 F. Supp. 2d 63 (D.D.C. 2009)
*In re al-Nashiri*, 791 F3d. 71 (D.C. Cir. 2015)
*In re* Guantánamo *Detainee Cases*, 355 F. Supp. 2d 443 (D.D.C. 2005)

*In re Omar Khadr*, No. 14-1227 (D.C. Cir. 2016)
*Johnson v. Eisentrager*, 339 U.S. 763 (1950)
*Khalid v. Bush*, 355 F. Supp. 2d 311 (D.D.C. 2005)
*Latif v. Obama*, 666 F.3d 746 (D.C. Cir. 2011)
*Padilla v. Bush*, 233 F. Supp. 2d 564 (S.D.N.Y. 2002)
*Padilla v. Hanft*, 423 F.3d 386 (4th Cir. 2005)
*Padilla v. Rumsfeld*, 243 F. Supp. 2d 42 (S.D.N.Y. 2003)
*Padilla v. Rumsfeld*, 352 F.3d 695 (2nd Cir. 2003)
*Rasul v. Bush*, 215 F. Supp. 2d 55 (D.D.C. 2002)
*Rasul v. Bush*, 542 U.S. 466 (2004)
*Rumsfeld v. Padilla*, 542 U.S. 426 (2004)
*Trump v. Hawaii*, 585 U.S. __ (2018)

## MILITARY COMMISSION CASES

*United States of America v. Ali Hamza Ahmad Suliman al Bahlul*, CMCR 09-001 (U.S.C.M.C.R. 2011).
*United States of America v. Omar Ahmed Khadr*, CMCR 07-001 (U.S.C.M.C.R. 2007).
*United States of America v. Omar Ahmed Khadr*, "Order on Jurisdiction." June 4, 2007.
*United States of America v. Salim Ahmed Hamdan*, CMCR 09-002 (U.S.C.M.C.R. 2011)
*United States of America v. Salim Ahmed Hamdan*, "Decision and Order—Motion to Dismiss for Lack of Jurisdiction Corrected Order." June 4, 2007.
*United States of America v. Salim Ahmed Hamdan*, "Ruling on Motion to Dismiss (Ex Post Facto)." July 14, 2008.
*United States of America v. Salim Ahmed Hamdan*, "Ruling on Motion to Suppress Statements Based on Fifth Amendment." July 20, 2008.

# *Bibliography*


Ackerman, Bruce. *The Decline and Fall of the American Republic.* Cambridge, MA: Belknap Press, 2010.

Alexander, Janet Cooper. "Military Commissions: A Place Outside the Law's Reach." *Saint Louis University Law Journal* 56, no. 4 (Summer 2012): 1115–1151.

Almasy, Steve, and Darran Simon. "A Timeline of President Trump's Travel Bans." CNN. March 30, 2017. https://www.cnn.com/2017/02/10/us/trump-travel-ban-timeline/index.html.

Anderson, Kenneth, and Benjamin Wittes. *Speaking the Law: The Obama Administration's Addresses on National Security Law.* Stanford, CA: Hoover Institution Press, 2015.

Anderson, Scott R. "Something Is Rotten with the State of the Military Commissions." Lawfare. March 2, 2018. https://www.lawfareblog.com/something-rotten-state-military-commissions.

Apuzzo, Matt. "Covert Inquiry by F.B.I. Rattles 9/11 Tribunals." *New York Times*, April 18, 2014.

———. "Guantánamo Conviction of Australian Is Overturned." *New York Times*, February 18, 2015.

Apuzzo, Matt, and James Risen. "Donald Trump Faces Obstacles to Resuming Waterboarding." *New York Times*, November 28, 2016.

Ashcroft, John. *Never Again: Securing America and Restoring Justice.* New York: Center Street, Hachette Book Group USA, 2006.

Associated Press. "9/11 Defendants Charged at Guantánamo with Terrorism and Murder." *New York Times*, May 31, 2011.

———. "Australian Is Charged in Terror Case." *New York Times*, March 2, 2007.

———. "Common Article 3 of the Geneva Conventions." Accessed June 5, 2020. https://archive.nytimes.com/www.nytimes.com/ref/us/AP-Guantanamo-Geneva-Conventions.html.

———. "New Charges Filed against Suspect in U.S.S. Cole Bombing." *New York Times*, April 20, 2011.

———. "Supreme Court Is Asked to Block Terror Tribunals." *New York Times*, August 9, 2005.

"At-a-glance: Guantanamo Bay Britons." BBC News. March 9, 2004. http://news.bbc.co.uk/2/hi/uk_news/3089395.stm.

Austen, Ian. "Sole Canadian Held at Guantánamo Bay Is Repatriated." *New York Times*, September 29, 2012.

Baker, Peter. "Trump Declares Suspect 'Should Get Death Penalty.'" *New York Times*, November 1, 2017.

Baker, Peter, and David M. Herszenhorn. "Obama Planning to Keep Tribunals for Detainees." *New York Times*, May 15, 2009.

Baker, Peter, and Charlie Savage. "Terror Attempt May Hinder Plans to Close Guantánamo." *New York Times*, December 31, 2009.

Barnes, Jeb. "Bringing the Courts Back In: Interbranch Perspectives on the Role of Courts in American Politics and Policy Making." *Annual Review of Political Science* 10 (2007): 25–43.

Barnes, Jeb, and Thomas F. Burke. *How Policy Shapes Politics: Rights, Courts, Litigation, and the Struggle over Injury Compensation*. New York: Oxford University Press, 2015.

Barnes, Jeb, and Mark C. Miller. "Putting the Pieces Together: American Lawmaking from an Interbranch Perspective." In *Making Policy, Making Law: An Interbranch Perspective*, edited by Mark C. Miller and Jeb Barnes, 3–12. Washington, DC: Georgetown University Press, 2004.

Barron, David J., and Martin S. Lederman. "The Commander in Chief at the Lowest Ebb—A Constitutional History." *Harvard Law Review* 121, no. 4 (February 2008): 941–1113.

———. "The Commander in Chief at the Lowest Ebb—Framing the Problem, Doctrine, and Original Understanding." *Harvard Law Review* 121, no. 3 (January 2008): 689–804.

Becker, Jo, and Scott Shane. "Secret 'Kill List' Proves a Test of Obama's Principles and Will." *New York Times*, May 29, 2012.

Bellia, Patricia L. "The Story of the *Steel Seizure* Case." In *Presidential Power Stories*, edited by Christopher H. Schroeder and Curtis A. Bradley, 233–285. New York: Thomson West Foundation Press, 2009.

Bennett, Wells. "Oral Argument Recap in Hamdan." Lawfare. May 4, 2012. https://www.lawfareblog.com/oral-argument-recap-hamdan.

Bennett, Wells, Larkin Reynolds, and Lawfare Staff. "Hamdan Oral Argument Preview." Lawfare. May 2, 2012. https://www.lawfareblog.com/hamdan-oral-argument-preview.

Bennett, Wells, and Benjamin Wittes. "Breaking News: D.C. Circuit Grants En Banc Rehearing in Al-Bahlul." Lawfare. April 23, 2013. https://www.lawfareblog.com/breaking-news-dc circuit-grants-en-banc-rehearing-al-bahlul.

Bickers, John M. "Too Little, Too Late? Why President Obama's Well-Intentioned Reforms of the Military Commissions May Not Be Enough to Save Them." *Whittier Law Review* 31, no. 3 (Spring 2010): 381–420.

Bogart, W. A. *Consequences: The Impact of Law and Its Complexity*. Toronto: University of Toronto Press, 2002.

Bonner, Raymond. "Marine Defends Guantánamo Detainee, and Surprises Australians." *New York Times*, March 28, 2004.

Bovarnick, Jeff A. "Detainee Review Boards in Afghanistan." *Army Lawyer*, Department of the Army Pamphlet 27-50-445 (June 2010): 9–49.

Bowley, Graham. "U.S. Puts Transfer of Detainees to Afghans on Hold." *New York Times*, September 9, 2012.

Bradley, Curtis A. "The Story of *Ex parte Milligan*: Military Trials, Enemy Combatants, and Congressional Authorization." In *Presidential Power Stories*, edited by

Christopher H. Schroeder and Curtis A. Bradley, 93–132. New York: Thomson West Foundation Press, 2009.

Bradley, Curtis A. and Jack L. Goldsmith. "Congressional Authorization and the War on Terrorism." *Harvard Law Review* 118, no. 7 (May 2005): 2047–2133.

Bravin, Jess. *The Terror Courts: Rough Justice at Guantanamo Bay*. New Haven, CT: Yale University Press, 2013.

Brinkley, Joel, and Eric Lichtblau. "U.S. Releases Saudi-American It Had Captured in Afghanistan." *New York Times*, October 12, 2004.

"Briton Condemns Proposed U.S. Trials." *New York Times*, June 26, 2004.

Burbank, Stephen B., and Sean Farhang. *Rights and Retrenchment: The Counterrevolution against Federal Litigation*. New York: Cambridge University Press, 2017.

Burke, Thomas F. *Lawyers, Lawsuits, and Legal Rights: The Battle over Litigation in American Society*. Berkeley: University of California Press, 2002.

Burke, Thomas F., and Jeb Barnes, eds. *Varieties of Legal Order: The Politics of Adversarial and Bureaucratic Legalism*. New York: Routledge, 2018.

Bush, George W. *Decision Points*. New York: Crown Publishers, 2010.

———. "Detention, Treatment, and Trial of Certain Non-Citizens in the War against Terrorism." *Federal Register* 66, no. 222 (November 16, 2001): 57831–57836. http://georgewbush-whitehouse.archives.gov/news/releases/2001/11/20011113-27.html.

———. "Humane Treatment of Taliban and al Qaeda Detainees." February 7, 2002. http://www.pegc.us/archive/White_House/bush_memo_20020207_ed.pdf.

———. "President Discusses Creation of Military Commissions to Try Suspected Terrorists." September 6, 2006. http://georgewbush whitehouse.archives.gov/news/releases/2006/09/20060906–3.html.

Cheney, Dick (with Liz Cheney). *In My Time: A Personal and Political Memoir*. New York: Threshold Editions, 2011.

Chesney, Robert. "The Expeditionary Targeting Force in Iraq: Putting the Short-Term Military Detention Model to the Test." Lawfare. March 2, 2016. https://www.lawfareblog.com/expeditionary-targeting-force-iraq-putting-short-term military-detention-model-test.

———. "Judicial Review of Decisions to Kill American Citizens under the AUMF: The Most Important Case You Missed Last Week." Lawfare. June 18, 2018. https://www.lawfareblog.com/judicial-review-decisions-kill-american-citizens-under aumf-most-important-case-you-missed-last-week.

———. "The Least Worst Venue." *Foreign Policy*, January 21, 2011. https://foreignpolicy.com/2011/01/21/the-least-worst-venue/.

———. "Military Commissions Compared to Civilian Prosecution in Federal Court: A Revealing Snapshot." Lawfare. February 26, 2018. https://www.lawfareblog.com/mili tarycommissions-compared-civilian-prosecution-federal-court-revealing-snapshot.

———. "Perhaps Guantánamo Won't Get New Detainees After All? An Update on Efforts to Capture Islamic State Leaders." Lawfare. June 26, 2017. https://www.lawfareblog.com/perhaps-guantanamo-wont-get-new-detainees-after-allupdate-efforts-capture-islamic-state-leaders.

Chong, Jane. "D.C. Circuit Upholds Security Policies in *Hatim v. Obama*." Lawfare. August 1, 2014. https://www.lawfareblog.com/dc-circuit-upholds-security-policies-hatim-v-obama.

"Close Guantánamo." American Civil Liberties Union. https://www.aclu.org/feature/close guantanamo.

Cloud, David S. "Terror Suspect Upsets Plan to Resume Trials in Cuba." *New York Times*, January 12, 2006.

Cloud, David S., and Sheryl Gay Stolberg. "White House Bill Proposes System to Try Detainees." *New York Times*, July 26, 2006.

Cooper, Helene. "Five Guantánamo Prisoners Are Released to Kazakhstan." *New York Times*, December 30, 2014.

Cooper, Helene, and William Glaberson. "At White House, Renewed Debate on Guantánamo." *New York Times*, June 23, 2007.

Cronogue, Graham. "A New AUMF: Defining Combatants in the War on Terror." *Duke Journal of Comparative and International Law* 22, no. 3 (April 2012): 377–406.

Davis, Morris D. "Guantánamo's Charade of Justice." *New York Times*, March 27, 2015.

"Declaration of Michael H. Mobbs, Special Advisor to the Under Secretary of Defense for Policy." *Frontline*. October 16, 2003. https://www.pbs.org/wgbh/pages/frontline/shows/sleeper/tools/mobbshamdi.html.

Denbeaux, Mark, Joshua Denbeaux, David Gratz, John Gregorek, Matthew Darby, Shana Edwards, Daniel Mann, Megan Sassaman, and Helen Skinner. "No-Hearing Hearings: An Analysis of the Proceedings of the Combatant Status Review Tribunals at Guantánamo." *Seton Hall Law Review* 41, no. 4 (2011): 1231–1268.

Denniston, Lyle. "Are the Guantanamo War Crimes Courts Now Doomed?" *Constitution Daily*, July 22, 2014.

Department of Defense. "The Manual for Military Commissions." January 18, 2007. https://www.mc.mil/Portals/0/manual_for_military_commissions_2007_signed.pdf.

———. "Military Commission Instructions." http://www.mc.mil/LEGALRESOURCES/MilitaryCommissionsDocuments/HistoricalDocuments.aspx.

———. "Military Commission Order No. 1." March 21, 2002. http://www.mc.mil/Portals/0/milcomord1.pdf.

———. "Military Commission Order No. 1" (revised). August 31, 2005. https://www.mc.mil/Portals/0/milcomord1%20(as%20amended).pdf.

———. "Military Commission Order No. 2." June 21, 2003. http://www.mc.mil/Portals/0/milcomord2.pdf.

———. "Military Commission Order No. 5." March 15, 2004. http://www.mc.mil/Portals/0/milcomord5.pdf.

Department of Justice. "Jose Padilla Re-Sentenced to 21 Years in Prison for Conspiracy to Murder Individuals Overseas, Providing Material Support to Terrorists." Press release. Updated October 7, 2014. https://www.justice.gov/opa/pr/jose-padilla-re-sentenced-21-years-prison-conspiracy-murder-individuals-overseas-providing.

Department of State. Memo to Senate Foreign Relations Committee Chairman Bob

Corker. August 2, 2017. https://assets.documentcloud.org/documents/3911844/8-2-17-Corker Response.pdf.

Dilanian, Ken. "U.S. Has Slashed Its Terrorism Interrogation Role." *Los Angeles Times*, April 10, 2011.

Diller, Paul A. "When Congress Passes an Intentionally Unconstitutional Law: The Military Commissions Act of 2006." *SMU Law Review* 61, no. 2 (Spring 2008): 281–336.

Donohue, Laura K. *The Cost of Counterterrorism: Power, Politics, and Liberty*. New York: Cambridge University Press, 2008.

Dorning, Mike. "U.S. Releases Details in Case against Padilla." *Chicago Tribune*, June 2, 2004.

Dratel, Joshua L. "How I Learned to Stop Worrying and Love the Military Commissions." *Seton Hall Law Review* 41, no. 4 (Fall 2011): 1339–1360.

Dycus, Stephen, William C. Banks, and Peter Raven-Hansen, eds. *Counterterrorism Law*. 2nd ed. New York: Wolters Kluwer Law & Business, 2012.

Edelson, Chris. *Emergency Presidential Power: From the Drafting of the Constitution to the War on Terror*. Madison: University of Wisconsin Press, 2013.

———. *Power without Constraint: The Post-9/11 Presidency and National Security*. Madison: University of Wisconsin Press, 2016.

Eggen, Dan, and Paul Kane. "Gonzales Hospital Episode Detailed." *Washington Post*, May 16, 2007.

Ely, Alex. "PRB Recommends Repatriation for One Saudi Detainee, Continued Detention for Another." Lawfare. October 21, 2014. https://www.lawfareblog.com/prb-recommends-repatriation one-saudi-detainee-continued-detention-another.

Epp, Charles R. *The Rights Revolution: Lawyers, Activists, and Supreme Courts in Comparative Perspective*. Chicago: University of Chicago Press.

Farmer, John J., and Edward F. Neafsey. "Trump and the Law on Torture." Lawfare. March 1, 2018. https://www.lawfareblog.com/trump-and-law-torture.

Feeley, Malcolm M., and Edward L. Rubin. *Judicial Policy Making and the Modern State: How the Courts Reformed America's Prisons*. New York: Cambridge University Press, 1998.

Fidell, Eugene R. "Charm Offensive in Lilliput: Military Commissions 3.1." *Saint Louis University Law Journal* 56, no. 4 (Summer 2012): 1177–1201.

"Final Report: Guantanamo Review Task Force." January 22, 2010. http://lostdocs.freegovinfo.info/2010/10/final-report-guantanamo-review-task-force-january-22-2010/.

Finn, Peter. "Guantanamo Detainee Majid Khan Pleads Guilty, Promises Cooperation." *Washington Post*, February 29, 2012.

"First Amendment—Establishment Clause—Judicial Review of Pretext—*Trump v. Hawaii*." *Harvard Law Review* 132, no. 1 (November 2018): 327–336.

"First Steps at Guantánamo." *New York Times*, January 22, 2009.

Fisher, Louis. *Constitutional Dialogues: Interpretation as Political Process*. Princeton, NJ: Princeton University Press, 1988.

———. *Military Tribunals and Presidential Power: American Revolution to the War on Terrorism*. Lawrence: University Press of Kansas, 2005.

Frakt, David J. R. "Mohammed Jawad and the Military Commissions of Guantánamo." *Duke Law Journal* 60, no. 6 (March 2011): 1367–1412.

———. "The Practice of Criminal Law in the Guantánamo Military Commissions." *Air Force Law Review* 67, no. 35 (2011): 35–88.

Gall, Carlotta. "U.S. Returns 18 Guantánamo Detainees to Afghanistan." *New York Times*, March 24, 2003.

Garcia, Michael John. "Guantanamo Detention Center: Legislative Activity in the 111th Congress." *Congressional Research Service*, January 13, 2011.

Gates, Robert M. *Duty: Memoirs of a Secretary at War*. New York: Alfred A. Knopf, 2014.

Gellman, Barton, and Jo Becker. "'A Different Understanding with the President.'" *Washington Post*, June 24, 2007.

Gerring, John. "Mere Description." *British Journal of Political Science* 42, no. 4 (October 2012): 721–746.

Gerstein, Josh. "GOP Revives 'Soft on Terror' Charge." *Politico*, January 30, 2010. https://www.politico.com/story/2010/01/gop-revives-soft-on-terror-charge-032250.

———. "Obama Signs Military Commissions Reforms." *Politico*, October 28, 2009. https://www.politico.com/blogs/under-the-radar/2009/10/obama-signs-military-commissions-reforms-022416.

Glaberson, William. "Australian to Serve 9 Months in Terror Case." *New York Times*, March 31, 2007.

———. "Bin Laden Driver Sentenced to a Short Term." *New York Times*, August 8, 2008.

———. "Claim of Pressure for Closed Guantánamo Trials." *New York Times*, October 20, 2007.

———. "Despite Ruling, Detainee Cases Facing Delays." *New York Times*, October 4, 2008.

———. "Detainee Convicted on Terrorism Charges." *New York Times*, November 3, 2008.

———. "Detainee Lawyers to Use Ruling for New Attacks." *New York Times*, June 14, 2008.

———. "Detainee's Lawyers Seek Removal of Prosecutor." *New York Times*, March 26, 2007.

———. "Detention Camp Remains, but Not Its Rationale." *New York Times*, June 13, 2008.

———. "Ex-Prosecutor Tells of Push by Pentagon on Detainees." *New York Times*, April 29, 2008.

———. "Former Prosecutor to Testify for Detainee." *New York Times*, February 28, 2008.

———. "Government Might Allow U.S. Trial for Detainee." *New York Times*, July 24, 2009.

———. "Hurdles Seen as Capital Charges Are Filed in 9/11 Case." *New York Times*, February 12, 2008.

———. "In Shift, Justices Agree to Review Detainees' Case." *New York Times*, June 30, 2007.

———. "Judge Declares Five Detainees Held Illegally." *New York Times*, November 20, 2008.

———. "Judge Orders 17 Detainees at Guantánamo Freed." *New York Times*, October 8, 2008.

———. "Judge's Guantánamo Ruling Bodes Ill for System." *New York Times*, May 11, 2008.

———. "Military Judges Dismiss Charges for 2 Detainees." *New York Times*, June 5, 2007.

———. "New Roadblocks Delay Tribunals at Guantánamo." *New York Times*, April 10, 2008.

———. "Panel Convicts bin Laden Driver in Split Verdict." *New York Times*, August 7, 2008.

———. "Unlikely Adversary Arises to Criticize Detainee Hearings." *New York Times*, July 23, 2007.

———. "U.S. Is Set to Release 3 Detainees from Base." *New York Times*, December 16, 2008.

———. "U.S. Judge Challenges Evidence on a Detainee." *New York Times*, July 23, 2009.

———. "U.S. Mulls New Status Hearings for Guantánamo Inmates." *New York Times*, October 15, 2007.

———. "U.S. Won't Label Terror Suspects as 'Combatants.'" *New York Times*, March 14, 2009.

Glaberson, William, and Margot Williams. "Next President Will Face Test on Detainees." *New York Times*, November 3, 2008.

Glaberson, William, and Robert F. Worth. "Yemen Dispute Slows Closing of Guantanamo." *New York Times*, April 24, 2009.

Glazier, David. "The Development of an Exceptional Court: The History of the American Military Commission." In *Guantánamo and Beyond: Exceptional Courts and Military Commissions in Comparative Perspective*, edited by Fionnuala Ní Aoláin and Oren Gross, 37–54. New York: Cambridge University Press, 2013.

———. "The Misuse of History: Conspiracy and the Guantánamo Military Commissions." *Baylor Law Review* 66, no. 2 (Spring 2014): 295–361.

———. "A Self-Inflicted Wound: A Half-Dozen Years of Turmoil over the Guantánamo Military Commissions." *Lewis & Clark Law Review* 12, no. 1 (Spring 2008): 131–204.

Glendon, Mary Ann. *Rights Talk: The Impoverishment of Political Discourse*. New York: Free Press, 1991.

Golden, Tim. "Administration Officials Split over Stalled Military Tribunals." *New York Times*, October 25, 2004.

———. "After Terror, a Secret Rewriting of Military Law." *New York Times*, October 24, 2004.

———. "Boycott Threat Roils Guantánamo Hearing." *New York Times*, April 6, 2006.

———. "Foiling U.S. Plan, Prison Expands in Afghanistan." *New York Times*, January 7, 2008.

Golden, Tim, and Eric Schmitt. "A Growing Afghan Prison Rivals Bleak Guantánamo." *New York Times*, February 26, 2006.

Goldman, Adam, and Eric Schmitt. "Benghazi Attacks Suspect Is Captured in Libya by U.S. Commandos." *New York Times*, October 30, 2017.

Goldman, Adam, and Benjamin Weiser. "How Civilian Prosecution Gave the U.S. a Key Informant." *New York Times*, January 27, 2017.

Goldsmith, Jack. "Bahlul: A Longer View." Lawfare. July 15, 2014. https://www.lawfareblog.com/bahlul-longer-view.

———. "Fire When Ready." *Foreign Policy*, March 20, 2012. https://foreignpolicy.com/2012/03/20/fire-when-ready/.

———. *Power and Constraint: The Accountable Presidency after 9/11*. New York: W. W. Norton, 2012.

———. "The Shell Game on Detainees and Interrogation." *Washington Post*, May 31, 2009.

———. *The Terror Presidency: Law and Judgment inside the Bush Administration*. New York: W. W. Norton, 2007.

Graber, Mark A. "The Nonmajoritarian Difficulty: Legislative Deference to the Judiciary." *Studies in American Political Development* 7, no. 1 (Spring 1993): 35–73.

Greenberger, Michael. "You Ain't Seen Nothin' Yet: The Inevitable Post-*Hamdan* Conflict between the Supreme Court and the Political Branches." *Maryland Law Review* 66, no. 3 (2007): 805–834.

Greenhouse, Linda. "Detainee Case Hits on Limits of Presidency." *New York Times*, January 10, 2006.

———. "Detainee Case Will Pose Delicate Question for Court." *New York Times*, March 27, 2006.

———. "Gitmo Fatigue at the Supreme Court." *New York Times*, April 6, 2011.

———. "Goodbye to Gitmo." *New York Times*, May 16, 2012.

———. "Justices, 5–3, Broadly Reject Bush Plan to Try Detainees." *New York Times*, June 30, 2006.

———. "Justices Let U.S. Transfer Padilla to Civilian Custody." *New York Times*, January 5, 2006.

———. "Lessons Maybe Learned." *New York Times*, September 7, 2011.

———. "A 2nd Case on Detainees Complicates Deliberations." *New York Times*, February 6, 2008.

———. "Supreme Court Denies Guantánamo Appeal." *New York Times*, April 3, 2007.

"The Guantánamo Docket." *New York Times*. Data last changed May 2, 2018. https://www.nytimes.com/interactive/projects/guantanamo.

Hirschl, Ran. *Towards Juristocracy: The Origins and Consequences of the New Constitutionalism*. Cambridge, MA: Harvard University Press, 2004.

Hirsh, Michael. "Slow Dance: Obama's Romance with the CIA." *Atlantic*, May 13, 2011.

Horowitz, Bernard, and Harvey Rishikof. "Enemy Combatant Detainees." In *Congress and the Politics of National Security*, edited by David P. Auerswald and Colton C. Campbell, 167–188. Cambridge: Cambridge University Press, 2012.

Hulse, Carl, Kate Zernike, and Sheryl Gay Stolberg. "How 3 G.O.P. Veterans Stalled Bush Detainee Bill." *New York Times*, September 17, 2006.

Huq, Aziz Z. "What Good Is Habeas?" *Constitutional Commentary* 26, no. 3 (Summer 2010): 385–432.

Ingber, Rebecca. "Interpretation Catalysts and Executive Branch Legal Decisionmaking." *Yale Journal of International Law* 38, no. 2 (Summer 2013): 359–421.

Issacharoff, Samuel, and Richard H. Pildes. "Between Civil Libertarianism and Executive Unilateralism: An Institutional Process Approach to Rights during Wartime." *Theoretical Inquiries in Law* 5, no. 1 (February 2004): 1–46.

Jehl, Douglas. "Pentagon Seeks to Transfer More Detainees from Base in Cuba." *New York Times*, March 11, 2005.

Johnsen, Dawn E. "The Story of *Hamdan v. Rumsfeld*: Trying Enemy Combatants by Military Commission." In *Presidential Power Stories*, edited by Christopher H. Schroeder and Curtis A. Bradley, 447–485. New York: Thomson West Foundation Press, 2009.

Johnston, David. "Compromise Is Reached on Detainees." *New York Times*, October 8, 2009.

———. "In Senate, Debate on Detainee Legal Rights." *New York Times*, July 7, 2009.

Johnston, David, and Neil A. Lewis. "U.S. Will Give Qaeda Suspect a Civilian Trial." *New York Times*, February 27, 2009.

Kagan, Robert A. *Adversarial Legalism: The American Way of Law*. Cambridge, MA: Harvard University Press, 2001.

———. "American Courts and the Policy Dialogue: The Role of Adversarial Legalism." In *Making Policy, Making Law: An Interbranch Perspective*, edited by Mark C. Miller and Jeb Barnes, 13–34. Washington, DC: Georgetown University Press, 2004.

———. "A Consequential Court: The U.S. Supreme Court in the Twentieth Century." In *Consequential Courts: Judicial Roles in Global Perspective*, edited by Diana Kapiszewski, Gordon Silverstein, and Robert A. Kagan, 199–232. New York: Cambridge University Press, 2013.

Kassem, Ramzi. "A View from Gitmo." *New York Times*, June 7, 2014.

Katyal, Neal Kumar. "*Hamdan v. Rumsfeld:* The Legal Academy Goes to Practice." *Harvard Law Review* 120, no. 1 (November 2006): 65–124.

———. "Internal Separation of Powers: Checking Today's Most Dangerous Branch from Within." *Yale Law Journal* 115, no. 9 (July 2006): 2314–2349.

Katyal, Neal K., and Laurence H. Tribe. "Waging War, Deciding Guilt: Trying the Military Tribunals." *Yale Law Journal* 111, no. 6 (April 2002): 1259–1310.

Keck, Thomas M. *Judicial Politics in Polarized Times*. Chicago: University of Chicago Press, 2014.

Klaidman, Daniel. *Kill or Capture: The War on Terror and the Soul of the Obama Presidency*. New York: Houghton Mifflin Harcourt, 2012.

Lake, Eli. "Somalia's Prisons: The War on Terror's Latest Front." *Daily Beast*, June 27, 2012.

Lee, Chisun. "Their Own Private Guantánamo." *New York Times*, July 22, 2009.

Levitsky, Steven, and Daniel Ziblatt. *How Democracies Die*. New York: Crown, 2018.
Lewis, Neil A. "Detainees from the Afghan War Remain in a Legal Limbo in Cuba." *New York Times*, April 24, 2003.
———. "Detainee Trials to Resume Soon, Rumsfeld Says." *New York Times*, July 18, 2005.
———. "First War-Crimes Case Opens at Guantánamo Base." *New York Times*, August 25, 2004.
———. "Guantánamo Detainees Gain in Ruling." *New York Times*, October 27, 2005.
———. "Guantánamo Detainees Make Their Case." *New York Times*, March 24, 2005.
———. "Hunger Strike by Detainees Goes to Court." *New York Times*, September 22, 2005.
———. "Lawyer Says Detainees Face Unfair System." *New York Times*, January 22, 2004.
———. "Officials Plan to Move Quickly for Terrorism Trials in Spring." *New York Times*, September 30, 2006.
———. "Officials See Qaeda Trials Using New Law in 2007." *New York Times*, November 3, 2006.
———. "Rules on Tribunal Require Unanimity on Death Penalty." *New York Times*, December 28, 2001.
———. "Suit Contests Military Trials of Detainees at Cuba Base." *New York Times*, April 8, 2004.
———. "Terror Tribunal Defendant Demands to Be Own Lawyer." *New York Times*, August 27, 2004.
———. "Try Detainees or Free Them, 3 Senators Urge." *New York Times*, December 13, 2003.
———. "Two Prosecutors Faulted Trials for Detainees." *New York Times*, August 1, 2005.
———. "U.S. Alters Rules for War Crime Trials." *New York Times*, September 1, 2005.
———. "U.S. Charges Two at Guantánamo with Conspiracy." *New York Times*, February 25, 2004.
———. "U.S. Is Readying Review for Detainees in Cuba." *New York Times*, July 17, 2004.
Lewis, Neil A., and Kate Zernike. "Measures Seek to Restrict Detainees' Access to Courts." *New York Times*, September 21, 2006.
Liptak, Adam. "Early Test of Obama View on Power over Detainees." *New York Times*, January 3, 2009.
———. "The 'Fill in the Blanks' Court Game of Indefinite Detention." *New York Times*, December 12, 2011.
———. "Justices Decline to Hear Appeal from Chinese Detainees." *New York Times*, April 18, 2011.
———. "Tribunal System, Newly Righted, Stumbles Again." *New York Times*, June 5, 2007.
Liptak, Adam, and Michael D. Shear. "Trump's Travel Ban Is Upheld by Supreme Court." *New York Times*, June 26, 2018.
Madison, James. "Helvidius Number IV." In *The Pacificus-Helvidius Debates of 1793–1794*, edited by Morton J. Frisch, 84–89. Indianapolis: Liberty Fund, 2007.

Margulies, Joseph. *Guantánamo and the Abuse of Presidential Power*. New York: Simon & Schuster, 2006.
Mazzetti, Mark. "C.I.A. Secretly Held Qaeda Suspect, Officials Say." *New York Times*, March 15, 2008.
Mazzetti, Mark, and William Glaberson. "Obama Issues Directive to Shut Down Guantánamo." *New York Times*, January 22, 2009.
Mazzetti, Mark, and Kate Zernike. "White House Says Terror Detainees Hold Basic Rights." *New York Times*, July 12, 2006.
McCord, Mary B. "Federal Prosecution Is a Viable Option for Enemy Combatants." Lawfare. July 24, 2017. https://www.lawfareblog.com/federal-prosecution-viable-option-enemy combatants.
Mintz, John. "6 Could Be Facing Military Tribunals; U.S. Says Detainees Tied to Al Qaeda." *Washington Post*, July 4, 2003.
Morrison, Trevor W. "Constitutional Alarmism." *Harvard Law Review* 124, no. 7 (May 2011): 1688–1749.
———. "The Story of *United States v. United States District Court (Keith)*: The Surveillance Power." In *Presidential Power Stories*, edited by Christopher H. Schroeder and Curtis A. Bradley, 287–325. New York: Thomson West Foundation Press, 2009.
Myers, Richard B. *Eyes on the Horizon: Serving on the Front Lines of National Security*. New York: Simon & Schuster, 2009.
Myers, Steven Lee. "Bush Decides to Keep Guantánamo Open." *New York Times*, October 21, 2008.
Myers, Steven Lee, and James Dao. "Marines Set Up Pens for Wave of Prisoners." *New York Times*, December 15, 2001.
Neustadt, Richard E. *Presidential Power and the Modern Presidents: The Politics of Leadership from Roosevelt to Reagan*. New York: Free Press, 1990.
Newman, Maria. "Reviews of Guantánamo Detainees to Begin Soon, Navy Says." *New York Times*, June 23, 2004.
Nordland, Rod. "Karzai Orders Afghan Forces to Take Control of American-Built Prison." *New York Times*, November 19, 2012.
Nordland, Rod, Michael R. Gordon, and Alissa J. Rubin. "Karzai Has Nothing but Praise for U.S. upon Bagram Prison Transfer." *New York Times*, March 25, 2013.
Nordland, Rod, and Charlie Savage. "U.S. Again Delays Transfer of Bagram Prison to Afghan Forces." *New York Times*, March 9, 2013.
Obama, Barack. "Ensuring Lawful Interrogations." *Federal Register* 74, no. 16 (January 27, 2009): 4891–4896.
———. "Presidential Policy Directive—Requirements of the National Defense Authorization Act." The White House: Office of the Press Secretary, February 28, 2012. https://obamawhitehouse.archives.gov/the-press-office/2012/02/28/presidential-policy directive-requirements-national-defense-authorizatio.
———. "Remarks by the President at the National Defense University." May 23, 2013. https://www.whitehouse.gov/the-press-office/2013/05/23/remarks-president-national defense-university.

———. "Remarks by the President on National Security." May 21, 2009. https://obamawhitehouse.archives.gov/the-press-office/remarks-president-national security-5-21-09.

———. "Statement by the President on H.R. 1540." The White House: Office of the Press Secretary, December 31, 2011. https://obamawhitehouse.archives.gov/the-press-office/2011/12/31/statement-president-hr-1540.

Office of the Director of National Intelligence (DNI). "Summary of the Reengagement of Detainees Formerly Held at Guantanamo Bay, Cuba," November 26, 2019. https://www.dni.gov/index.php/newsroom/reports-publications/item/2079-summary-of the-reengagement-of-detainees-formerly-held-at-guantanamo-bay-cuba.

O'Hagan, Maureen. "Yemeni's Lawsuit Contends Special Tribunal Violates Constitution." *Seattle Times*, May 19, 2004.

Oyez. "2003–2004 Term." Accessed May 18, 2020. https://www.oyez.org/cases/2003.

Panetta, Leon. *Worthy Fights: A Memoir of Leadership in War and Peace*. New York: Penguin Books, 2014.

Pearlman, Adam R. "Meaningful Review and Process Due: How Guantanamo Detention Is Changing the Battlefield." *Harvard National Security Journal* 6, no. 1 (February 2015): 255–298.

Philbin, Patrick F. "Legality of the Use of Military Commissions to Try Terrorists." November 6, 2001. https://nsarchive2.gwu.edu/torturingdemocracy/documents/20011106.pdf.

Philbin, Patrick F., and John C. Yoo. "Memorandum for William J. Haynes, II, General Counsel, Department of Defense." December 28, 2001. http://nsarchive.gwu.edu/torturingdemocracy/documents/20011228.pdf.

Philipps, Dave. "Many Say He's the Least Qualified Lawyer Ever to Lead a Guantánamo Case. He Agrees." *New York Times*, February 5, 2018.

Preston, Julia. "Judge Orders U.S. to Supply Prisoner Names." *New York Times*, January 24, 2006.

Priest, Dana, Devlin Barrett, and Matt Zapotosky. "Case of Suspected American ISIS Fighter Captured in Syria Vexes U.S." *Washington Post*, October 29, 2017.

Purdy, Matthew. "Bush's New Rules to Fight Terror Transform the Legal Landscape." *New York Times*, November 25, 2001.

"Reneging on Justice at Guantánamo." *New York Times*, November 19, 2011.

Reuters. "Bush Speaks of Closing Guantánamo Prison." *New York Times*, May 8, 2006.

Reynolds, Larkin, The Harvard Law School National Security Research Committee, Benjamin Wittes, and Robert M. Chesney. "The Emerging Law of Detention 2.0: The Guantánamo Habeas Cases as Lawmaking." April 2012. https://www.brookings.edu/research/the-emerging-law-of-detention-2-0-the-guantanamo-habeas-cases-as-lawmaking/.

Rice, Condoleezza. *No Higher Honor: A Memoir of My Years in Washington*. New York: Crown Publishers, 2011.

Risen, James. "35 Guantánamo Detainees Are Given to Pakistan." *New York Times*, September 19, 2004.

"Room for Debate: Prosecuting Terrorists in Federal Court." *New York Times*, November 18, 2010.

Rosenberg, Carol. "Guantánamo Parole Board Clears Another 'Forever Prisoner.'" *Miami Herald*, March 18, 2015.

———. "Judge Cancels 9/11 Pretrial Hearing, Considers It Productive." *Miami Herald*, October 15, 2014.

———. "Pentagon Scraps Judges' Guantánamo Move Order; 9/11 Case Unfrozen." *Miami Herald*, February 27, 2015.

———. "Pentagon Throws Out Foot Soldier's Guantánamo War Court Conviction." *Miami Herald*, January 9, 2015.

———. "Something's Wrong with War Court Prosecutor's Charges in Southeast Asia Terror Plots." *Miami Herald*, December 20, 2017.

Rosenberg, Gerald N. *The Hollow Hope: Can Courts Bring About Social Change?* Chicago: University of Chicago Press, 1991.

Rosenberg, Matthew. "With Release of Prisoners, Afghan Leader Again Defies U.S. Wishes." *New York Times*, January 9, 2014.

Rozenshtein, Alan. "An Explainer on *Hamdan II*, *Al-Bahlul*, and the Jurisdiction of the Guantánamo Military Commissions." Lawfare. April 26, 2013. https://www.lawfareblog.com/explainer-hamdan-ii-al-bahlul-and-jurisdiction guant%C3%A1namo-military-commissions.

Rubin, Alissa J. "U.S. Readies New Facility for Afghan Detainees." *New York Times*, November 16, 2009.

Rubin, Alissa J., and Sangar Rahimi. "Bagram Detainees Named by U.S." *New York Times*, January 16, 2010.

Rudalevige, Andrew. *The New Imperial Presidency: Renewing Presidential Power after Watergate*. Ann Arbor: University of Michigan Press, 2005.

Ruiz, Rebecca R., Adam Goldman, and Matt Apuzzo. "Terror Suspect Brought to U.S. for Trial, Breaking from Trump Rhetoric." *New York Times*, July 21, 2017.

Rumsfeld, Donald. *Known and Unknown: A Memoir*. New York: Sentinel, 2011.

Ryan, Missy. "Qatari Man, Once Held As Enemy Combatant, Is Quietly Released from Supermax Prison." *Washington Post*, January 20, 2015.

———. "Senior Official Resigns after Flap over Relocating Judges to Guantanamo." *Washington Post*, March 18, 2015.

Saad, Aisha I., and Zoe A. Y. Weinberg. "Remember Guantánamo?" *New York Times*, March 15, 2018.

Sales, Nathan Alexander. "Self-Restraint and National Security." *Journal of National Security Law & Policy* 6, no. 1 (2012): 227–290.

Sanger, David E., and Scott Shane. "Court's Ruling Is Likely to Force Negotiations over Presidential Power." *New York Times*, June 30, 2006.

Savage, Charlie. "5 Guantánamo Inmates Are Sent to Eastern Europe." *New York Times*, November 20, 2014.

———. "9 Guantánamo Prisoners from Yemen Are Sent to Saudi Arabia." *New York Times*, April 16, 2016.

———. "10 More Detainees Are Transferred from Guantánamo Prison." *New York Times*, January 16, 2017.
———. "15 Guantánamo Detainees Are Sent to Emirates in Largest Obama-Era Transfer." *New York Times*, August 15, 2016.
———. "Appeals Court Allows Challenges by Detainees at Guantánamo Prison." *New York Times*, February 11, 2014.
———. "Appeals Court Bars U.S. from Transferring American ISIS Suspect." *New York Times*, May 9, 2018.
———. "Closing Guantánamo Fades as a Priority." *New York Times*, June 25, 2010.
———. "Despair Drives Guantánamo Detainees to Revolt." *New York Times*, April 24, 2013.
———. "Donald Trump 'Fine' with Prosecuting U.S. Citizens at Guantánamo." *New York Times*, August 12, 2016.
———. "Fired Pentagon Official Was Exploring Plea Deals for 9/11 Suspects at Guantánamo." *New York Times*, February 10, 2018.
———. "Frustrated in Efforts to Close Guantánamo Prison, Officials Look to Reduce Population." *New York Times*, December 2, 2015.
———. "Frustrated Military Tribunal Judge Indefinitely Halts Cole Bombing Case." *New York Times*, February 16, 2018.
———. "Ghailani Verdict Reignites Debate over the Proper Court for Terrorism Trials." *New York Times*, November 18, 2010.
———. "G.O.P. Pushes Military Custody for Terror Suspects." *New York Times*, October 27, 2011.
———. "Guantánamo Defendant Is Sentenced, in Rare Success for Military Commission." *New York Times*, October 13, 2017.
———. "Guantánamo Detainee Pleads Guilty in 2002 Attack on Tanker Off Yemen." *New York Times*, February 20, 2014.
———. "Guantánamo Population Drops to 93 after 10 Prisoners Go to Oman." *New York Times*, January 14, 2016.
———. "Guantánamo Prisoner Is Repatriated to Sudan." *New York Times*, July 11, 2012.
———. "Harsher Security Tactics? Obama Left Door Ajar, and Donald Trump Is Knocking." *New York Times*, November 13, 2016.
———. "In a Reversal, Military Trials for 9/11 Cases." *New York Times*, April 4, 2011.
———. "ISIS Detainees May Be Held at Guantánamo, Document Shows." *New York Times*, February 8, 2017.
———. "Judge Bars Statements Made by Guantánamo Detainees during F.B.I. Interrogations." *New York Times*, August 17, 2018.
———. "Judge Overrules Censors in Guantánamo 9/11 Hearing." *New York Times*, January 30, 2013.
———. "Lawyers for a Guantánamo Detainee Cite Failing Health in Seeking His Release." *New York Times*, April 7, 2014.
———. "Levin and McCain Strike Deal over Detainee Handling." *New York Times*, November 15, 2011.

———. "Military Ordered to Notify A.C.L.U. before Transferring American ISIS Suspect." *New York Times*, January 24, 2018.
———. "New Measure to Hinder Closing of Guantánamo." *New York Times*, January 7, 2011.
———. "Obama May Bypass Guantánamo Rules, Aides Say." *New York Times*, January 3, 2011.
———. "Obama Transfers 4 From Guantánamo, Leaving 41 There as Term Ends." *New York Times*, January 19, 2017.
———. "Panel Recommends Transferring Yemeni From Guantánamo." *New York Times*, January 9, 2014.
———. "Pentagon Denies Money for Guantánamo Overhaul." *New York Times*, September 24, 2013.
———. *Power Wars: Inside Obama's Post-9/11 Presidency*. New York: Little, Brown, 2015.
———. "Reversal Upholds Detention of Yemeni at Guantánamo." *New York Times*, July 13, 2010.
———. "Senate Declines to Clarify Rights of American Qaeda Suspects Arrested in U.S." *New York Times*, December 1, 2011.
———. "Senator Proposes Deal on Handling of Detainees." *New York Times*, March 3, 2010.
———. "Sessions Says Guantánamo Is a 'Very Fine Place' for New Suspects." *New York Times*, March 9, 2017.
———. "Sudanese Detainee to Be Sent Home from Guantánamo." *New York Times*, December 4, 2013.
———. *Takeover: The Return of the Imperial Presidency and the Subversion of American Democracy*. New York: Back Bay Books, 2007.
———. "Two Guantánamo Detainees Are Involuntarily Repatriated to Algeria." *New York Times*, December 5, 2013.
———. "Two Guantánamo Detainees Freed, the First in 15 Months." *New York Times*, April 19, 2012.
———. "Two Saudi Prisoners Sent Home from Guantánamo." *New York Times*, December 16, 2013.
———. "U.S. Frees Last of the Chinese Uighur Detainees from Guantánamo Bay." *New York Times*, December 31, 2013.
———. "U.S. Legal Officials Split over How to Prosecute Terrorism Detainees." *New York Times*, January 7, 2013.
———. "U.S. Tests New Approach to Terrorism Cases on Somali Suspect." *New York Times*, July 6, 2011.
———. "U.S. to Press Fight of Detainee's Appeal." *New York Times*, January 9, 2013.
———. "U.S. to Send 2 at Guantánamo Back to Algeria, Saying Security Conditions Are Met." *New York Times*, July 26, 2013.
———. "U.S. Transfers First Guantánamo Detainee under Trump, Who Vowed to Fill It." *New York Times*, May 2, 2018.

———. "Vote Hurts Obama's Push to Empty Cuba Prison." *New York Times*, December 22, 2010.
———. "White House Postpones Picking Site of 9/11 Trial." *New York Times*, March 5, 2010.
Savage, Charlie, Rukmini Callimachi, and Eric Schmitt. "American ISIS Suspect Is Freed After Being Held More Than a Year." *New York Times*, October 29, 2018.
Savage, Charlie, and Helene Cooper. "Under Pressure, Hagel Promises to Act on Guantánamo Transfers." *New York Times*, May 29, 2014.
Savage, Charlie, and Steven Erlanger. "Shaker Aamer Is Released from Guantánamo Prison after 13 Years." *New York Times*, October 30, 2015.
Savage, Charlie, and Adam Goldman. "Following Trump's Lead, Republicans Grow Quiet on Guantánamo." *New York Times*, November 4, 2017.
Savage, Charlie, and Matthew Rosenberg. "Republican Report Criticizes Transfers from Guantánamo." *New York Times*, February 9, 2012.
Savage, Charlie, and Eric Schmitt. "U.S. to Prosecute a Somali Suspect in Civilian Court." *New York Times*, July 5, 2011.
Savage, Charlie, and Peter Shane. "Experts Urge Keeping Two Options for Terror Trials." *New York Times*, March 8, 2010.
Savage, Charlie, and Jonathan Weisman. "NSA Collection of Bulk Data Is Ruled Illegal." *New York Times*, May 7, 2015.
Scheppele, Kim Lane. "The New Judicial Deference." *Boston University Law Review* 92, no. 1 (January 2012): 89–170.
Schlesinger, Arthur M. Jr. *The Imperial Presidency*. Boston: Houghton Mifflin, 1973.
Schmitt, Eric. "U.S. to Expand Detainee Review in Afghan Prison." *New York Times*, September 13, 2009.
Schmitt, Eric, and Tim Golden. "Lawmakers Back Use of Evidence Coerced from Detainees." *New York Times*, December 17, 2005.
Schmitt, Eric, and Charlie Savage. "American Held as ISIS Suspect, Creating a Quandary for the Trump Administration." *New York Times*, October 6, 2017.
Schwarz, Frederick A. O. Jr., and Aziz Z. Huq. *Unchecked and Unbalanced: Presidential Power in a Time of Terror*. New York: New Press, 2007.
Seelye, Katharine Q. "Believed to Be a U.S. Citizen, Detainee Is Jailed in Virginia." *New York Times*, April 6, 2002.
———. "Criticized, U.S. Brings Visitors to Prison Camp." *New York Times*, January 26, 2002.
———. "For America's Captives, Home Is a Camp in Cuba, with Goggles and a Koran." *New York Times*, January 20, 2002.
———. "Move Likely for Inmate Who May Be American." *New York Times*, April 5, 2002.
———. "Rumsfeld Defends U.S. Treatment of Detainees in Cuba." *New York Times*, January 23, 2002.
———. "Some Guantánamo Prisoners Will Be Freed, Rumsfeld Says." *New York Times*, October 23, 2002.

———. "U.S. to Hold Taliban Detainees in 'the Least Worst Place.'" *New York Times*, December 28, 2001.

Shah, Reema, and Sam Kleiner. "Running Out of Options: Expiring Detention Authority and the Viability of Prosecutions in the Military Commissions under *Hamdan II*." *Yale Law & Policy Review* 32, no. 2 (Spring 2014): 465–504.

Shane, Peter M. *Madison's Nightmare: How Executive Power Threatens American Democracy*. Chicago: University of Chicago Press, 2009.

Shane, Scott. "Judge Blocks the Transfer of 13 Detainees from Guantánamo." *New York Times*, March 13, 2005.

Shane, Scott, and William Glaberson. "Courts Clear the Way for First Trial at Guantánamo." *New York Times*, July 18, 2008.

Shane, Scott, and David Johnston. "U.S. Acts to Avert Tactic Expected in Qaeda Trial." *New York Times*, February 13, 2008.

Shane, Scott, and Mark Landler. "Obama Clears Way for Guantánamo Trials." *New York Times*, March 7, 2011.

Shane, Scott, and Benjamin Weiser. "U.S. Drops Plan for a 9/11 Trial in New York City." *New York Times*, January 29, 2010.

Shane, Scott, and Margot Williams. "Yemenis Freed after Transfer from Secret Prisons, Report Says." *New York Times*, April 5, 2006.

Shanker, Thom. "Barring Evidence from Torture Is Considered." *New York Times*, March 23, 2006.

———. "Pentagon Plans to Tell Names of Detainees." *New York Times*, February 26, 2006.

Shanker, Thom, and David Johnston. "Legislation Could Be Path to Closing Guantánamo." *New York Times*, July 3, 2007.

Shapiro, Martin. "Political Jurisprudence." Reprinted in *On Law, Politics, and Judicialization*, edited by Martin Shapiro and Alec Stone Sweet, 19–54. New York: Oxford University Press, 2002.

Shear, Michael D. "New Order Indefinitely Bars Almost All Travel from Seven Countries." *New York Times*, September 24, 2017.

Shenon, Philip. "Britain Defends U.S. Treatment of Detainees at Guantánamo." *New York Times*, January 22, 2002.

———. "Suit to Be Filed on Behalf of Three Detainees in Cuba." *New York Times*, February 19, 2002.

Silliman, Scott L. "Prosecuting Alleged Terrorists by Military Commission: A Prudent Option." *Case Western Reserve Journal of International Law* 42, no. 1–2 (Winter 2009): 289–298.

Silverstein, Gordon. *Imbalance of Powers: Constitutional Interpretation and the Making of American Foreign Policy*. New York: Oxford University Press, 1997.

———. *Law's Allure: How Law Shapes, Constrains, Saves, and Kills Politics*. New York: Cambridge University Press, 2009.

Sitaraman, Ganesh, and Ingrid Wuerth. "The Normalization of Foreign Relations Law." *Harvard Law Review* 128, no. 7 (May 2015): 1897–1979.

Soufan, Ali. "Tribunal and Error." *New York Times*, February 11, 2010.
Staszak, Sarah. *No Day in Court: Access to Justice and the Politics of Judicial Retrenchment*. New York: Oxford University Press, 2015.
Stout, David. "House Backs Detainee Transfers." *New York Times*, October 16, 2009.
———. "Justices, 6–3, Sidestep Ruling on Padilla Case." *New York Times*, April 3, 2006.
———. "Senate Blocks Detainees' Rights Bill." *New York Times*, September 19, 2007.
Sulmasy, Glenn. "*Ex parte Quirin* and Military Commissions under the Obama Administration." *University of Toledo Law Review* 41, no. 4 (Summer 2010): 767–782.
Sundquist, James L. *The Decline and Resurgence of Congress*. Washington, DC: Brookings Institution Press, 1981.
Tate, C. Neal, and Torbjörn Vallinder, eds. *The Global Expansion of Judicial Power*. New York: New York University Press, 1995.
Thrush, Glenn. "Trump's New Travel Ban Blocks Migrants from Six Nations, Sparing Iraq." *New York Times*, March 6, 2017.
"Timeline of the Muslim Ban." ACLU Washington. Accessed June 29, 2020. www.acluwa.org/pages/timeline-muslim-ban.
Toner, Robin. "Lawmakers Seek Action after Ruling on Detainees." *New York Times*, July 3, 2006.
Tushnet, Mark. "The Political Constitution of Emergency Powers: Some Lessons from *Hamdan*." *Minnesota Law Review* 91, no. 5 (May 2007): 1451–1472.
U.S. Library of Congress. Congressional Research Service. *The Department of Defense Rules for Military Commissions: Analysis of Procedural Rules and Comparison with Proposed Legislation and the Uniform Code of Military Justice*, by Jennifer Elsea. RL31600. 2005.
———. *The Military Commissions Act of 2006: Analysis of Procedural Rules and Comparison with Previous DOD Rules and the Uniform Code of Military Justice*, by Jennifer Elsea. RL33688. 2006.
———. *The Military Commissions Act of 2009 (MCA 2009): Overview and Legal Issues*, by Jennifer Elsea. R41163. 2014.
"The U.S. Military Commissions: Looking Forward." Report by the American Bar Association Standing Committee on Law and National Security and the George Washington University Law School, May 2018. https://www.americanbar.org/content/dam/aba/administrative/law_national_security/ABAMilitaryCommissionsWorkshopFINAL.authcheckdam.pdf.
Vázquez, Carlos Manuel. "The Military Commissions Act, the Geneva Conventions, and the Courts: A Critical Guide." *American Journal of International Law* 101, no. 1 (January 2007): 73–98.
Vladeck, Stephen I. "Exceptional Courts and the Structure of American Military Justice." In *Guantánamo and Beyond: Exceptional Courts and Military Commissions in Comparative Perspective*, edited by Fionnuala Ní Aoláin and Oren Gross, 163–180. New York: Cambridge University Press, 2013.
———. "Four Big Questions Heading into the Hamdan Argument." Lawfare. May 1, 2012. https://www.lawfareblog.com/four-big-questions-heading-hamdan-argument.

———. "My Three Takeaways from the Hamdan Argument." Lawfare. May 3, 2012. https://www.lawfareblog.com/my-three-takeaways-hamdan-argument.

———. "One Huge Difference between Kavanaugh and Kennedy: Their Guantanamo Records." *Washington Post*, July 11, 2018.

———. "Three (Early) Observations on Judge Kavanaugh's Analysis in Hamdan." Lawfare. October 16, 2012. https://www.lawfareblog.com/three-early-observations-judge kavanaughs-analysis-hamdan.

———. "The True Significance of Judge Tatel's Opinion in the Force-Feeding Appeal." Just Security. February 11, 2014. https://www.justsecurity.org/7016/true-significance-judge tatels-opinion-force-feeding-appeal/.

Weiser, Benjamin. "Top Terror Prosecutor Is a Critic of Civilian Trials." *New York Times*, February 19, 2010.

Weisman, Jonathan, and Jennifer Steinhauer. "Court Ruling on N.S.A.'s Data Collection Jolts Both Defenders and Reformers." *New York Times*, May 8, 2015.

Welna, David. "'Torture Report' Reshapes Conversation in Guantánamo Courtroom." NPR, *Morning Edition*, February 25, 2015.

Wheeler, Darren A. *Presidential Power in Action: Implementing Supreme Court Detainee Decisions*. New York: Palgrave Macmillan, 2008.

White, Josh, and William Branigin. "Former Bin Laden Driver Hamdan to Leave Guantanamo Bay for Yemen." *Washington Post*, November 25, 2008.

Wilbur, Del Quentin, and Peter Finn. "U.S. Retires 'Enemy Combatant,' Keeps Broad Right to Detain." *Washington Post*, March 14, 2009.

Wilson, James Q. *Bureaucracy: What Government Agencies Do and Why They Do It*. New York: Basic Books, 1989.

Winograd, Ben. "Hamdan Military Commission Coverage." *SCOTUSblog*. July 22, 2008. http://www.scotusblog.com/2008/07/hamdan-military-commission-coverage/.

Wittes, Benjamin. *Detention and Denial: The Case for Candor after Guantánamo*. Washington, DC: Brookings Institution Press, 2011.

———. "Interesting New Habeas Argument in the D.C. Circuit." Lawfare. July 11, 2014. https://www.lawfareblog.com/interesting-new-habeas-argument-dc-circuit.

———. *Law and Long War: The Future of Justice in the Age of Terror*. New York: Penguin Books, 2008.

———. "The Lawfare Podcast, Episode #84: Bahlul, Bahlul, Bahlul." Podcast. Lawfare. July 19, 2014. https://www.lawfareblog.com/lawfare-podcast-episode-84-bahlul-bahlul-bahlul.

Wolfowitz, Paul. "Memorandum for the Secretary of the Navy, Subject: Order Establishing Combatant Status Review Tribunal." July 7, 2004. https://www.law.utoronto.ca/documents/Mackin/MuneerAhmad_ExhibitV.pdf.

Woodward, Bob. "Guantanamo Detainee Was Tortured, Says Official Overseeing Military Trials." *Washington Post*, January 14, 2009.

Yoo, John. "Federal Courts as Weapons of Foreign Policy: The Case of the Helms-Burton Act." *Hastings International and Comparative Law Review* 20, no. 4 (Summer 1997): 747–776.

———. "Foreign Affairs Federalism and the Separation of Powers." *Villanova Law Review* 46, no. 5 (December 2001): 1341–1348.
Zeleny, Jeff. "Democrats Hope to Expand Rights at Guantánamo." *New York Times*, June 6, 2007.
Zernike, Kate. "White House Prods Congress to Curb Detainee Rights." *New York Times*, July 13, 2006.
Zernike, Kate, and Neil A. Lewis. "Plan for Tribunals Would Hew to the First Series." *New York Times*, September 7, 2006.

# Index


*Aamer v. Obama*, 87
Abbasi, Feroz, 101
Abdulmutallab, Umar Farouk, 76
Abraham, Stephen, 54
ACLU. *See* American Civil Liberties Union
Addington, David, 95
administrative review boards (ARBs)
  creation of, 19, 30–31, 39
  Detainee Treatment Act and, 47, 48
  Guantánamo Bay detainees and, 19, 30–31, 50, 65
  revamped as periodic review boards, 68, 82–83, 91
  John Roberts's dissent in *Boumediene v. Bush* and, 61
adversarial legalism
  combatant status review tribunals and, 37–38
  detention litigation and the reshaping of detention policy, 2–10, 23–31, 35–41, 91–92, 158
  drawbacks and unintended consequences of, 7–9, 69, 80–82
  explanations for the importance of in shaping post-9/11 national security policy, 10–14
  interrogation policy and, 161–162
  reshaping of military commissions, 2–10, 94, 103–111, 112–113, 120–121, 134, 147–152
  reshaping of post-9/11 national security policy, 1–10, 164–166
  restraints on presidential unilateralism and, 4–5
  John Roberts's dissent in *Boumediene v. Bush* and, 60–61
  Trump administration travel ban policy and, 163–164
  *See also* habeas corpus litigation
Afghanistan, 75, 85–86, 104. *See also* Bagram detention facility
*Al-Adahi v. Obama*, 79
Alito, Samuel, 59, 117
Allred, Keith, 129, 131
*Al Maqaleh v. Gates*, 72–74
al-Qaeda
  Abd al-Rahim al-Nashiri and, 139
  Al-Adahi and, 79
  Ali al-Marri and, 69–70
  Ali Hamza al Bahlul and, 132
  Salim Hamdan and, 104
  initial US detention policy decisions after 9/11 and, 20–23
  ISIS and, 89
  March 13 Standard and, 71, 84
  Jose Padilla and, 24
  post-9/11 armed conflict and, 2
Al-Qaeda in the Arabian Peninsula (AQAP), 76, 83, 162
Al Shabab, 83, 162
Alsheikh, Abdulrahman Ahmad, 89–90
Altenburg, John, Jr., 100, 107
American Civil Liberties Union (ACLU), 7, 8, 13, 75, 90, 115, 186n52
AQAP. *See* Al-Qaeda in the Arabian Peninsula
ARBs. *See* administrative review boards
Article III courts
  *al-Marri* litigation and, 70
  *Bahlul* litigation and, 145, 146, 148, 149
  combatant status review tribunals and, 50, 61
  convergence with military commissions, 156–157
  criminal prosecution of terrorist enemy combatants and, 9, 156
  *Hamdan v. Gates* and, 130
  hybrid model of detention and prosecution, 83–84, 159–160
  Obama administration's use of, 78, 89
  Obama's preference for, 132, 135, 138
  transfer of Guantánamo Bay detainee cases to blocked by Congress, 138–139
  Trump administration's use of, 152–153
Ary, Vaughn, 152

Ashcroft, John, 95, 160
AUMF. *See* Authorization for Use of Military Force
Authorization for Use of Military Force (AUMF; 2001)
detention litigation by the Obama DOJ and, 71–72
detention policy and, 20
*Hamdan v. Rumsfeld* and, 108, 117, 119
*Hamdi v. Rumsfeld* and, 29, 33, 34, 35
interbranch shaping of detention policy and, 46
*Khalid v. Bush* and, 43
*Padilla v. Bush* and, 26, 29, 30
significance in post-9/11 national security policy, 2
targeted killing policy and, 162, 207n12
Awlaki, Anwar al-, 162, 207n12

Bagram detention facility
closing of, 85–86
enemy combatant review boards and, 50
impact of the *Boumediene* ruling on detention litigation in, 67
increased use of as a consequence of detention litigation, 39, 55, 65
Obama administration and, 71, 72–75, 85–86
Bahlul, Ali al, 101, 102–103, 132
*Bahlul* litigation
DC Circuit Court and, 143–150, 151
Supreme Court denial of certiorari, 151
Barnes, Jeb, 1, 4, 15, 31, 165
Barron, David, 201n12
Bates, John, 71, 72–74, 75
battlefield exception, 136, 201–202n12
Becker, Jo, 95
Begg, Moazzam, 101
Berenson, Bradford, 120
bin Laden, Osama, 79
*Bismullah v. Gates*, 55–57
Borch, Fred, 112
Bosaso prison, 81
*Boumediene v. Bush*
*Al Maqaleh v. Gates* and, 73
DC Circuit Court and, 48, 53, 68, 80
DC District Court decision, 51–53, 80
DC District Court habeas corpus lawsuits in the Obama administration and, 75, 78–80
detention policy and litigation trends in the immediate aftermath of, 62–64
influence of *Bismullah v. Gates* on, 57
origin and overview of, 42–43, 48
ramifications for military commissions, 129–130, 133–134, 136
Supreme Court case, 42–43, 53–54, 57–62, 65, 129–130
Bravin, Jess, 106, 110, 126
Breyer, Stephen
*Boumediene v. Bush*, 53, 57
*Hamdan v. Rumsfeld*, 117, 121
*Hamdi v. Rumsfeld*, 33
*Rumsfeld v. Padilla*, 35
Brown, Janice Rogers, 145–146, 149
Brown, Scott, 187n58
Brownback, Pete, 102, 106–107
*Brown v. Board of Education*, 12
Burke, Thomas, 1, 12
Bush, George W.
defense of the CIA's rendition, detention, and interrogation program, 51
designation of Jose Padilla as an enemy combatant, 26
desire to close the Guantánamo Bay detention facility, 50
Detainee Treatment Act and, 46
Executive Order 13425 restarting military commissions, 126
initial detention policy decisions after 9/11, 20, 21
internal administration divisions over Guantánamo Bay and, 63
presidential power and the enactment of post-9/11 enemy combatant policies, 3, 4
presidential unilateralism and the creation of military commissions, 93, 94–97, 111, 154
surveillance policy and, 160
transfer of CIA detainees to Guantánamo Bay in 2006, 51, 181–182n29

Bush administration (2001–2004)
challenges in the implementation of military commissions, 100–103
detention litigation in the circuit courts, 28–31
detention policy changes following Supreme Court rulings, 31, 35–36
development of rules and regulations for military commissions, 97–100
early detention litigation in federal district courts, 23–28
initial detention policy decisions after 9/11, 20–23
overview of detention policy and litigation in, 19–20, 39–41
*Padilla v. Bush* and, 69–70 (see also *Padilla v. Bush*)
presidential unilateralism and the creation of military commissions, 93, 94–97, 111, 154
responses to Supreme Court detention case rulings, 36–41
response to the DC District Court ruling in *Hamdan v. Rumsfeld*, 107
Supreme Court detainee cases and, 30, 31–36
surveillance policy and, 160
Bush administration (2005–2008)
Congress, detention policy, and the Detainee Treatment Act, 46–48
DC Circuit Court decision in *Hamdan v. Rumsfeld* and the reshaping of military commissions, 109–111
detention policy and litigation trends in the immediate aftermath of *Boumediene v. Bush*, 62–64
habeas corpus litigation in the DC District Court, 43–45
interbranch relations in the shaping of detention policy, 48–57
internal divisions over Guantánamo Bay, 54, 62–64
internal email leak concerning military commissions and, 110
military commission proceedings and challenges following the MCA reforms, 126–132
Military Commissions Act and the reform of military commissions, 121–126
overview of detention policy and litigation in, 42–43, 64–66
release of detainees from Guantánamo Bay and, 45
transfer of CIA detainees to Guantánamo Bay in 2006, 51, 181–182n29

Card, Andrew, 160
Carter, Ashton, 87
CCR. *See* Center for Constitutional Rights
Center for Constitutional Rights (CCR), 7, 8, 13, 23, 115
Central Intelligence Agency (CIA)
rendition, detention, and interrogation program, 20, 39, 51, 147, 161
transfer of CIA detainees to Guantánamo Bay in 2006, 51, 181–182n29
Chambliss, Saxby, 81
Cheney, Dick, 51, 54
Chesney, Robert, 156
Christmas Day terrorist attack (2009), 76, 78, 138
Chutkan, Tanya, 90
CIA. *See* Central Intelligence Agency
circuit courts
detention litigation in, 28–31
*See also individual circuit courts*
civil rights movement, 12
Classified Information Procedures Act, 136
CMCR. *See* Court of Military Commission Review
Coalition of Clergy, Lawyers, and Professors, 23
*Coalition of Clergy v. Bush*, 23–24, 28–29
coercion provision, of the Detainee Treatment Act, 47–48
combatant status review tribunals (CSRTs)
*Al Maqaleh v. Gates* and, 73
*Boumediene v. Bush* and, 53, 54, 59
creation and purpose of, 20, 36–38, 40
Detainee Treatment Act and, 42, 47, 48
Freedom of Information Act litigation and, 51

combatant status review tribunals (CSRTs), *continued*
  Guantánamo Bay detainees and, 36–38, 50, 51, 55–57, 65
  *Hamdan v. Rumsfeld* and, 104
  *In re Guantánamo Detainee Cases* and, 44, 45
  judicial review by the DC Circuit Court, 42, 47, 55–57, 59, 65
  military commission proceedings against Salim Hamdan and Omar Khadr and, 127–128, 129
  John Roberts's dissent in *Boumediene v. Bush* and, 61
Comey, James, 160
Common Article 3 (Geneva Conventions), 51, 104–105, 117–118, 119, 123, 161
Congress
  Detainee Treatment Act and, 42, 46–48, 115–116
  detention policy changes in response to litigation in the courts, 30, 31
  Guantánamo Bay closure and detainee resettlement issue, 76, 77–78
  hybrid model of detention and prosecution, 83–84
  interbranch dynamics in the shaping of detention policy and, 82–86, 91–92
  Military Commissions Act and, 49, 114–115, 121–126, 135–137
  response to George W. Bush's creation of military commissions, 96–97
  surveillance policy and, 161
  transfer of Guantánamo Bay detainee cases to civilian courts blocked by, 138–139
conspiracy offense
  *Bahlul* litigation and, 141, 143, 144–145, 146, 147–150
  criminal prosecution of terrorist enemy combatants and, 9
  *Hamdan v. Rumsfeld* and, 118–119
Conyers, John, 96
Court of Military Commission Review (CMCR)
  2009 reforms of the MCA and, 133, 137
  *Bahlul* litigation and, 141, 151
  creation and purpose of, 124–125
  review of Salim Hamdan's conviction for material support, 140–141, 142
  ruling on CSRT "enemy combatant" classifications, 128
courts-martial, 106, 107, 109, 117, 126, 137
Crawford, Susan, 128–129
CSRTs. *See* combatant status review tribunals

Damache, Ali, 89
Darbi, Ahmed Muhammed Haza al-, 88, 154
Davis, Morris, 129
death sentences, 98
Defense Intelligence Agency, 27
Define and Punish Clause
  *Bahlul* litigation, 148, 149, 150
  *Hamdan* litigation, 140–141, 142
Dellinger, Walter, 119–120
de novo review, *Bahlul* litigation and, 146, 147–148, 150
detainee review boards (DRBs), 74
Detainee Treatment Act (DTA; 2005)
  *Bismullah v. Gates* and, 55–57
  *Boumediene v. Bush* and, 57, 58–59
  coercion provision, 47–48
  creation and provisions of, 42
  *Hamdan v. Rumsfeld* and, 49
  interrogation policy and, 46, 115, 161
  military commissions and, 115–116
  reshaping of detention policy and, 46–48
  Supreme Court ruling in *Hamdan v. Rumsfeld* and, 117
detention policy and law
  adversarial legalism and the reshaping of detention policy, 2–10, 23–31, 35–41, 91–92, 158
  case of Ali al-Marri, 69–70
  Congress and the Detainee Treatment Act, 46–48
  DC District Court habeas corpus lawsuits following the *Boumediene* ruling, 75, 78–80
  detentions outside the purview of federal courts, 20, 38–39
  early litigation in federal district courts, 23–28
  future of detention, 158–160

hybrid model of detention and prosecution, 83–84, 159–160
initial policy decisions after 9/11, 20–23
litigation in the circuit courts, 28–31
overseas detention in Afghanistan, 50–51
overview of trends in the Bush administration (2001–2004), 19–20, 36–41
overview of trends in the Bush administration (2005–2008), 42–43, 48–57, 64–66
periodic review boards, 82–83
policy changes following Supreme Court rulings, 31, 35–41
proxy detention, 8–9, 69, 81–82, 92
Supreme Court cases, 30, 31–36
trends in the immediate aftermath of *Boumediene v. Bush*, 62–64
trends in the Obama administration, 67, 68–69, 70–72, 75–78, 82–88, 91
Trump administration and, 88–90, 91–92
unintended consequences of adversarial legalism and, 8–9, 69, 80–82
DOD. *See* US Department of Defense
*Doe v. Mattis*, 90
DOJ. *See* US Department of Justice
domestic common law of war, 142, 143, 146
Donilon, Tom, 72
Doumar, Robert, 24–26
Dratel, Joshua, 101–102
drone strikes. *See* targeted killing policy
DTA. *See* Detainee Treatment Act
Due Process Clause
*Hamdi v. Rumsfeld* and, 33, 34–35
*In re Guantánamo Detainee Cases* and, 44
Obama administration's interpretation of the *Boumediene* decision and, 135–136
Dunham, Frank, 24–25

ECRBs. *See* enemy combatant review boards
enemy combatant policies
criminal prosecution in Article III courts and, 9
interbranch dynamics and restraint on presidential unilateralism, 3–6
overview of the role of courts and litigation in shaping, 2–10
*See also* detention policy and law; military commissions; national security policy
enemy combatant review boards (ECRBs), 50
enemy combatants
designation of Jose Padilla as, 26
discontinued use of the term by the Obama administration, 71
Guantánamo Bay detainees defined as, 22–23
*Hamdi v. Rumsfeld* and, 25–26
England, Gordon, 37
enhanced interrogation techniques, 128
entrepreneurial lawyering
adversarial legalism and, 7 (*see also* adversarial legalism)
detention litigation in the Obama administration and, 68
overview of detention litigation in the early Bush administration, 40
transfers of Guantánamo Bay detainees and, 87–88
Epp, Charles, 12, 13
Establishment Clause, 163
Eviatar, Daphne, 146
executive branch
interbranch dynamics and the shaping of enemy combatant policies, 5
interbranch dynamics in the development of military commissions, 93–94, 111–112
rules and regulations for military commissions and, 97–100
*See also specific administrations*
executive orders
George W. Bush and creation of military commissions, 93, 94–97, 111
Executive Order 13425, 126
*Ex parte Quirin*, 95, 148, 150
Ex Post Facto Clause, 141, 144, 145

federal district courts
early detention litigation in, 23–28
*See also individual district courts*
Feeley, Malcolm, 13

Fifth Amendment. *See* Due Process Clause
Fisher, Louis, 173n19
FOIA. *See* Freedom of Information Act
force-feeding procedures, 45, 87
Freedom of Information Act (FOIA), 50–51, 75

Garland, Merrick, 144
Gates, Robert, 54, 63, 65, 126
Gellman, Barton, 95
Geneva Conventions
- *Hamdan v. Rumsfeld* and, 51, 104–105, 108–109, 117–118, 119, 161
- Military Commissions Act and, 123

Ghailani, Ahmed Khalfan, 78, 139, 202–203n25
Ginsburg, Douglas, 56
Ginsburg, Ruth Bader
- *Boumediene v. Bush*, 53, 57
- *Hamdan v. Rumsfeld*, 117
- *Hamdi v. Rumsfeld*, 34–35
- *Rumsfeld v. Padilla*, 35

Goldsmith, Jack, 5–6, 99, 146–147, 207n12
Gonzales, Alberto, 54, 95, 160
Graber, Mark, 13, 84
Graham, Lindsey, 30, 77, 82, 114, 122–123, 138
Green, Joyce Hens, 44–45
Greenberger, Michael, 38
Greenhouse, Linda, 57, 80, 120
Griffith, Thomas, 144, 149, 151
Guantánamo Bay detention facility
- administrative review boards, 19, 30–31, 50, 65 (*see also* administrative review boards)
- arrival of first detainees at, 22
- availability of review mechanisms to detainees, 50, 51
- Bush administration's decision to employ as a detention facility, 21–22
- closure and detainee resettlement issue in the Obama administration, 67, 75–78, 85, 86–88
- combatant status review tribunals and, 36–38, 50, 51, 55–57, 65 (*see also* combatant status review tribunals)
- critics of, 91
- desire and failure of US presidents to close, 50, 65–66, 76–77
- detainee hunger strikes, 45, 85, 87
- detainee population figures, 28, 68
- Detainee Treatment Act and habeas corpus litigation, 115–116
- detention cases in the Supreme Court, 31–33, 36
- detention policy and litigation trends in the Bush administration (2001–2004), 19–20
- detention policy and litigation trends in the Bush administration (2005–2008), 42–43, 54, 62–66
- detention policy and litigation trends in the Obama administration, 71–72, 75, 78–80
- detention policy changes in response to litigation in the courts, 30–31, 36–41
- early detention litigation in federal district courts, 23–24, 28–29
- future of detention and military commissions and, 158–159
- habeas corpus jurisdiction and the Military Commissions Act, 49, 125
- habeas corpus litigation and *Boumediene v. Bush* and, 57–62, 129–130
- habeas corpus litigation and the Suspension Clause, 49–50
- habeas corpus litigation in the DC District Court, 43–45
- *Hamdan v. Rumsfeld* and, 48–49
- Yaser Hamdi and, 24, 28
- military commission trials and, 101–103 (*see also* military commissions)
- policy changes and trends in 2002–2003, 28
- releases of detainees from, 38, 40, 45, 54–55, 63–64, 113
- transfer of CIA detainees to in 2006, 51, 181–182n29
- Trump administration and, 67–68, 92

habeas corpus litigation
- Abdulrahman Ahmad Alsheikh and, 90
- at Bagram in the Obama administration, 71, 72–74
- *Boumediene v. Bush* and, 42–43, 48, 52–53, 57–62, 129–130

- in the circuit courts, 29
- Detainee Treatment Act and, 46–47, 115–116
- in the early Bush administration, 20
- in federal district courts, 23–28, 43–45, 62, 75, 78–80 (*see also* US District Court for the District of Columbia)
- following the *Boumediene* ruling, 75, 78–80
- in the immediate aftermath of *Boumediene v. Bush*, 62–63
- impact of the *Boumediene* ruling on detention litigation in Afghanistan, 67
- Military Commissions Act and, 49, 52–53, 125
- policy changes following Supreme Court detention cases, 36, 39–41
- Supreme Court detention cases and, 31–35
- Suspension Clause and, 49–50

Hafetz, Jonathan, 90
Hagel, Chuck, 87
Hamdan, Salim
- argument in *Hamdan v. Rumsfeld*, 48–49
- conspiracy offense and, 101
- material support offense and, 140–141, 142–143
- military commission proceedings against, 101, 102, 103, 113, 127–128, 129, 130, 131, 132, 140–142

*Hamdan II*, 142–143
*Hamdan v. Gates*, 130, 131
*Hamdan v. Rumsfeld*
- adversarial legalism and the reshaping of military commissions, 112, 120–121
- background to, 48–49
- Common Article 3 of the Geneva Conventions and, 51
- DC Circuit Court review of *Bahlul* and, 145
- DC Circuit Court ruling in, 107–110
- DC District Court ruling in, 103–106
- impact of the DC District Court ruling on military commission proceedings, 106–107, 113
- impact on detention policy, 49, 51
- influence on the Military Commissions Act, 121, 122, 123
- Manual for Military Commissions and, 126
- ramifications for interrogation policy, 161
- reaction to the Supreme Court ruling in, 119–120
- Supreme Court case, 48, 49, 115–119

Hamdi, Yaser, 24, 28, 38, 40
*Hamdi v. Rumsfeld*
- Bush administration responses to the ruling in, 40
- CIA's RDI program and, 39
- circuit court case, 29
- combatant status review tribunals and, 20, 37, 38
- federal district court case, 24–26, 27
- *In re Guantánamo Detainee Cases* and, 44, 45
- John Roberts's dissent in *Boumediene v. Bush* and, 61
- Supreme Court case, 30, 33–35, 36

*Hamlily v. Obama*, 71
Hartmann, Thomas, 129
Haynes, William, 22–23, 100
Henderson, Karen LeCraft, 56, 144–145, 149
Henley, Stephen, 135
Hicks, David, 23, 101, 102, 126–127, 151
Holder, Eric, 70, 139, 144
Huvelle, Ellen Segal, 135
hybrid model of detention and prosecution, 83–84, 159–160

Imam, Mustafa al-, 89, 152
Ingber, Rebecca, 99
*In re Guantánamo Detainee Cases*, 44–45, 48
International Committee of the Red Cross, 22
international law of war, *Bahlul* litigation and, 148, 149
interrogation policy
- adversarial legalism and, 45, 128–129, 161–162
- case of Mohammed al-Qahtani and, 128–129

interrogation policy, *continued*
  CIA's rendition, detention, and interrogation program, 20, 39, 51, 147, 161
  Common Article 3 of the Geneva Conventions and, 105, 118, 161
  Detainee Treatment Act and, 46, 115, 161
  *Hamdan v. Rumsfeld* and, 105
  hybrid model of prosecution and, 83
Iqbal, Asif, 23
Iraqi, Abdul Hadi al, 153
ISIS detainees, 88–89

JAGs. *See* judge advocates general
Jawad, Mohammed, 135
JCS. *See* Joint Chiefs of Staff
Jeffress, Amy, 70
Johnsen, Dawn, 98
Johnson, Jeh, 162
*Johnson v. Eisentrager*
  *Boumediene v. Bush* and, 52, 58
  *Coalition of Clergy v. Bush* and, 23, 24, 29
  *Khalid v. Bush* and, 44
  *Rasul v. Bush* and, 31–32
Joint Chiefs of Staff (JCS), 98, 99
judge advocates general (JAGs), 37, 93, 95, 126

Kagan, Robert, 7, 12
Kassem, Ramzi, 91
Katyal, Neal, 7, 30, 103, 107, 115, 120
Kavanaugh, Brett
  *Bahlul*, 145, 146, 149, 150
  *Bismullah III*, 56
  elevation to the Supreme Court, 183n69
  *Hamdan II*, 142
Keck, Thomas, 12
Kennedy, Anthony, 143
  *Boumediene v. Bush*, 53–54
  *Hamdan v. Rumsfeld*, 118–119
  *Hamdi v. Rumsfeld*, 33
  *Rasul v. Bush* and, 32
Kessler, Gladys, 45, 79
Khadr, Omar, 127–128, 138
*Khalid v. Bush*, 43–44, 45, 48
Khan, Majid Shoukat, 139, 154
Klaidman, Daniel, 70, 81, 162
Koh, Harold, 162
Kollar-Kotelly, Colleen, 24
Kris, David, 140

Lasnik, Robert, 103
*Latif v. Obama*, 79–80
Leahy, Patrick, 96–97
legalization, 12–14
Leon, Richard, 43–44, 64
Levin, Carl, 48, 84
Libya, 152
Lieberman, Joseph, 138
*Limburg* terrorist attack, 151
Lindh, John Walker, 127
Luttig, Michael, 70

Madison, James, 3
mandatory military custody, 84–85
Manual for Military Commissions, 126
March 13 Standard, 71, 72, 74–75, 84
Marri, Ali al-, 69–70
Martins, Mark, 143
material support offense
  *Bahlul* case and, 141, 144, 145
  criminal prosecution of terrorist enemy combatants and, 9
  *Hamdan* case and, 140–141, 142–143
*Mathews v. Eldridge*, 34
Matz, A. Howard, 23–24
MCA. *See* Military Commissions Act
McCain, John, 30, 46, 65, 122, 138
MCIs. *See* military commission instructions
MCOs. *See* Military Commission Orders
McRaven, William, 82
military commission instructions (MCIs), 100–101
Military Commission Orders (MCOs)
  No. 1, 97–100, 105–106, 110
  No. 2, 100
  No. 10, 111
military commissions
  2009 reforms to the Military Commissions Act and, 133–134, 135–137
  adversarial legalism and the reshaping of, 2–10, 94, 103–111, 112–113, 120–121, 134, 147–152
  *Bahlul* litigation, 143–151

battlefield exception and, 136, 201–202n12
Bush administration's internal email leak concerning, 110
case of Mohammed Jawad, 135
challenges in the implementation process, 100–103
convergence with Article III courts, 156–157
conviction of Ali Hamza al Bahlul, 132
conviction of David Hicks, 126–127
DC Circuit Court and the judicial review of, 116, 133, 134, 137, 142–150, 151, 155
DC Circuit Court ruling in *Bahlul* and, 143–147
dismissal of charges against Mohammed al-Qahtani, 128–129
first round of pretrial hearings at Guantánamo Bay, 102–103
future of, 158–160
*Hamdan II* and, 142–143
*Hamdan v. Rumsfeld* and (see *Hamdan v. Rumsfeld*)
interbranch dynamics in the development of, 93–94, 111–112
Manual for Military Commissions and, 126
Military Commissions Act and the reform and reshaping of, 114–115, 121–126
Obama administration and, 132, 133–135, 137–138, 139
overview of the forces shaping and the current status of, 153–157, 158
presidential unilateralism and the creation of, 93, 94–97, 111, 154
proceedings against Salim Hamdan, 101, 102, 103, 113, 127–128, 129, 130, 131, 132, 140–142
ramifications of *Boumediene v. Bush* for, 129–130, 133–134, 136
reformed proceedings, 126–132
response of Congress to Bush's creation of, 96–97
rules and regulations for, 97–100
rulings of the Court of Military Commission Review, 140–142
transfer of prosecutions to civilian courts blocked by Congress, 138–139
Trump administration and, 133, 152–153, 157
unlawful enemy combatant issue and, 127–128
Military Commissions Act (MCA; 2006)
2009 reforms to, 133–134, 135–137
*Bahlul* litigation and, 144, 145, 148, 149, 150
*Boumediene v. Bush* and, 58
material support offense and, 141
reshaping and reform of military commissions, 114–115, 121–126
revocation of habeas corpus jurisdiction over Guantánamo Bay and, 49, 52–53
Miller, Mark, 4, 31
Millett, Patricia, 150
Mobbs, Michael, 25–26
Mobbs Declaration, 25–26, 29
Mohammed, Khalid Sheikh, 42, 51, 78
Monaco, Lisa, 143
Mori, Michael, 102
Moussaoui, Zacarias, 78
Muhammed, Noor Uthman, 138, 151
Mukasey, Michael, 26–27, 37

NAACP. *See* National Association for the Advancement of Colored People
Nashiri, Abd al-Rahim al-, 139, 151, 153, 154, 156, 203n28
National Association for the Advancement of Colored People (NAACP), 12
National Defense Authorization Act (NDAA)
of 2010, 136
of 2011, 77–78, 84
of 2014, 86
National Security Agency, 160–161
National Security Council, 28
national security policy
adversarial legalism and the shaping of, 1–10
explanations for the importance of adversarial legalism in shaping, 10–14
interbranch perspective on the shaping of, 14–16, 164–166

national security policy, *continued*
*See also* detention policy and law; military commissions
NDAA. *See* National Defense Authorization Act
Neustadt, Richard, 4, 91
Newman, Donna, 26
Non-Detention Act (1971), 30, 34, 35

Obama, Barack
critical view of military commissions, 132, 157
detention policy adjustments accomplished by, 91
interrogation policy and, 161
mandatory military custody and Presidential Policy Directive 14, 84–85
periodic review boards and, 82–83
views of detention litigation, 70
Obama administration
Bagram detention facility and, 71, 72–75, 85–86
*Bahlul* review by the DC Circuit Court and, 143–144
case of Ali al-Marri, 69–70
DC District Court habeas lawsuits following the *Boumediene* ruling, 75, 78–80
detention policy and litigation, 67, 68–69, 70–72, 75–78, 82–88, 91
Guantánamo Bay closure and detainee resettlement issue, 65, 66, 67, 75–78, 85, 86–88
hybrid model of detention and prosecution, 83–84, 159–160
ISIS detainees and, 89
mandatory military custody and Presidential Policy Directive 14, 84–85
military commissions and, 132, 133–135, 137–138, 139
periodic review boards and, 82–83
preference for civilian trials of enemy combatant detainees, 135, 138, 139
pursuit of post-9/11 armed conflict and, 2
targeted killing policy and, 72, 80–82, 162
unintended consequences of detention litigation and, 80–82
O'Connor, Sandra Day, 33–35, 44
Office of Legal Counsel (OLC), 21–22, 95, 96, 140, 160
Office of Military Commissions (OMC), 101, 107, 110, 126, 128
OLC. *See* Office of Legal Counsel
OMC. *See* Office of Military Commissions

Padilla, Jose, 24, 35, 69–70, 84, 185n17
*Padilla v. Bush*
background and comparison to the *al-Marri* litigation, 69–70
circuit court case, 29–30
evidence for enemy combatant classification and, 27, 37
federal district court case, 26–27
issue of American citizens taken into custody on American soil and, 84
Supreme Court case, 30, 35, 36
periodic review boards (PRBs), 68, 82–83, 85, 86, 87, 91
Philbin, Patrick, 95
Pillard, Cornelia, 150
plain error review, 144–146
Pohl, James, 152
Powell, Colin, 95, 123
PRBs. *See* periodic review boards
Presidential Policy Directive 14, 84–85
presidential unilateralism
Article II of the Constitution and, 4
creation of military commissions and, 93, 94–97, 111, 154
detention policy in the early Bush administration and, 19
interbranch dynamics and the restraint on, 3–6
presumption of innocence, military commissions and, 98
prisoner of war status, 104
proxy detention, 8–9, 69, 81–82, 92

Qahtani, Mohammed al-, 128–129
Qala-i-Jangi, 21
*Qassim v. Trump*, 187n68
Qosi, Ibrahim al, 101, 137–138

Randolph, A. Raymond, 52, 56, 108
Rasul, Shafiq, 23, 180n83
*Rasul v. Bush*
  *Boumediene v. Bush* and, 52–53
  Bush administration's responses to the Supreme Court ruling in, 39–40
  CIA's RDI program and, 39
  combatant status review tribunals and, 20
  DC District Court case, 24
  Detainee Treatment Act and, 46, 116
  impact of the Supreme Court ruling in on habeas corpus litigation, 36, 43, 44
  Supreme Court case, 30, 31–33, 49
RDI. *See* rendition, detention, and interrogation
Rehnquist, William, 32, 33
Reid, Richard, 78
rendition, detention, and interrogation (RDI), 20, 39, 51, 147, 161
Rice, Condoleezza, 21, 51, 63, 95
Rice, Susan, 87
rights revolution, 12–13
Rishikof, Harvey, 153
Rizzo, John, 39
Roberts, John, 59, 60–62, 63, 108, 116
Robertson, James, 103–106, 107, 108, 109, 130, 131, 139–140
Rogers, Judith, 52–53, 145, 147–148, 150
Rogers, Mike, 81
Romero, Anthony, 88
Rosenberg, Gerald, 3
Rubin, Edward, 13
Rumsfeld, Donald
  initial detention policy decisions after 9/11 and, 20–21
  military commissions and, 97, 98–99, 100
  *Padilla v. Bush* and, 26
  release of Guantánamo Bay detainees and, 38
  transfer of high-value detainees to Guantánamo Bay in 2006 and, 51
*Rumsfeld v. Padilla*, 35

Saipov, Sayfullo, 152–153
Saudi Arabia, 90
Savage, Charlie, 5, 72, 79, 84–85, 142, 154, 162, 202n25, 202n38
Scalia, Antonin
  *Boumediene v. Bush*, 59–60, 61–62
  *Hamdan v. Rumsfeld*, 117
  *Hamdi v. Rumsfeld*, 35
  *Rasul v. Bush*, 32
  *Rumsfeld v. Padilla*, 35
secretary of defense
  Guantánamo Bay detainee transfer issue and, 77
  initial detention policy decisions after 9/11 and, 21
  military commissions and, 96
Senate Armed Services Committee, 123
Senate Intelligence Committee, 81, 147
Sentelle, David, 52, 56
Sessions, Jeff, 152
Shapiro, Martin, 1
Silverstein, Gordon, 5, 8, 172–173n12
Snowden, Edward, 161
solicitation offense, *Bahlul* case and, 141, 143, 144, 145
Somalia, 81, 83
Souter, David
  *Boumediene v. Bush*, 53, 57
  *Hamdan v. Rumsfeld*, 117
  *Hamdi v. Rumsfeld*, 34–35
  *Rumsfeld v. Padilla*, 35
Spath, Vance, 153
Specter, Arlen, 97, 122
*Steel Seizure Case*, 120
Stevens, John Paul
  *Boumediene v. Bush*, 53–54, 57
  *Hamdan v. Rumsfeld*, 116–117, 118, 119
  *Hamdi v. Rumsfeld*, 35
  *Rasul v. Bush*, 31–32
  *Rumsfeld v. Padilla*, 35
Sudan, 138
Sundel, Philip, 102
surveillance policy, 160–161
Suspension Clause, 49–50, 52, 58, 62, 129, 136
Swift, Charles, 103, 131

Taliban
  Yaser Hamdi and, 24
  initial US detention policy decisions after 9/11 and, 20–23

Taliban, *continued*
John Walker Lindh and, 127
March 13 Standard and, 84
post-9/11 armed conflict and, 2
targeted killing policy
AUMF and, 162, 207n12
costs and benefits of, 9, 82, 92
effect of courts and litigation on, 162–163
Obama administration and, 72, 162
as an unintended consequence of detention litigation, 8, 69, 80–82
Tate, C. Neal, 12
Tatel, David, 80, 144, 147, 148, 150, 187n68
Thomas, Clarence
*Boumediene v. Bush*, 59
*Hamdan v. Rumsfeld*, 117, 119
*Hamdi v. Rumsfeld*, 33, 34
*Rasul v. Bush*, 32
Tocqueville, Alexis de, 12
torture, 111, 129
travel ban policy, 163–164
Trump administration
detention policy and, 88–90, 91–92
Guantánamo Bay and, 67–68, 92
interrogation policy and, 161–162
military commissions and, 133, 152–153, 157
pursuit of post-9/11 armed conflict and, 2
travel ban policy and, 163–164

UCMJ. *See* Uniform Code of Military Justice
UECRBs. *See* unlawful enemy combatant review boards
Uighurs, 63–64
Uniform Code of Military Justice (UCMJ)
George W. Bush's executive order creating military commissions and, 96
DC Circuit Court review of *Bahlul* and, 145
*Hamdan II* and, 142
*Hamdan v. Rumsfeld* and, 104, 106, 108, 109, 117, 118–119
unlawful enemy combatant review boards (UECRBs), 73, 74
unlawful enemy combatants, 22, 127–128, 129
Urbina, Ricardo, 64
USA Freedom Act, 161
US Army Regulation 190–8, 104, 109
US Constitution
Article II and George W. Bush's assertion of presidential power, 4
Article II and George W. Bush's creation of military commissions, 95, 96, 106, 109–110, 119
Article III and *Bahlul* litigation, 147–150
Define and Punish Clause and *Bahlul* litigation, 148, 149, 150
Define and Punish Clause and *Hamdan* litigation, 140–141, 142
Establishment Clause, 163
Ex Post Facto Clause, 141, 144, 145
Suspension Clause and habeas corpus litigation, 49–50, 52, 58, 62, 129, 130
US Court of Appeals for the District of Columbia Circuit
adversarial legalism and the reshaping of military commissions, 112, 143–151
*Al-Adahi v. Obama*, 79
*Bahlul* litigation, 143–150, 151
*Bismullah v. Gates*, 55–57
*Boumediene v. Bush*, 48, 53, 68, 80
*Coalition of Clergy v. Bush*, 29
Court of Military Commission Review and, 125
detention litigation in the Obama administration and, 79–80
groin searches of Guantánamo Bay detainees and, 88
*Hamdan II*, 142–143
*Hamdan v. Rumsfeld*, 107–110, 112
judicial review of CSRT decisions, 42, 47, 55–57, 59, 65
judicial review of military commissions and, 116, 133, 134, 137, 142–150, 151, 155
*Latif v. Obama*, 79–80
US Court of Appeals for the Fourth Circuit, 24, 25, 29, 69–70
US Court of Appeals for the Ninth Circuit, 28–29, 103, 163
US Court of Appeals for the Second Circuit, 29–30, 70, 161

US Department of Defense (DOD)
- Abdulrahman Ahmad Alsheikh and, 89–90
- creation of military commissions and, 95, 96
- detention of Jose Padilla and Yaser Hamdi, 24
- detention policy changes in response to litigation in the courts, 30–31
- Guantánamo Bay detention facility and, 22–23, 28 (*see also* Guantánamo Bay detention facility)
- interbranch dynamics in the evolution of military commissions and, 94
- Manual for Military Commissions and, 126
- Mobbs Declaration, 25–26
- rules and regulations for military commissions, 97–100

US Department of Justice (DOJ)
- detention litigation in the Obama administration and, 71–72
- *Hamdi v. Rumsfeld* and, 25–26
- Manual for Military Commissions and, 126
- Military Commission Order No. 10 on, 111
- Jose Padilla and, 24
- structure of military commissions and, 98

US Department of State, 98, 107

US District Court for the District of Columbia
- *Aamer v. Obama*, 87
- adversarial legalism and the reshaping of military commissions, 112
- *Al-Adahi v. Obama*, 79
- *Al Maqaleh v. Obama*, 75
- Abdulrahman Ahmad Alsheikh and, 90
- *Boumediene v. Bush*, 51–53, 80
- case of Mohammed Jawad, 135
- groin searches of Guantánamo Bay detainees and, 88
- habeas corpus litigation, 20, 29, 43–45, 62, 71, 75, 78–80
- *Hamdan v. Gates*, 130
- *Hamdan v. Rumsfeld* and, 49, 103–106, 112, 139–140 (see also *Hamdan v. Rumsfeld*)
- *Rasul v. Bush*, 24
- release of Guantánamo detainees into the US, 63–64

US District Court for the Eastern District of Virginia, 24–26

US District Court for the Southern District of New York, 26–27

USS *Cole* terrorist attack, 139, 151, 154

US Supreme Court
- *al-Marri* litigation and, 69, 70
- *Boumediene v. Bush*, 42–43, 53–54, 57–62, 65, 129–130 (see also *Boumediene v. Bush*)
- denial of certiorari to Ali al Bahlul, 151
- detention litigation, 19–20, 30, 31–36
- executive branch responses to detention case rulings, 36–41
- *Ex parte Quirin*, 95, 148, 150
- *Hamdan v. Rumsfeld*, 48, 49, 114, 115–121 (see also *Hamdan v. Rumsfeld*)
- *Johnson v. Eisentrager*, 23, 24 (see also *Johnson v. Eisentrager*)
- Brett Kavanaugh and, 183n69
- *Rasul v. Bush*, 30, 31–33, 49
- reshaping of post-9/11 national security policy and, 1
- Trump administration travel ban policy and, 163, 164

*U.S. v. Nixon*, 120

Vallinder, Torbjörn, 12
Verrilli, Donald, 144
Vladeck, Stephen, 146

War Crimes Act, 51
Warner, John, 122
war on terror, 1, 2
Warsame, Ahmed Abdulkadir, 83
waterboarding, 161
Wilkins, Robert, 150
Williams, Stephen, 108–109
Wilson, James Q., 5, 99
Wittes, Benjamin, 80, 125
Wolfowitz, Paul, 30–31, 36, 100
Work, Robert, 152

Yemen, 76, 79, 131
Yemeni detainees, 45, 76, 79, 86, 88
Yoo, John, 174n23